Russian History

An Enthralling Overview of Russia's Past and the Romanovs

Free limited time bonus

Stop for a moment. We have a free bonus set up for you. The problem is this: we forget 90% of everything that we read after 7 days. Crazy fact, right? Here's the solution: we've created a printable, 1-page pdf summary for this book that you're reading now. All you have to do to get your free pdf summary is to go to the following website:

https://livetolearn.lpages.co/enthrallinghistory/

Once you do, it will be intuitive. Enjoy, and thank you!

We forget 90% of everything that we've read in 7 days...

Get the free printable pdf summary of the book you've read AND much, much more... shhhh...

Enter Your Most Frequently Used Email to Get Started

DOWNLOAD FREE PDF SUMMARY

© Enthralling History

Table of Contents

PART 1: HISTORY OF RUSSIA...1

INTRODUCTION 2

SECTION ONE: EARLY SLAVIC KINGDOMS AND THE
MONGOL INVASION (800–1480 CE) 4

CHAPTER 1: THE EARLY EAST SLAVS AND KIEVAN RUS' 5

CHAPTER 2: THE CHRISTIANIZATION OF KIEVAN RUS'
AND THE MONGOL INVASION (980–1340) 18

SECTION TWO: THE RISE OF THE RUSSIAN EMPIRE
(1480–1917 CE) 30

CHAPTER 3: FROM THE GRAND DUCHY OF MOSCOW TO
PETER THE GREAT 31

CHAPTER 4: CATHERINE THE GREAT AND 18TH-CENTURY
RUSSIA..42

CHAPTER 5: FROM NAPOLEON TO THE CRIMEAN WAR............54

CHAPTER 6: TSAR ALEXANDER II'S REFORMS AND TSAR
ALEXANDER III'S SETBACK TO AUTOCRACY...............................64

SECTION THREE: WWI AND THE RUSSIAN REVOLUTION
(1914–1922) 75

CHAPTER 7: TSAR NICHOLAS II AND THE FEBRUARY
REVOLUTION..76

CHAPTER 8: THE OCTOBER REVOLUTION AND THE
RUSSIAN CIVIL WAR 87

SECTION FOUR: THE JOURNEY FROM COMMUNIST
RUSSIA TO THE RUSSIAN REPUBLIC (1922–2022) 98

CHAPTER 9: THE UNION OF SOVIET SOCIALIST REPUBLICS (USSR) 99

CHAPTER 10: THE GREAT PATRIOTIC WAR AND THE COLD WAR..109

CHAPTER 11: DE-STALINIZATION TO THE REPUBLIC OF RUSSIA..120

CHAPTER 12: RUSSIAN ARTS, LITERATURE, AND SCIENCE 133

CONCLUSION..150

PART 2: THE ROMANOVS 152

INTRODUCTION 153

CHAPTER 1: BEFORE THE ROMANOVS..................................156

CHAPTER 2: THE LAST OF THE RURIKIDS...............................166

CHAPTER 3: THE FIRST ROMANOVS 181

CHAPTER 4: PETER THE GREAT 190

CHAPTER 5: THE AGE OF ENLIGHTENED DESPOTISM............206

CHAPTER 6: 19TH-CENTURY ROMANOVS 217

CHAPTER 7: NICHOLAS II, THE LAST ROMANOV.....................236

CONCLUSION..246

HERE'S ANOTHER BOOK BY ENTHRALLING HISTORY THAT YOU MIGHT LIKE..248

FREE LIMITED TIME BONUS 249

BIBLIOGRAPHY...250

SOURCES 266

Part 1: History of Russia

An Enthralling Overview of Major Events in Russian History

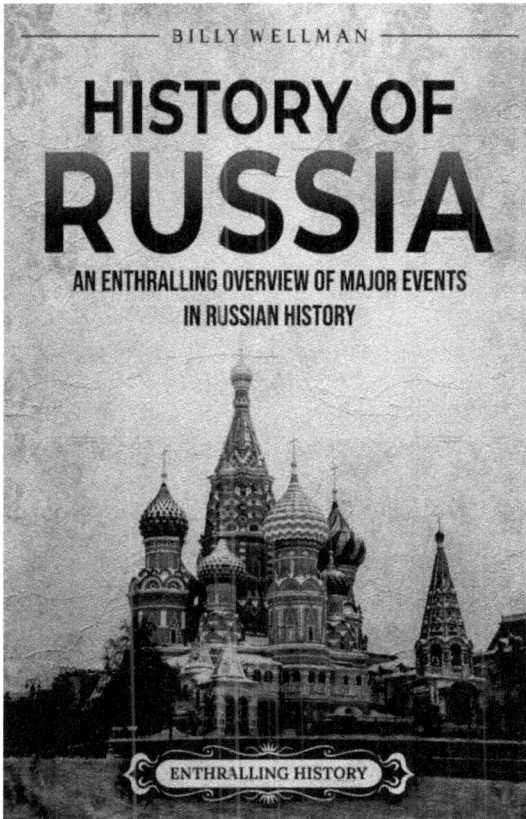

BILLY WELLMAN

HISTORY OF
RUSSIA

AN ENTHRALLING OVERVIEW OF MAJOR EVENTS
IN RUSSIAN HISTORY

ENTHRALLING HISTORY

Introduction

Attempting to document the history of Russia is a formidable task. As the largest country in the world, Russia encompasses almost 11 percent of the world's landmass and is the home of many different cultures. There's a lot of history to cover, and documenting the entire history of Russia would fill a number of books. Russian history contains many controversial and famous figures, such as Catherine the Great, the Romanov family, Vladimir Lenin, and Joseph Stalin. Besides the main events in Russian history, there are also changes in culture, literature, and science that will fascinate any lover of history. A comprehensive guide to Russian history is difficult to compile, but this introductory guide will put you on the right path.

The history of Russia begins with the early Slavic kingdoms, such as the first major Slavic state, Kievan Rus'. According to legend, the state was founded by a Viking named Oleg of Novgorod, but historians dispute this. For years, Kiev (today's Kyiv) acted as the capital of the Slavic state. Prince Vladimir set about ruling the Rurik dynasty and converted many Slavs from paganism to Orthodox Christianity. Unfortunately, Russia was later invaded by the Mongols, who destroyed Moscow and Kiev, the latter of which had become a center of culture and politics in Eastern Europe. These events are the subject of the first part of the book and lay a powerful foundation for the rest of Russian history.

Ivan the Great forced the Mongols out of Russia and established Muscovite rule. While this was initially good news for the Russian people, the Muscovite line produced Ivan the Terrible, who reigned with an iron fist and terrorized the nobility. When he died, Russia was plunged into instability and only began to recover under the Romanov dynasty, which would rule Russia for a little over three hundred years. The second part of this book will explore the rise and fall of the Romanov dynasty. It includes the story of colorful figures like Catherine the Great, Napoleon Bonaparte, and various influential tsars.

Eventually, the Romanov dynasty declined as the world began preparing for the First World War. Russia was rocked by the war, which eventually led to the February Revolution and the October Revolution. Part three of this book will take a look at the climactic events that would have long-lasting effects on modern history.

The Romanov dynasty was replaced by communist leaders who sought to lead Russia into an enlightened and modern era. This eventually led to the formation of the Union of Soviet Socialist Republics (USSR). The USSR brought new economic policies and cultural changes to its people. During this period, Russia fought different wars, including the Great Patriotic War and the Cold War. While the USSR stood for lofty ideals, it eventually stagnated. Despite Russia's stagnation, it was able to emerge as a front-runner during the Space Race and developed an enviable space program.

In time, the USSR was dissolved, and leaders like Boris Yeltsin were able to pioneer a new era in Russian society. The fourth and final part of the book covers the events from the First World War to the controversial reforms brought about by Vladimir Putin.

While the full history of Russia would fill hundreds of books, this comprehensive guide will help readers become acquainted with some of the most important events and time periods in Russian history.

SECTION ONE:
Early Slavic Kingdoms and the Mongol Invasion (800–1480 CE)

Chapter 1: The Early East Slavs and Kievan Rus'

The early Slavs lived in Central and Eastern Europe approximately between the 5th and 10th centuries. Unfortunately, few historical records still exist from the early Slavs, which means a lot of the information about them is saturated with theories and legends. Scholars believe the Slavs originated in Eastern Europe in Polesia (a region that spans parts of modern Central and Eastern Europe).

Map of Polesia.
https://commons.wikimedia.org/wiki/File:Polesia_map_-_topography.jpg

The Byzantine Empire was among the first to acknowledge the Slavs, and their records play a vital part in untangling their mysterious story. In time, the Slavs met the Vikings, who would go on to form Kievan Rus', a vast territory that would eventually form a large part of Russia.

"Barbarian" Enemies of Rome

Slavs are an ethnic group of people who all speak Slavic languages. Writing was only incorporated into the Slavic culture when the Slavs converted to Christianity around the 9th and 10th centuries. Some authors claim the Slavs were nomads, while others suggest they originally lived in states located in forests. It seems the Slavs occupied a large amount of territory and shared common cultural elements instead of being completely united under one ruler. There is a lot of debate over how the early Slavs were organized. Some accounts state the Slavs were ruled by a king, while others suggest they used a primitive form of democracy.

According to archaeological evidence, proto-Slavic cultures lived in parts of modern-day western Poland and Belarus by 1500 BCE. Interestingly, scholars have been able to detect traces of Iranian and Germanic languages in Slavic languages. This means that at some point, the Slavs came into contact with Iranian and Germanic tribes.

Archaeologists have uncovered some clues about early Slavic culture. Apparently, the Slavs worshiped a god named Perun, who was considered the supreme god by some Slavic cultures. Perun was similar to the Norse god Thor, who was a thunder god. Another Slavic god was Yarilo, who was the god of youth and spring. He was a high-ranking god, as was his consort, Lada, the goddess of love. It appears as though these two gods died every year and were resurrected, which would have connected them to fertility.

Pendant of the god Perun.

Historians know the Slavs were enemies of the Romans during the later stages of the Roman Empire. The Romans were biased against all of their enemies and deemed most non-Romans as savage and uncivilized. In the 5th century, the Slavs made it difficult for the Romans to keep their borders along the Balkans. Throughout the century, the Slavs engaged in several campaigns against the Romans. In the 550s CE, the Slavs devastated the region of the Hebrus River and destroyed several cities. After the destruction, the Slavs turned the women and children into slaves but killed all the men. Accounts report that the Slavs wanted to capture Thessalonica but were thwarted by the Roman army. In 585, the Slavs marched on Constantinople, but the Romans were able to drive them off. However, during this time, the Slavs were able to establish permanent footholds in Greece.

In 626, the Slavs joined forces with the Avars and Bulgars and once again set their sights on Constantinople. The Slavs were almost able to accomplish their goal but were repelled by the Romans. Since the Slavs were able to occupy parts of Greece, they would frequently butt heads with the emerging Byzantine Empire.

The Byzantine Empire and the Slavs

The Slavs frequently raided the Byzantine Empire's Danube border. Byzantine writers referred to the Slavs as the "Veneti." The Veneti were divided into two distinct groups: the Sclavenes and the Antes. It is important to note that one Byzantine writer, Procopius of Caesarea, wrote the Sclavenes and Antes spoke the same language. This likely means that while the two groups lived in different areas, they still shared many common traits.

Byzantine historians also reported the Slavs were ruled by the strongest and most cunning among them. Slavic society was dominated by village elders who were viewed as wise men and were tasked with passing their knowledge to the younger generation. The Slavs engaged in raids against the Byzantine Empire, and the Byzantines claimed the Slavs intentionally caused chaos to take over the lands they wanted. Once the Slavs settled into a new territory, they integrated the existing people into their own culture. It appears as though the Slavs originated in Eastern Europe and then slowly migrated to Central Europe and the Balkans, where they incorporated the Scythians, Alans, and Sarmatians into their culture.

This integration allowed the Slavic fighting style, armor, weapons, and warfare to become increasingly diverse. When the Byzantine Empire fell, the Slavs organized themselves into kingdoms and were able to keep the Mongol hordes at bay.

The Khazars

The Khazars were a Turkic people who originated in Central Asia. They eventually converted to Judaism and spread into the Northern Caucasus. As time passed, they controlled a lot of lands in Eastern Europe. During the height of their power, they controlled much of modern-day southern Russia, as well as parts of Kazakhstan, Ukraine, Dagestan, Georgia, and Azerbaijan. They had a mostly peaceful relationship with the Byzantine Empire and helped the Byzantines against the Sassanids. The Khazars likely prevented an Arab invasion of Eastern Europe by fighting against the Arab caliphates.

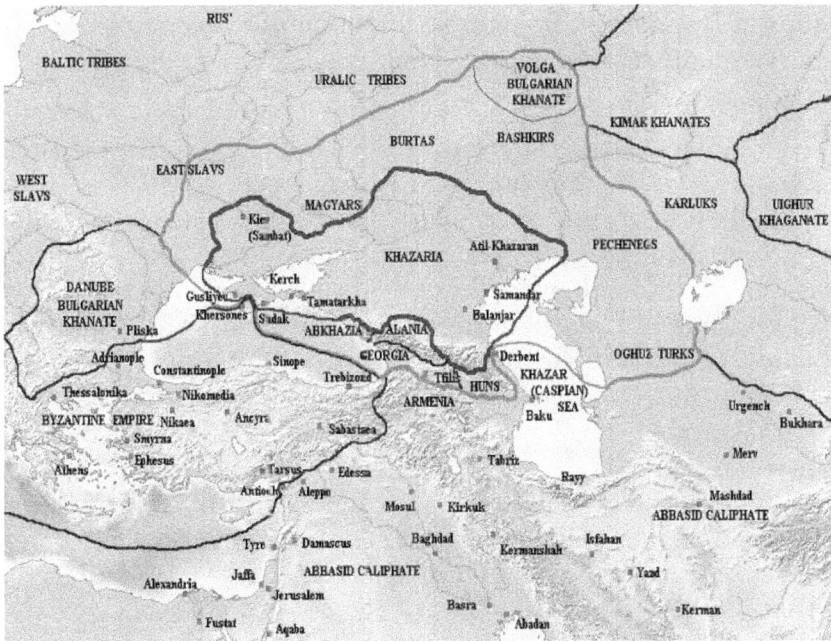

Map showing the Khazar Empire.

Briangotts; This file is licensed under the Creative Commons Attribution-Share Alike 3.0 Unported license; https://commons.wikimedia.org/wiki/File:Khazar_map1.PNG

It appears as though the Khazars were ruled by a khagan and the bek (or a khagan bek). It is believed the khagan was a spiritual ruler who had limits placed on his power, while the bek controlled the military and administration. According to Arab sources, the khagan typically lived on an island in the Volga River. The khagan had numerous wives, as he received one daughter from each client ruler, but this may be an exaggeration.

The Khazars were located in a prime trading location, as goods were brought through Khazar states from Western Europe to Asia and the East. The Muslim world was forced to trade with Northern Europe through Khazar intermediaries, and the Khazars placed a levy on all goods that went through their borders. The Khazars traded a vast number of goods, namely honey, wool, millet, fish, slaves, and furs. The Khazars also allowed the Radhanites (a guild of Jewish merchants) to use a trade route that went through their empire. This may have led to the Khazars' conversion to Judaism.

Eventually, their alliance with the Byzantine Empire began to collapse in the 900s, and the Byzantines began making alliances with the Rus' and Pechenegs in the hope of isolating the Khazar state further. Khazar imperial power was defeated in the 960s.

Vikings in Russia

It appears as though the Vikings first appeared in Russia in the 6th century. During this time, the Khazars were still ruling, which means the two groups often butted heads. The Vikings might not have been looking to conquer the territory; their initial goal might have been to trade with the people of Eastern Europe. The Norwegians and Danish mostly stayed in Western Europe, but the Swedes began looking further than that and eventually began trading in the Baltic and regions located in modern-day Russia. The Vikings eventually became the rulers of Slavic territories in Novgorod and Kiev. These Vikings were known as the Rus' to the Slavs. The Rus' (they were also referred to as Varangians) associated freely with the Slavs and created a series of clans. Viking princes took control of Kiev (modern-day Kyiv) and Novgorod in the late 800s.

At first, the Khazars had a good relationship with the Rus', and it seems the Rus' were influenced by Khazar culture. The Khazars even allowed the Rus' to use a trading route along the Volga River. However, when the Rus' began attacking Arab lands, the relationship between the Arabs and Khazars began to sour. As a result, the Khazars were forced to end their alliance with the Rus'.

Much of the information about the Rus' and their eventual Slavic state, Kievan Rus', is derived from the *Russian Primary Chronicle*, which was likely completed in 113 CE. While it provides a lot of historical information, many of the stories seem to have been exaggerated or influenced by legends. However, archaeological evidence supports some of the information in the *Chronicle*. According to the *Russian Primary Chronicle*, the region of Kievan Rus' was given to Noah's son, Japheth. This alludes to the Great Flood described in the Bible. For those unfamiliar with the story, a global flood destroyed all of mankind except for the faithful man Noah, who survived along with his wife, his three sons, and his sons' wives.

Accordingly, the Slavs who lived in the land given to Japheth were eventually subdued by the Khazars and the Varangians. In time, the Slavs drove the Varangians away but found the Khazars had become increasingly harsh. The Slavs were unable to govern themselves and decided to appeal to the Varangians for help. The *Chronicle* states the Slavs went to the lands of the Varangians (it doesn't mention where these lands were located) and asked the Varangians to return and rule over the Slavs again. Three noble brothers responded to this appeal.

Three Noble Brothers

The *Russian Primary Chronicle* states that three brothers decided to return to the land of the Slavs and establish themselves as kings. The oldest, Rurik, decided to take the region surrounding Novgorod, while the second, Sineus, chose Beloozero. The final brother, Truvor, chose Izborsk. While many have rejected the *Chronicle*'s claims, some Norse artifacts were found at a site at Novgorod, which means there may be some truth in the *Chronicle*'s reports. Archaeologists have found Scandinavian settlements near the Volkhov River from as early as 750 CE. It doesn't appear as if the Vikings wanted to raid the areas, as there was very little to steal, so it's likely they wanted to take advantage of Russia's resources.

That first settlement experienced a population fluctuation, which adds credence to the *Chronicle*'s claims that the Slavs expelled the Rus' only to ask them to return later. The *Chronicle* continues the story of the three brothers and claims that Sineus and Truvor eventually died, which allowed Rurik to assimilate their regions into his lands. Two of his men, Askold and Dir, were allowed to leave and find their own lands. They were originally supposed to go to Constantinople but found a prosperous city named Kyiv or Kiev (the difference in the spelling results from the English translation of two different languages; Kyiv is the English translation of the Ukrainian word, while Kiev is from Russian). Askold and Dir conquered the city and used it as a base for raids on surrounding cities, which allowed them to amass large amounts of wealth.

In time, Rurik died, leaving behind a young son, Igor. However, Igor was still too young to rule, so Rurik entrusted his son to one of his men, Oleg, who ruled over Rurik's lands.

Prince Oleg of Novgorod

Oleg of Novgorod immediately began expanding the lands he had been given. He conquered surrounding regions and incorporated them into his domain. As his territory kept growing, he eventually found Askold and Dir at Kiev. They had managed to secure massive fortunes for themselves through their frequent raids. Oleg recognized the value of Kiev, but instead of forming an alliance, he managed to get Askold and Dir out of the city and killed them, allowing him to take full control. This made him the founder of Kievan Rus'. According to the *Russian Primary Chronicle*, Oleg became the ruler of Novgorod around 879. By 882, he had captured Kiev and Smolensk. Since Kiev was located in a prime location along the Dnieper River, he made Kiev his capital.

At this time, the Khazars were still a formidable ruling power and demanded tribute from surrounding states. Once Oleg captured Kiev, he began convincing surrounding states and tribes to pay tribute to him instead. Besides Oleg's military victories, he also made several lucrative treaties, including a trade deal with Constantinople. The *Chronicle* also states that Oleg was called Oleg the Priest (or prophet) and details a disturbing prophecy that Oleg received.

According to the prophecy, Oleg was going to be killed by a horse that he owned. Oleg immediately ordered the horse be sent away but made arrangements to make sure it was always well cared for. In time, Oleg became confident in his own reign and scoffed at the prophecy. When he was told his horse had died, he ordered the bones be brought to him. He loudly mocked the prophecy and went to crush the horse's skull beneath his feet, but when he stepped on the skull, he disturbed a snake that had been hiding under it. The snake immediately bit him, and he died from the poison.

Prince Oleg stepping on his horse's skull.

During his reign, Oleg dutifully raised Rurik's son, Igor of Kiev, who became Oleg's successor.

Rise of Kievan Rus'

According to historical sources, the Vikings first visited Constantinople around 830. They must have been impressed by what they saw because they besieged the city in 860 and then again in 907. While the Vikings were powerful enough to present a serious threat to Constantinople, they weren't able to capture the city. In time, the relationship between the Rus' and Constantinople became more positive, and they were able to make trade deals and treaties. The Rus' supplied Constantinople with a steady supply of slaves, honey, and furs, while Constantinople gave the Rus' luxury items in return.

Principalities of Kievan Rus' (1054 CE).

Oleg expanded Kievan Rus' from Kiev to the Dnieper River and had a series of forts that eventually reached the Baltic. This put him in direct opposition with the Khazars, who felt he was encroaching on their territory. While the Khazars were originally allies of the Rus', this relationship eventually soured.

Oleg decided to attack the Khazars. The Byzantines often interfered with this conflict, as it benefited them since the Khazars and Rus' both presented various threats to the Byzantine Empire. According to a historical record called the Schechter Letter, Oleg fought against the Khazar Empire around 941, going up against the Khazar general Pesakh. Oleg lost the fight.

Grand Prince Sviatoslav I of Kiev was responsible for conquering the Khazars. In the 960s, he captured the Khazar strongholds of Tamantarkhan and Sarkel. Finally, the Khazar capital of Atil fell to the Rus'. According to a contemporary source, the Rus' sacked the city so thoroughly that nothing was left. With the Khazars out of the way, the Kievan Rus' state was able to grow to new heights.

Olga of Kiev

While the *Russian Primary Chronicle* provides many helpful details that clarify the history of Kievan Rus', it was also heavily influenced by legends. For example, while the story of Oleg's death is fascinating and entertaining, it is likely based more on fiction than reality. Another figure in the *Chronicle* who fell victim to such exaggeration was Olga of Kiev. She may have been a real person, but it is unlikely that she perpetrated all the acts that are described in the *Chronicle*.

According to the *Chronicle*, Igor of Kiev succeeded Oleg of Novgorod. By that time, Igor had married a woman named Olga. Like Oleg, Igor collected tributes from conquered regions. He was also a good warrior and conquered new lands. However, he became greedy and began charging larger tributes. He became so oppressive that a tribe called the Drevlians decided to assassinate him. Their plot was successful, and Olga was left to take care of their young son, Sviatoslav I. Since Sviatoslav was still too young to rule, Olga ruled as regent in his place.

Olga immediately decided to avenge her husband's murder. The Drevlians decided to opt for diplomacy and sent emissaries to arrange a marriage between Olga and their prince, Mai. Olga tricked the emissaries into getting into a boat, which was then carried around. The unsuspecting emissaries were then thrown into a pit and buried alive. However, Olga wasn't done yet. She invited the Drevlian wise men to visit her. When they arrived, she ordered that they bathe before they came to her. Once they were in the bathhouses, she had the bathhouses set on fire, burning the wise men alive. Finally, she claimed she would forgive the Drevlians if they arranged a funeral feast in Igor's honor. They agreed, and at the feast, everyone ate well and got drunk. As soon as the Drevlians were inebriated, Olga ordered her men to kill them all.

A painting of Olga of Kiev's baptism by Sergei Kirillov.
Sergei Kirillov, CC BY-SA 3.0 <https://creativecommons.org/licenses/by-sa/3.0>, via Wikimedia Commons; https://commons.wikimedia.org/wiki/File:Kirillov_knyaginya_olga.jpg

The Drevlians realized Olga was never going to spare them and retreated to the city of Iskorosten. Olga besieged the city but was unable to capture it. Eventually, she promised to stop attacking the city if each household gave her three pigeons and sparrows. The Drevlians complied and gave her the birds. Once she had her tribute, she and her soldiers attached hot sulfur threads to the birds and released them. The birds returned to their nests in the houses of the city. The city caught fire, and Olga either killed or enslaved the survivors.

While most of Olga's story is rooted in legend, the real Olga might have played a part in spreading Christianity throughout Kievan Rus'. The Christian Church later denied all the violent parts of Olga's history and made her a saint due to her missionary work. Despite Olga's efforts, Vladimir the Great would be the one to turn Kievan Rus' from paganism to Orthodox Christianity.

Chapter 2: The Christianization of Kievan Rus' and the Mongol Invasion (980–1340)

When the Vikings arrived in Russia initially, they likely wanted to establish trade routes with the Slavs and other cultures. However, in time, the Vikings became known as the Rus', and they set up Kievan Rus', which became a dominant power in the region. With the fall of the Khazars, Kievan Rus' became increasingly powerful. They exacted tribute from the Slavs, and their Eastern Roman neighbors viewed them as "barbarians." Efforts were made to convert the Rus' to Christianity, but that only came to fruition through the work of Prince Vladimir I.

Map of Kievan Rus' in 1237.

The Eastern Orthodox Church had an indelible effect on Slavic culture. Christianity wouldn't be the only new influence on the Slavs and Rus', as a new threat loomed in the East. The Mongols eventually overran Kievan Rus' and turned it into a part of the Golden Horde. In time, the Mongols would be driven out of Russia, but the Mongol invasion would have lasting consequences on Russian history.

Prince Vladimir I

Prince Vladimir was the youngest son of Sviatoslav, the son of the famous Olga of Kiev. Sviatoslav appointed his oldest son, Yaropolk, as the heir to Kiev, while Vladimir was appointed as the prince of Novgorod around 969. A few years later, Sviatoslav died, and the kingdom descended into a period of political instability. Tensions between the brothers escalated until Yaropolk murdered his younger brother Oleg around 976. Vladimir was able to escape to Scandinavia and avoided the same fate.

Vladimir I.
https://commons.wikimedia.org/wiki/File:Vladimir_I_The_Saint.jpg

Thankfully, Vladimir had family in Norway, and the ruler of Norway, Haakon Sigurdsson, took in Vladimir. Together, they plotted against Yaropolk. Vladimir was able to return in 978 and defeat his brother. He had Yaropolk executed on the charge of treason and was able to gain control of his father's kingdom. As the new ruler of Kievan Rus', Vladimir looked for ways to strengthen and expand his territory. According to records, he spent a decade fortifying his borders and strengthening his army. During this time,

Kievan Rus' was still primarily pagan. According to the *Russian Primary Chronicle*, Vladimir decided to send envoys to neighboring countries to investigate their religions. The thunder god, Perun, was massively popular in Kievan Rus' and had several shrines and cults that worshiped him. When the envoys returned, they reported the Orthodox Christian religion practiced in Constantinople was impressive, which may have aided in Vladimir's decision to convert to Christianity.

Orthodox Christianity

There are three main groups of Christianity, namely the Orthodox Church, the Roman Catholics, and the Protestants. Most Orthodox churches are either self-governing or have their own head but are united through tradition and theology. Many Orthodox churches have incorporated elements of Middle Eastern, Greek, Slavic, and Russian culture. A lot of Orthodox tradition is based on geography, which means many of the churches are unique and reflect local cultures and traditions. Orthodox Christianity developed from the Christianity practiced by the Eastern Roman Empire. The Orthodox churches share many similarities with other Christian churches, namely the belief that Jesus Christ was God himself and the resurrection and crucifixion of Jesus. However, there are a few notable differences in the Orthodox theology and way of living when compared to other Christian churches.

There are many different Orthodox churches, such as the Eastern Orthodox Church, which traditionally was led by the patriarch of Constantinople. However, most Orthodox churches have their own patriarchs or are led by archbishops. Originally, there was no difference between the Eastern and Western churches; however, over the centuries, schisms developed, with Christian doctrines being decided through various councils. There were five main patriarchal sees; they were located in Rome, Alexandria, Constantinople, Jerusalem, and Antioch. After the split from Rome, Orthodox Christianity became known as the "Eastern" church and became the main Christian force in Asia Minor, Russia, the eastern Mediterranean, and the Balkans.

Around 787, the Western and Eastern churches were almost completely divided. The Eastern Church chafed at the Western

Church's attempt to claim the papacy had the right to control both churches. There were also differences in opinion regarding various theological matters. Most Orthodox believe the great split between Western and Eastern Christianity occurred during the sack of Constantinople during the Fourth Crusade in 1204. The sacking eventually allowed Muslim Ottomans to take control of the historic city in 1453. This capital offense was never forgiven by the Eastern Orthodox Church and cemented the massive gap between the Eastern Church and Rome (the seat of power of the Western Church.

The Baptism of Kiev

There are various versions of how the Rus' was converted to Christianity. One version of events centers around the claim that Prince Vladimir's envoys returned from investigating the religions of surrounding territories and reported on the grandeur of the Orthodox Church. The envoys said the festivities and churches in Constantinople were the most beautiful they had ever seen. These reports convinced Prince Vladimir to adopt the new religion due to the church's beauty and prestige.

However, others claimed that Basil II of Byzantine faced an uprising near Constantinople and needed an ally. He approached Prince Vladimir, who used the situation to demand a royal marriage alliance with Constantinople. To sweeten the deal, Vladimir promised to convert the Rus' in return for the marriage alliance. Another version states that Vladimir fell in love with Basil II's sister, Anna, and converted to Christianity to gain her hand in marriage.

While scholars may never know the real reason for Vladimir's conversion, they know he brought his new wife with him to Kiev in 988. There was a marked difference in Vladimir, as he immediately destroyed all the local pagan temples. He then went on to build the Church of the Tithes, which was the first stone church in Kiev. Kievan Rus' also enjoyed a long-lasting alliance with the Byzantine Empire.

Vladimir didn't stop with the construction of the church. Upon his return to Kiev in 988, he had his twelve sons and other officials baptized. All the citizens of Kiev were summoned to the banks of the Dnieper River, where they were baptized while Orthodox priests prayed over the scene. These actions were meant to turn Orthodoxy into the new state religion, and the mass baptism became known as the "Baptism of Kiev."

Despite Vladimir's efforts, many communities within Kievan Rus' strongly opposed the new religion, which led to many brutal and violent uprisings. Vladimir died around 1015 and became the figurehead of Russian Orthodoxy. After his death, parts of his body were sent to various churches to serve as holy relics.

The Rise of the Mongols

Like so many other states, Kievan Rus' was only as strong as its rulers. In 1054, Yaroslav the Wise died, and Kievan Rus' was left without its great leader. As a result, the state began to break apart as smaller factions struggled for power. For decades, princes squabbled over territories, which weakened their power. As power was divided between local principalities, cities and territories were left to fend for themselves. To make matters worse, the Byzantine Empire was weakening, so Kievan Rus' couldn't rely on its strongest ally. All of these factors would lead to a much more serious threat: the Mongols.

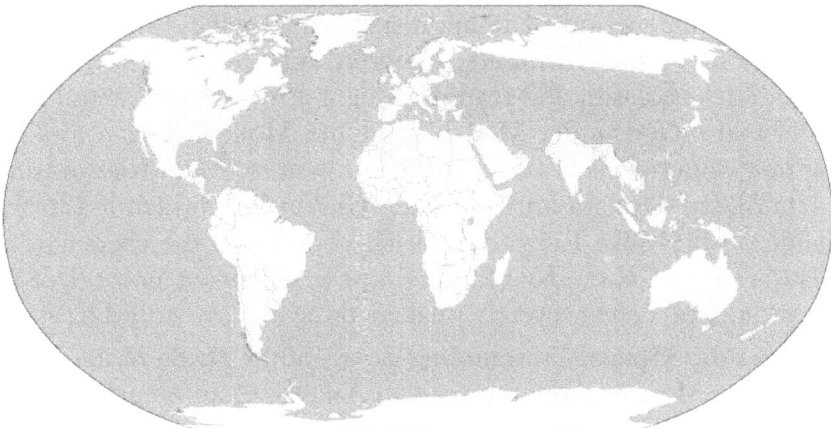

Map of the great Mongol Empire.
Canuckguy and many others, CC BY-SA 4.0 <https://creativecommons.org/licenses/by-sa/4.0>, via Wikimedia Commons; https://commons.wikimedia.org/wiki/File:Great_Mongol_Empire_map.svg

The Mongol Empire was founded by the formidable Genghis Khan and lasted from 1206 to 1368. During that time, it ruled over most of Eurasia. The Mongols had a gigantic army of trained soldiers and the most advanced warfare technology of the time at their disposal. Before the rise of Genghis Khan, the Mongols were forced to maintain a nomadic lifestyle, as their farms and flocks required a steady supply of grass and water. Since droughts and famines were common, the Mongols lived with frequent insecurity.

In 1206, Genghis Khan (previously known as Temüjin, the son of a local chieftain) assumed power and united the Mongol tribes. He reformed laws, established a new type of government, improved trade, and encouraged the advancement of technology, such as leather armor, gunpowder, stirrups, and composite bows. Genghis Khan also embraced a policy of religious freedom.

The Mongol army quickly became incredibly successful. They engaged in psychological warfare, built up large arsenals, and used guerilla warfare tactics, such as hit-and-runs and arrow storms. Thanks to a policy of aggressive expansion, the Mongol Empire's borders quickly expanded. As the Mongol army marched, it spread terror, as reports of their brutal tactics spread throughout surrounding territories. However, the Mongol Empire also fostered a brief period of peace, which allowed for new trading opportunities and safe traveling.

Invasion of Kievan Rus'

During the period of political instability in the 12th century in Kievan Rus', the fractured kingdom was forced to face the incredibly successful and feared Mongol army. Once Central Asia had been united under Mongol rule, the Mongols began looking for new opportunities. They quickly set their sights on Kievan Rus'. In 1223, the Mongol army attacked Kievan Rus' which led to the Battle of the Kalka River. The battle ended with the execution of Mstislav III of Kiev. Kievan Rus' lost a significant portion of its army, and the defeat severely weakened the already struggling state.

After the Mongols' resounding victory at the Battle of the Kalka River, the Mongol army returned to Asia to rejoin Genghis Khan. The Rus' lived in fear of the Mongol forces, which proved to be well-founded as the Mongols returned in 1237. Batu Khan, one of Genghis Khan's grandsons, led the Mongol forces into Kievan Rus' and burned down Kolomna and Moscow. Between 1237 and 1238, he attacked each principality in Kievan Rus'. There was such widespread destruction that thousands of Rus' were forced to flee to the harsh north, where they struggled to make a living due to the scarcity of resources. Very few cities were spared during the invasion. In 1240, Batu Khan finally captured the city of Kiev, and his victory over Kievan Rus' was complete.

The Tatars and the Golden Horde

The European territories that belonged to the Mongol Empire were called the Golden Horde. Mongol tradition states that before Genghis Khan died, he left his empire to his four sons. His son Jochi was allowed to rule the lands around and beyond the Ural Mountains. Later, Jochi's son, Batu Khan, would establish the Golden Horde. Another one of Genghis Khan's sons, Ögedei Khan, ordered the Mongol army to invade Europe, but Batu Khan finished the job.

Once Kievan Rus' had been defeated, the Mongols marched westward to defeat the Polish and Hungarians. The rest of Europe was spared since Ögedei died soon after the defeat of the Hungarian army at the Battle of Mohi (also known as the Battle of the Sajó River). While the Golden Horde remained a fixed Mongolian territory for the next two centuries, the Mongol army never got that far into Europe again. However, the Mongols left a lasting mark on Europe, with the Europeans calling the Mongols "Tatars." This was likely due to the fact that one Mongol clan was called the Tatars, but it also referred to Tartarus, which was the deepest part of the underworld. It was believed the Mongols had arrived straight from hell to wreak havoc on Europe.

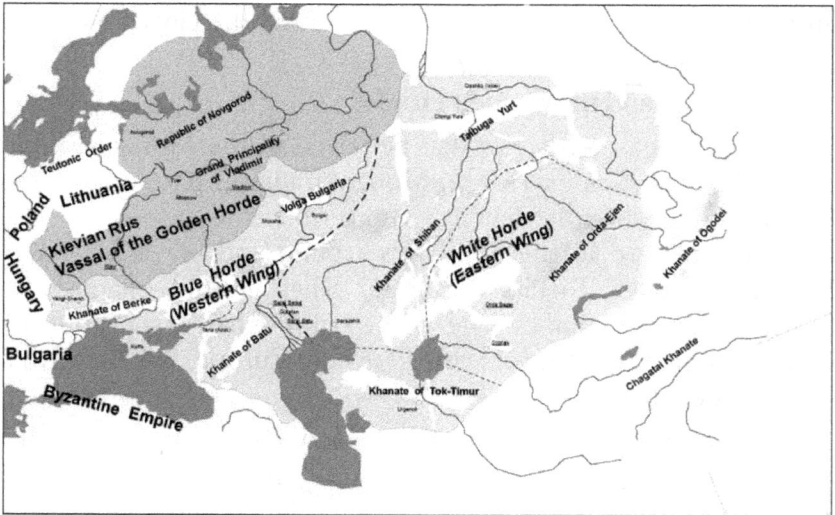

Map of the Golden Horde.

Afil, CC BY-SA 3.0 <https://creativecommons.org/licenses/by-sa/3.0>, via Wikimedia Commons; https://commons.wikimedia.org/wiki/File:Golden_Horde_2.png

After the Mongols took control of Kievan Rus', they built their capital at Sarai, which was located near the Volga River. Russian princes were then forced to pay tribute to the Mongols. Despite the harsh realities of the Mongol invasion, the period of the Tatar yoke (which refers to the economic and cultural rule of the Mongols) was surprisingly peaceful. The Mongols didn't force the Rus' to convert or adopt Mongolian practices. The Rus' were largely left in peace as long as they paid their taxes.

Alexander Nevsky

Alexander Nevsky was born in 1221 and was the prince of Novgorod and Kiev and the grand prince of Vladimir. For years, the Novgorodians had been encroaching on Swedish land in Finnish territory, which led to a Swedish invasion in 1240. Alexander was able to defeat the Swedes, which earned him the honorific of "Nevsky." (Nevsky means "of Neva," referring to his victory in the Battle of Neva.) However, his military prowess didn't hold lasting merit, as the Novgorodians expelled him for getting involved in city affairs.

Alexander Nevsky.

Soon after the Swedish invasion, the pope of the time, Pope Gregory IX, convinced the Teutonic Knights (a Catholic-sanctioned military society that was originally formed to protect and help Christians who made pilgrimages to the Holy Land) to "Christianize" the Baltic. This would prove to be an ironic move since the territories were already predominantly Christian. Alexander was asked to return to Novgorod to defeat this new threat. During a battle on the frozen waters of Lake Peipus in 1242, Alexander defeated the Teutonic Knights.

Unfortunately, the Mongol armies were already in Kievan Rus' and were quickly conquering many Russian principalities. Alexander's father submitted to the Mongol rulers in 1246 but died soon after. Alexander and his brother Andrew appealed to Batu Khan to help them settle the matter of succession. However, since Alexander was Batu's favorite, the great khan made Andrew the grand prince (at the time, the great khan was displeased with Batu Khan). Andrew tried to conspire against the Mongols, but

Alexander revealed the plot to Batu Khan's son, who retaliated and defeated Andrew. Alexander was then appointed as the grand prince.

Alexander chose to pay tribute to the Mongols instead of trying to defeat them, which drew heavy criticism from his peers and the Rus'. While many viewed Alexander's acceptance of Mongol rule as cowardly, he was able to rebuild Russian infrastructure by building churches and fortifications and passing laws. This would not have been possible if he had been deposed by the Mongols.

Alexander continued to protect Kievan Rus' during his reign. He quelled rebellions before the Mongols could react brutally and managed to get the Rus' exempted from a military draft. Alexander's actions garnered support from the Russian Orthodox Church, and he was declared a saint in 1547. Once Alexander died, Kievan Rus' quickly splintered into principalities, but his son, Daniel, was able to establish the house of Moscow.

Impact of the Mongol Invasion

Kievan Rus' was left in a state of ruin after the onslaught of the Mongol invasion, and years of forced taxation meant the Rus' were unable to repair their cities. The Rus' focused on rebuilding Kiev and Pskov, but it took years before the cities were restored. In the meantime, new cities, such as Tver and Moscow, were able to flourish. Novgorod also managed to escape most of the destruction and continued to prosper.

While the years under the Tatar yoke were relatively peaceful, the Rus' still lived with the constant threat of invasion, which happened a few times and always led to heavy burdens for the local population since they were forced to repair the destruction.

The Tatars also built a massive postal road system and introduced new military tactics and organizational methods. Over the years, Mongolian culture began to affect local populations. Russian noblemen began adopting the Mongolian language and changed their names. These cultural elements would have linguistic and aesthetic influences on Russian culture. The Mongol rule also caused the split between the East Slavs and led to the formation of three modern nations: Russia, Belarus, and Ukraine.

By the 14th century, some Mongol leaders had converted to Islam, with rulers of the Golden Horde either practicing Buddhism or Mongolian pagan beliefs. When the Black Death struck in the 14th century, the Golden Horde was severely weakened, and matters were worsened by the outbreak of a civil war. Between 1359 and 1382, the Mongol grip began to weaken on Eastern Europe. In 1380, the Russians were able to secure their first major victory against the Mongols at the Battle of Kulikovo. Eventually, the Golden Horde splintered into distinct khanates, which would slowly be forced into extinction.

Rise of Moscow

In the early years of Russia's history, Moscow was a relatively small trading post that belonged to the principality of Vladimir-Suzdal. In the years of Mongol rule, Moscow was sheltered in the north and mostly spared from the near-constant power struggles and raids that crippled other Russian cities. Cities like Kiev financially struggled since they were forced to rebuild after destructive Mongol raids.

Around 1288, Ivan I was born. He would later become the prince of Moscow and convince many people to move to the city since it was comparatively safer than other cities in Russia. Thanks to Ivan I's savvy politics, he was able to turn Moscow into a prosperous and safe city during the instability of Mongolian leadership. During this time, Moscow became the seat of power of the Russian Orthodox Church.

SECTION TWO:
The Rise of the Russian Empire
(1480–1917 CE)

Chapter 3: From the Grand Duchy of Moscow to Peter the Great

When the Mongols invaded Kievan Rus', they ripped through the territory as if nothing could stop them. Kievan Rus' was then turned into the Golden Horde, the European part of the extensive Mongol Empire. The two centuries of Mongol rule are perceived as relatively peaceful, but the Rus' lived in near-constant fear of destructive raids, which would result in expensive damage. Finally, as the Mongol Empire weakened, the Rus' were able to take back their lands, which was largely possible due to the efforts of Ivan III, who would become the "Grand Duke of all the Russias" and Ivan the Great.

Ivan the Great unified Russia and established Moscow as an important Russian city. However, not all his descendants would follow his example, as his grandson, Ivan IV, would become one of the most feared rulers in history and earn the title "Ivan the Terrible." Eventually, the Romanovs took the throne and established an enduring dynasty that would produce the likes of Peter the Great.

Ivan the Great

Ivan III was born in 1440 to Vasili II of Russia. In 1450, Ivan became co-regent with his father and finally succeeded his father in

1462. He proved to be a cautious ruler but had the goal of unifying the Russian states. For decades, Moscow had been a Mongol ally. The city was perched along profitable trade routes between the Volga River and Novgorod. This advantageous geographical position allowed Moscow to flourish, and Ivan III's predecessors were able to greatly expand Moscow's borders. However, Ivan III wasn't satisfied with Moscow's position and decided to find a way to end Mongol rule over the city.

In 1476, he refused to pay the normal tribute to the Mongols. Four years later, Khan Ahmed attacked the city but was forced to retreat to the inner part of the Mongol Empire. By that point, the Mongol Empire was fractured and divided, which meant the Mongol rulers were unable to keep their hold on the Golden Horde.

Ivan III of Russia.
https://commons.wikimedia.org/wiki/File:Ivan_III_of_Russia_(Granovitaya_palata,_1881-2).jpg

Once the Mongols were no longer a problem, Ivan III set his sights on unifying Russia. For years, Moscow and Novgorod had been enemies, but Ivan III was able to defeat the rival city and bring it under his rule. In time, he was able to gain control of Yaroslav, Rostov, Vyatka, and Tver, which brought an end to the autonomous rule of distinct Russian principalities.

Ivan III also made an alliance with the Russian Orthodox Church, which increased his power. The former autonomous Russian princes became part of the nobility, and if a conquered state rebelled, members of its royal family were taken to Moscow or sent to distant lands, which effectively ended most rebellions. Ivan III also created a new legal code called the Muscovite Sudebnik. He later went on to marry Sophia Paleologue of Constantinople, who brought many Byzantine influences into the Russian court.

Ivan the Great was determined to turn Moscow into the next Constantinople. He invited master craftsmen to Moscow and oversaw the construction of many lavish buildings like cathedrals and palaces. Previously, Russia had been ruled through patriarchal systems of governments that were heavily influenced by members of the nobility called boyars. However, Ivan III introduced an autocratic system of government similar to the Byzantine system and made the position of monarch sacred. Boyars were reduced to ministers who depended heavily on the king's will, which sowed seeds of discord among the nobility. Ivan III died in 1505, leaving his son, Vasili III, as the new ruler of Moscow.

Vasili III

Before Ivan III's marriage to Sophia Paleologue, he was married to Maria of Tver. When she died in 1467, Ivan III married Sophia Paleologue, the niece of the last Byzantine emperor, Constantine XI. At first, the condition of their marriage was that Maria's child would inherit the throne. However, Sophia had considerable influence over her husband and encouraged his imperialistic ideals. She was known for being a formidable woman, and it was her son, Vasili III, who inherited Ivan III's throne instead of Maria of Tver's son, Ivan the Young.

Vasili III was born in 1479 and inherited the Muscovite state in 1505. He expanded Moscow's borders by conquering

Volokolamsk, Ryazan, Novgorod-Seversky, Pskov, and Smolensk. The capture of Smolensk was one of his greatest achievements since it was Lithuania's stronghold. While Vasili III's military and political feats were impressive, he was known for being an oppressive ruler. He brutally punished anyone who disobeyed him and cut the power of the boyars, especially those who came from conquered principalities. Vasili III died in 1533, leaving behind his three-year-old son, who would eventually succeed him and become Ivan the Terrible.

Ivan the Terrible

Ivan IV was only eight years old when his mother died, leaving him and his deaf-mute brother Yuri in the hands of the nobility, who resented Ivan's father and grandfather for greatly reducing their power. Some reports claim that Ivan and Yuri were treated terribly as children and were frequently left without food or proper clothes. This treatment at the hands of the nobility fostered a deep mistrust and eventual hatred of the nobles in Ivan. Apparently, when he was thirteen, Ivan IV was with the Shuisky family. In 1453, while at a feast, Ivan had the most powerful Shuisky, Prince Andrei, arrested for mismanaging the country. Prince Andrei was put to death shortly after, likely beaten to death by his jailers.

Ivan IV of Russia.
https://commons.wikimedia.org/wiki/File:Ivan_the_Terrible_(cropped).JPG

When he was sixteen, Ivan IV was crowned "Tsar of all Russias." Shortly thereafter, he married Anastasia Romanovna. The marriage cemented his alliance with the formidable Romanov family. While Ivan IV gained an infamous reputation, the early years of his rule went relatively well. He established a standing army and a Russian parliament. He brought the first printing press to Russia, constructed St. Basil's Cathedral in Moscow, and established new church regulations.

Unfortunately, in the 1560s, Russia went through a difficult time due to Tatar invasions, a sea blockade initiated by the Swedes and Poles, and a terrible drought. To make matters worse, Anastasia died in 1560, likely from poison. These events caused Ivan IV to struggle mentally, and he fled from Moscow in 1564. He was persuaded to return on the condition he would be granted absolute power. Ivan IV went on to harass the boyars by executing, exiling, and forcibly removing them from their positions of power.

Despite his increasing reputation as a mentally unstable leader, he had many impressive achievements. He made a profitable trade agreement with England and defeated the Kazan Khanate, the Crimean horde, and many Siberian regions. Unfortunately, he also made several reckless decisions, such as the Livonian War, which lasted for twenty-four years and drained Russia of necessary resources. During the war, Russia fought against the Polish-Lithuanian Commonwealth and the Swedish Empire.

Ivan IV died in 1584 of a stroke. Ivan IV had murdered his eldest son in a fit of passion, so the throne passed to Feodor Ivanovich, a man who was not mentally capable of ruling.

Time of Troubles

Unfortunately, Feodor Ivanovich died in 1598 without an heir, which left Russia in a state of dynastic crisis. The Zemsky Sobor, or Great National Assembly, appointed Boris Godunov as Feodor's successor. According to reports, Feodor had been mentally challenged, and Boris was the boyar who effectively assisted Feodor during his reign. However, many other noble families viewed Boris as low-ranking before his appointment as tsar and refused to follow him. Thus, Boris had a short and troubled reign, which ended in 1605.

From 1601 to 1603, a devastating famine afflicted Russia and caused the deaths of about two million Russians. The famine was caused by a volcanic eruption in Peru a year earlier. Unfortunately, the eruption caused temperatures to remain colder than usual during the day and plummeted to freezing at night, which killed vast amounts of crops. Residents desperately went to Moscow, looking for food while straining the city's resources.

Once the famine was over, things only got worse. Before Boris's reign, Feodor Ivanovich's younger brother had died after being reportedly stabbed (it is not known whether it was self-inflicted). However, many believed Feodor's younger brother, Dmitri, had escaped. As a result, a few pretenders came forward. For years, Russia was beset by the False Dmitris, with pretenders rising up and gaining followers to invade Russia. The first pretender was supported by the Lithuanians, Cossacks, and Russian exiles. False Dimitri I ascended to the throne in 1605 after Boris's death and the short reign of his son. However, Vasili Shuisky dethroned and killed the pretender before taking the throne for himself. He ruled from 1606 to 1610.

During Shuisky's rule, another false Dimitri appeared with the support of the Poles and Lithuanians. Around 1605, the Polish-Muscovite War began, lasting until 1618 and further straining Moscow's resources. Meanwhile, the boyars squabbled amongst themselves as they tried to take power for themselves.

Finally, Michael Romanov was elected as the tsar of Russia in 1613 by the Grand National Assembly.

Michael I Romanov

Michael I was born in 1596 to an important boyar named Feodor Nikitich Romanov, who had been exiled by Boris Godunov in 1600. However, the Romanovs rose to prominence during the Time of Troubles. Feodor had been forced to take monastic vows and became known as Patriarch Filaret. Michael was a popular choice for the throne since he was distantly related to Ivan the Terrible and Feodor Romanov. While the boyars were satisfied with the outcome, Michael's future was incredibly uncertain due to the political atmosphere that lingered due to the Time of Troubles.

Michael I proved to be a competent leader who managed to reinvigorate Moscow. He also developed the Razryadny Prikaz (provincial administration office) and the Posolsky Prikaz (the foreign office). He also managed to establish the Romanov dynasty, which would rule over Russia for the next few centuries. Michael I died in 1645, and his son, Alexis, succeeded him.

Michael I Romanov.
https://commons.wikimedia.org/wiki/File:Michael-I-Romanov-Wedekind.jpg

Alexis I had to deal with several riots in prominent cities like Novgorod and Pskov. During his reign, he also engaged in wars against Sweden and Poland. Despite all the trouble, he was known for being a peaceful ruler. He managed to enact a new legal code (the Sobornoye Ulozheniye), which led to the creation of a serf class and made official state documentation necessary to travel within the country. During this time, the Orthodox Church created new customs under the Great Moscow Synod, which led to the division of the church between those who adhered to the new traditions and the people who clung to the old traditions. Alexis I died in 1676 after about three decades of being on the throne.

Dynastic Dispute

Unfortunately, Alexis I's death caused another dynastic dispute, which would have consequences for the entire kingdom. The dispute began when the children of Alexis I's first wife and second wife began fighting over who had the right to the throne. At first, the fight was between Feodor III, Sofia Alekseyevna, and Ivan V, who were Alexis I's children from his first marriage, and Peter Alekseyevich, who was the son of Alexis I's second wife. Feodor III became the tsar but died after six years of ruling due to illness.

Ultimately, Ivan V and Peter were forced to share the Russian throne, an arrangement that would last until 1696, when Ivan V died.

Peter the Great

Peter Alekseyevich was born in 1672 to Alexis I and Natalya Kirillovna Naryshkina. When he inherited the throne in 1696 (after ruling beside his half-brother), he found that Russia was severely underdeveloped compared to other European countries. Russia was mostly cut off from the Western world and had rejected any attempts to connect with the West, which meant Russia was cut off from modern movements like the Renaissance and Reformation. Peter wanted more for Russia and almost immediately instituted massive reforms to modernize the country. He reorganized the Russian army, involved himself in the Russian Orthodox Church, reorganized the territorial divisions of the country, and separated schools from religious control.

Peter the Great.
Jean-Marc Nattier, Public domain, via Wikimedia Commons;
https://commons.wikimedia.org/wiki/File:Jean-Marc_Nattier,_Pierre_Ier_(1717)_-002.jpg

Unfortunately, Peter faced a lot of opposition from the nobility, as his reforms touched on every aspect of Russian life. He was able to move past the opposition and brought experts to Russia to advance technology. Peter founded the first Russian newspaper, refined the gentry, and updated the alphabet. He proved that he was a progressive thinker and worked hard to turn Russia into a great nation.

Peter was also a capable politician who appointed a senate, regulated state administration, and made great strides in foreign policy. He managed to gain more territories in Latvia, Finland, and Estonia and even defeated the Swedish Army in 1709. During the battle with the Swedish Army, Peter proved his military capabilities when he routed the Swedish troops to the city of Poltava during an especially brutal winter. Peter managed to secure access to the Black Sea after several wars with Turkey. He also commissioned the city of St. Petersburg along the Neva River, which would eventually be called the "window to Europe" and Russia's capital.

During his reign, he visited England to learn more about shipbuilding and navigation, which helped him build Russia's navy. King William III of England assisted Peter, as he was hoping for a way to increase trade with Russia. In 1703, Peter achieved his goal when a fleet was established in the Baltic Sea, allowing Russia to become a formidable naval power.

Peter the Great encouraged industrial growth, allowing the economy to flourish, and introduced many progressive policies that ushered Russia into a new age and brought it up to speed with European advancements.

Russo-Persian War

The Russo-Persian War is also known as Peter the Great's Persian campaign. Peter wanted to prevent the Ottoman Empire from taking land in the Caucasus and Caspian regions as Safavid Iran weakened. For years, Peter had been reforming his army and introducing new technologies to the Russian people. He also built a modern navy, something Russia had never had before.

It became clear that Peter's reforms had been successful since he secured a victory over Safavid Iran. The victory gave Russia control of areas in the North and South Caucasus, including the cities of Baku and Derbent. Russia also received the provinces of Gilan, Shirvan, Astarabad, and Mazandaran, as outlined in the Treaty of St. Petersburg.

Russia continued to control the Iranian territories for about a decade. However, during the Treaty of Resht of 1732 and the Treaty of Ganja of 1735, the lands were given back to Iran. Even though the lands were eventually returned to Iran, the Russo-Persian War was one of Peter the Great's last achievements and likely a source of great pride for the aging monarch since he personally participated in the campaigns.

Thanks to Peter the Great's victories, he was able to gain territories around the Baltic Sea, bringing an end to Swedish control of the Baltic. Peter the Great's reforms, foreign policies, and successful wars turned Russia into one of the most formidable European powers.

Tsar Peter the Great's Legacy

Peter the Great inherited a struggling nation that was completely behind its European peers. He sought to modernize Russia and turn it into one of the greatest nations on earth. For the most part, he was able to achieve his goals and earned his title of Peter the Great. While he had many achievements, his reign was not without its problems. Like many of his predecessors, he was known for being a tyrant who imposed cruel punishments on those who wronged him. His various reforms often led to an increase in taxes, but any rebellions or riots were immediately repressed.

Peter married twice and fathered about eleven legitimate children. Unfortunately, many of his children didn't survive infancy. He was a tall and handsome man who indulged in excessive tendencies and could be quite violent. While his reign was full of impressive achievements, he had a difficult personal life. His eldest son, Alexei, was found guilty of treason. Peter sentenced his son to death but sought any information that could exonerate him, even if the means of extracting that information meant torture. Alexei died after being interrogated in 1718.

Peter the Great died in 1725 and was entombed in St. Petersburg. He has been called the greatest Russian ruler, and his efforts certainly turned Russia into one of the great European nations. His efforts weren't always well received, and he often had to overcome formidable opposition from his own people as he reformed most parts of Russian life. Russia would be forever changed, and Peter the Great's legacy continues to be a source of pride for the Russian people.

Chapter 4: Catherine the Great and 18ᵗʰ-Century Russia

During the 18ᵗʰ century, Russia went through numerous major changes. Peter the Great built Russia's formidable navy and modernized the entire country. Once he died, his legacy would be continued by an unlikely source: a foreign woman. Catherine the Great rose to prominence during the 18ᵗʰ century and had a lasting impact on imperial Russia. She started off as a young princess in a strange court who eventually overthrew her own husband and took control of the country.

At this time, Russian explorers were making expeditions into the great unknown in the north while the Russian Enlightenment spread steadily throughout the vast country. The Russian Empire had been increasingly growing for years, but in the 18ᵗʰ century, it would finally reach its peak when it administered over five million square miles.

The Issue of Succession

Peter the Great was an excellent monarch who had many achievements. Unfortunately, he failed in one of the most vital aspects of his duties. He failed to name an heir before his death. His family life was somewhat complicated. Peter the Great was first married to Eudoxia Lopukhina, the daughter of a minor Russian noble, in 1689. However, the marriage wasn't a happy one, and he divorced Eudoxia in 1698. The couple had three children together, but only one survived childhood: the Tsarevich of Russia, Alexei Petrovich. Peter the Great then married his mistress, Marta Helena Skowrońska, a Polish-Lithuanian peasant who converted to Russian Orthodoxy and changed her name to Catherine. The couple had several children, but few survived childhood.

Peter was greatly disappointed by the young tsarevich, who didn't share his imposing stature and propensity for war. In 1715, Peter the Great threatened to cut Alexei from the line of succession. The threat worked better than Peter had expected, as Alexei offered to relinquish his right to the throne. Alexei didn't share many of Peter's progressive ideas, and there was a good chance that once Peter died, Alexei would undo much of his father's work. Peter retaliated by ordering his son to either become a monk or a worthy successor. There were concerns that Alexei would draw Peter's enemies to his side and become a serious threat. Alexei agreed to become a monk but fled the country with his mistress and sought refuge in Austria.

Alexei was forced to return to Russia in 1718, where he was put on trial for treason. His father publicly disowned him. Alexei was imprisoned and brutally tortured. While under torture, Alexei admitted to plotting his father's demise. Peter oversaw the torture but hesitated to execute his son. Alexei died in prison. Eudoxia was also punished on the false charge of adultery and publicly flogged. She was then confined in a monastery. In 1724, Peter crowned his second wife as empress, but by then, all his male children were dead.

Struggle for Power

When Peter the Great died in 1725, his failure to name an heir became extremely serious since the Russian people wondered who to look to for leadership. Russian law dictated that the monarch had the right to name his heir, which meant that his next of kin wasn't automatically eligible for the throne. As soon as Peter died, his wife, Catherine I, took the throne, but she became a puppet for Peter's ministers. Peter's chief advisor, Prince Aleksandr Danilovich Menshikov, made most of the pertinent decisions in the empire, but the other nobles soon caught wind of what he was doing and forced him to share power with others.

Once Catherine I died, the nobles made Peter's grandson, Peter II, the new tsar in 1727. He was very young when he took the throne; he was only around eleven years old. Peter II was Tsarevich Alexei's son through his marriage to a German princess. Nobles vied for power, and Peter II was used as a pawn. Menshikov aimed to marry the young tsar to his sixteen-year-old daughter Maria. However, Menshikov became sick, and Peter II was quickly influenced by other nobles who convinced the young tsar to exile Menshikov. Peter II complied but died in 1730.

The throne went to Peter the Great's niece, Anna. Anna's rule supported the old ways of doing things, undoing some of the progress made by Peter I, especially in regard to how the nobles were treated. She attempted to put her heir on the throne but was thwarted by the nobles who supported Peter I's daughter, Elizabeth. She gladly took the throne and continued many of her father's reforms.

Elizabeth I of Russia.
https://commons.wikimedia.org/wiki/File:Elizabeth_of_Russia_by_anonim_after_Caravaq
ue_(18_c,_priv.coll).jpg

Elizabeth I was a capable ruler who opened Russia's first university and won several notable battles. However, Elizabeth remained childless. Unlike her father, Elizabeth took care to name her heir. She chose her nephew, Peter, to succeed her and arranged his marriage to Princess Sophie of Anhalt-Zerbst. Elizabeth died in 1762.

The Great Northern Expedition

The Great Northern Expedition was one of the greatest exploration efforts in history. It was initiated by Peter the Great, who commissioned Vitus Bering to explore the Asian Pacific coast. The first and second expeditions resulted in the mapping of most of Siberia and some parts of North America, which had previously been unknown. The First Kamchatka Expedition lasted from 1725 to 1731, while the Second Kamchatka Expedition lasted from 1733 to 1743. The Second Kamchatka Expedition was incredibly successful and was later called the Great Northern Expedition.

Originally, Peter the Great wanted to find a North Sea route from Europe to the Pacific for the Russian Navy. The expedition was funded by the Admiralty College in St. Petersburg, and over three thousand people were involved. It was one of the largest projects of its kind in history.

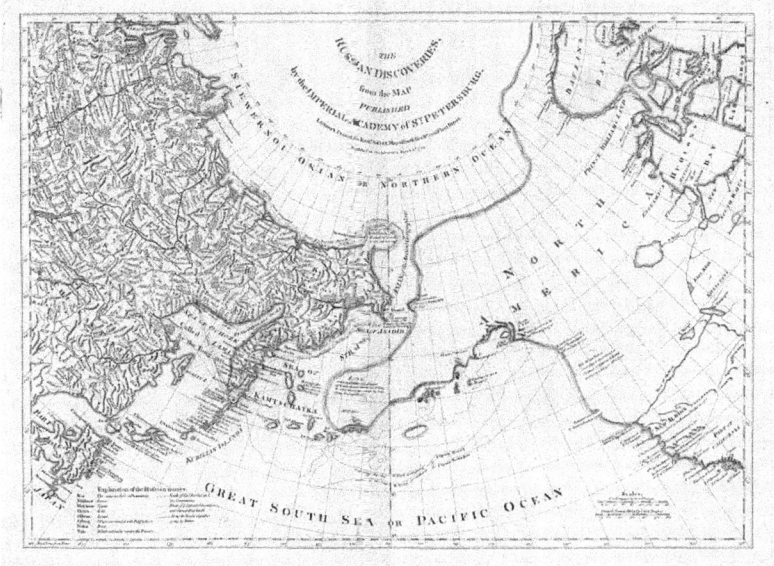

Russia's discoveries (Map published by the Imperial Academy of St. Petersburg).
https://commons.wikimedia.org/wiki/File:Jefferys_-_The_Russian_Discoveries.jpg#file

The expedition led to the discovery of Alaska, the Commander Islands, Bering Island, and the Aleutian Islands. It also resulted in detailed cartographical information of the northern coast of the Kuril Islands and Russia. For years, it was believed there was another landmass in the North Pacific, but this expedition helped to clear up that myth. It also resulted in extensive scientific research on Kamchatka and Siberia. Unfortunately, the expedition failed to find the Northeast Passage.

The Great Northern Expedition was a product of the Russian Enlightenment, and while it was one of Peter I's dreams, Empress Anna and Elizabeth I made the expedition a reality.

Peter III

Peter was born in the Duchy of Holstein-Gottorp to the duke of Holstein-Gottorp, Charles, and Anna Petrovna, the daughter of Peter the Great. Unfortunately, his mother died when he was still an infant, and his father died a few years later, leaving the young boy an orphan. His aunt, Elizabeth I, called him to Russia in 1742, where she proclaimed him as her heir. Elizabeth I also arranged his marriage to his second cousin. Sophia converted to the Russian Orthodox Church and changed her name to Catherine. However, their marriage was extremely unhappy. Reports indicate that Peter was an abrasive young man who made Catherine's life difficult. It should be noted that most of the information about Peter is derived from Catherine's memoirs.

Peter III and Catherine II of Russia.
https://commons.wikimedia.org/wiki/File:Peter_III_and_Catherine_II_of_Russia_(Anna_Rosina_Lisiewska)_-_Nationalmuseum_-_15939.tif

When Elizabeth I died, Peter took the throne, but he wasn't popular with the Russian people, who viewed him as a foreign ruler. Peter might have been Russian, but he was born in Germany and barely spoke any Russian. He also endorsed foreign policies and thinking. Peter was a pro-Prussian ruler who withdrew troops from the Seven Years' War. He also planned to go to war against Denmark but was overthrown before he could.

Peter showed a profound lack of understanding of his own country, as he endorsed the Lutheran religion. While this may have been an attempt to introduce religious freedom, his decisions were viewed as anti-Orthodox, which alienated him from his subjects. Peter and Catherine had one son together named Paul.

The Seven Years' War

The Seven Years' War has been called the first real "world war," as it involved an alliance of Russia, France, Sweden, Austria, and Saxony against Hanover, Great Britain, and Prussia. The war took place between 1756 and 1763. It took on an international component, as Britain and France fought against each other in India and North America.

The war can be traced back to 1748. The War of the Austrian Succession ended with the Treaty of Aix-la-Chapelle, which many viewed as a temporary measure. Austria lost the region of Silesia to Prussia, which was a wealthy land. Tensions brewed between the two countries, and their allies began preparing for war. Russia was worried about the increasing strength of Prussia and was willing to become allies with Austria to stop them.

In 1756, Frederick II of Prussia attacked Saxony, breaking its alliance with Austria. Eventually, Austria's allies attacked Prussia from all sides. The Prussians were forced to retreat in the face of the Franco-Russo-Austrian alliance. While the Prussians won a few battles, they needed something to change. Elizabeth I was notoriously anti-Prussian, but her successor, Peter III, didn't have the same views. Eventually, Russia entered into negotiations, and by 1763, most of Europe was feeling the financial strain of fighting the war. In 1763, the Treaty of Paris was signed, settling many issues between Britain, France, and Spain. The war led to the increased prestige of Prussia and Russia, while Spain and Holland were greatly reduced.

Rise of Catherine the Great

In 1762, Peter had been ruling for six months and had vastly underestimated his wife's hatred. During this time, he took a holiday to Oranienbaum while Catherine was left in St. Petersburg. She arranged a military regiment to protect her from Peter, and the clergy ordained her as the Russian ruler. She then arrested Peter and forced him to abdicate. Peter was assassinated a few days later by Alexei Orlov. While the timing of his death is suspicious, there is no evidence that Catherine murdered her husband.

Catherine the Great.
https://commons.wikimedia.org/wiki/File:Catherine_II_by_F.Rokotov_after_Roslin_(178 0s,_Hermitage).jpg)

Peter had proven that he didn't understand his own people, but Catherine was not like her husband. Catherine learned Russian almost as soon as she arrived in Russia and even spoke with a Russian accent while her husband could barely speak the language. During her marriage to Peter, she had taken the time to ingratiate herself with many powerful figures in the court. Once she sat on the throne, she quickly focused on expanding Russia's borders and continued many of Peter the Great's reforms. Catherine added the territories of Belarus, Lithuania, and Crimea to Russia. After making arrangements with Prussia and Austria, she received many lands in Central Europe.

Catherine instituted financial reforms and worked hard to improve Russia's economy. She was intensely interested in public health and opened several hospitals. The army was forced to update its medical practices under her reign. She even had herself inoculated against smallpox, which was a controversial procedure at the time. When the procedure worked, she promoted inoculations throughout the empire. Catherine's husband had ruled for about six months, but Catherine would go on to rule for over three decades and earn the title of "Catherine the Great."

Notable Features of the Catherinian Era

One of Catherine's goals was to incorporate Russia's culture and economy into Europe. She was an avid reader of philosophical books and particularly enjoyed the works of Diderot and Voltaire. In her opinion, Russia needed to catch up to Europe. She gave the press creative freedom, managed the economy well, and opened spaces where learned people could meet. All of these factors contributed to the Russian Enlightenment and intellectual life.

Catherine was responsible for a number of progressive reforms, including the Statute on the Provinces of 1775, which aimed to improve the government and institute more orphanages, schools, and hospitals. She set rules for provincial and municipal services and encouraged the nobles to take better care of their serfs. In Russia, serfs were people owned by noble landowners. They gave away their rights in exchange for protection and support during difficult times. They worked on the nobles' lands and were required to pay a portion of their grain as taxes to the nobles. Serfs had limited rights, but Catherine afforded them new rights. For example, if a noble wasn't taking care of their serfs, the serfs were allowed to make a complaint. This gave serfs bureaucratic status they previously didn't have. Serfs also became more educated, as some nobles chose to send certain serfs to schools opened by Catherine. They would return as skilled employees whom the nobles could employ.

Catherine stimulated the economy by lowering grain prices to increase exports and decreased the regulation of manufacturing. Her reforms brought about a golden age in Russian history, which would survive after her death in 1796.

The Russian Enlightenment

Catherine the Great considered herself to be one of Europe's most enlightened rulers, and many historians are inclined to believe this claim. The Russian Enlightenment was inspired by ideas pioneered in Western Europe. It first found prominence under Peter the Great but reached a new high under Catherine the Great. The Enlightenment was a period of cultural change that brought about developments in fields like architecture, mathematics, and fashion. Enlightenment ideals were centered around innovation, the search for knowledge, and progress. Russian leaders held absolute power and used this to either encourage or hinder the Russian Enlightenment.

St. Petersburg quickly became the capital of the Russian Enlightenment, and the movement reached the nobles first. Children of nobles were sent to Western European schools, where they learned about mathematics, science, and literature. The Enlightenment also helped modernize the Russian army, as Peter the Great's reforms aimed to greatly improve the army according to Western European standards. Peter the Great was so eager to modernize Russia that he imposed a beard tax on Russians, forcing them to shave to look more like Western Europeans. Beards had traditionally been a sign of manliness in Russian culture, but that didn't matter in Peter the Great's quest to modernize the country. Soon, the noble court began wearing Western European fashions, especially French fashion.

Catherine the Great continued Peter the Great's efforts to modernize Russia. Her efforts led to Russia's golden age.

The Peasant Uprising of 1773

In 1773, Yemelyan Pugachev led what would become one of the most influential rebellions in Russian history. While Catherine the Great brought about reforms that benefited the serfs, most didn't feel the benefits. To secure the nobles' cooperation, she increased the nobles' authority over the serfs, which led to increasing unrest. Between 1762 and 1769, more than fifty rebellions broke out. Unrest grew to a fevered pitch.

Pugachev gained support from the peasants and Cossacks because he promised to secure more rights for the serfs, including lands of their own. In the past, serfs could appeal to the monarch if they were abused by nobles, but Catherine the Great cut off this communication when she decreed that serfs could make formal complaints with the government instead. This angered many serfs. Pugachev was able to rally thousands of rebels until he led an army of about 100,000.

At the time, Russia was locked in a war against Turkey. However, Catherine the Great was forced to resolve that quickly in order to have enough troops to bring an end to the rebellions.

The Cossacks were known for being skilled and brutal warriors who were obligated to help the Russian army. Pugachev was a Cossack who ended up defecting from the army. The Russian government alienated numerous Cossacks when they revoked many of the Cossacks' privileges, which caused many Cossacks to join Pugachev's cause.

Pugachev took on the name of Peter III and issued a manifesto that gave serfs freedom and the right to own their land. The rebellion dragged on for over a year and spread like wildfire. Rebels were encouraged to kill nobles, and it is estimated that hundreds of nobles were murdered. The government killed thousands of rebels, while others were branded and sent to Siberian prisons.

The rebellion was finally suppressed in 1774, and Pugachev was executed. However, Pugachev's rebellion inspired new ideas in the minds of serfs, and imperial Russia was impacted by the echoes of the rebellion until its fall in 1917.

The Russian Army in the 18th Century

During the 18th century, the Russian army experienced a "golden age." Thanks to Peter the Great's efforts, the Russian army became one of the best forces in the world, as it managed to defeat Poland, Sweden, and the Ottoman Empire. The army and navy were highly organized, and progressive reforms gave Russian soldiers access to new technologies and tactics. At the time, the Imperial Russian Army was a prestigious institution that was only surpassed by the church and the royals. Most social classes were involved in the army in one way or another.

Badge of the Russian Imperial Army.

Peter the Great introduced conscription in 1699. Peasants were conscripted according to population numbers, and in the 18th century, conscription was for life. At first, commoners were able to rise through the ranks of the army and were given titles. However, this practice was abolished during Catherine the Great's reign. A notable general from this period was Alexander Suvorov, who fought in Crimea and the Caucasus. He also fought during the Russo-Turkish War, which lasted from 1787 to 1792. He won many victories for the Russian army and was highly decorated.

The Imperial Russian Army was a formidable power that would serve Russia well when Napoleon decided to invade.

Chapter 5: From Napoleon to the Crimean War

The 18th century ushered in a golden age in Russian history, with progressive leaders introducing reforms that modernized the army and stimulated the economy. This meant Russia was in a good position in the years leading up to Napoleon's invasion. The 19th century brought more changes, and Russian monarchs strived to live up to the legacy of their predecessors. It was a time marked by revolts and opposing ideas that would eventually lead to the end of the Russian golden age.

In time, Russia would become embroiled in the Crimean War, a grueling military engagement that would have disastrous consequences for the Imperial Russian Army.

Napoleon's Invasion of Russia

In 1799, Napoleon Bonaparte took power in France and became a serious threat to Europe. He took Belgium, Holland, parts of Italy, Germany, and Croatia. It seemed the French emperor was invincible, as his power grew to include parts of Poland, Spain, and Switzerland. No one seemed to be able to beat Napoleon.

At the time, the Russians were experiencing the negative impacts of Napoleon's reign since trade declined sharply. Tsar Alexander I, who ruled Russia at the time, decided to push back against Napoleon by enforcing a strict tax on French products and refused to give one of his sisters to Napoleon in marriage. Russia was also trading with Britain, the latter of which was one of France's biggest rivals.

Napoleon wanted to teach Alexander I a lesson and amassed a massive army to invade Russia in June 1812. He had every reason to be confident, as his Grande Armèe numbered around 450,000, while the Russian army numbered around 200,000. Napoleon expected to defeat the Russians quickly and force Alexander I into negotiations.

The Russians had another plan. The Grande Armèe captured the city of Vilna a few days after the initial invasion, and to their surprise, the Russians put up very little fight. As Napoleon advanced, the Russians pulled back into the interior. To make matters worse, Russian roads were in a deplorable state, making it impossible for supply carts to reach the French army in time. Winter was setting in, and thousands of French soldiers and horses died from exposure. As the Russians retreated, they set fire to fields and supplies that could aid the French. The Russians employed a scorched-earth policy, which caused the French to become increasingly desperate. Soon, the French soldiers were afflicted with diseases like typhus and dysentery, which decimated their ranks.

Finally, in September 1812, the Russians made a stand, leading to the Battle of Borodino, which led to significant losses on both sides. When the Grande Armèe entered Moscow a few days later, they found the Russians had set fire to the historic city. There were large amounts of liquor left behind but no food. Napoleon was forced to retreat soon after due to the winter. It had become apparent the Grande Armèe couldn't maintain its position.

The Grande Armèe was pressed for food and supplies. The massive army's numbers had dwindled down to about 100,000 men. The Russian army constantly attacked the Grande Armèe's rearguard, which led to even more casualties. As winter progressed, thousands more died from the cold. Reports state that some men cut open dead animals and crawled inside for warmth, while others say soldiers stacked dead bodies over windows and doors to keep the cold out.

By December, Napoleon had to return to Paris, as rumors of a coup reached him. It took a few more days for the French to leave Russia completely. The disastrous invasion was the beginning of the end for Napoleon.

The Defeat of Napoleon

The invasion of Russia left Napoleon in a weakened state, and Prussia, Sweden, and Austria decided to help Britain and Russia defeat Napoleon once and for all. Napoleon quickly assembled a new army. While it was almost as large as his previous army, the soldiers lacked battle experience. In October 1813, he suffered a massive defeat at the Battle of Leipzig. A few months later, Paris was captured, and Napoleon was exiled to Elba.

However, Napoleon was far from ready to give up. He was able to escape Elba in 1815 and immediately returned to France, where he set up his government. Allied troops quickly responded to his escape, but Napoleon won significant victories against the Prussians. His goal was to prevent Europe from uniting. In June, Napoleon led his troops to meet Arthur Wellesley, Duke of Wellington, at the village of Waterloo in Brussels. Napoleon made a series of fatal mistakes, and the Duke of Wellington proved to be a formidable enemy. The French army was defeated, and Napoleon was forced to retreat. He later abdicated in favor of his son and surrendered to the British. Napoleon was exiled to the remote island of St. Helena, where he died a few years later of stomach cancer.

The Decembrist Revolt of 1825

Tsar Alexander I died unexpectedly on December 1ˢᵗ, 1825, and his royal guards quickly rallied around his brother, Constantine Pavlovich. However, Constantine had renounced his rights to the throne, so Alexander I's younger brother, Nicholas, decided to take the throne for himself.

Meanwhile, some imperial officers decided to create a society known as the Union of Salvation in 1816. In 1825, the society split into Southern and Northern factions. The Northern Society wanted a constitutional monarchy, equality in the law, and the abolishment of serfdom. The Southern Society was more radical and wanted to create a republic that redistributed lands between the state and the peasants, as well as abolish the monarchy. Many officers belonging to the Union of Salvation were indignant about the injustices faced by peasants and rejected courtly traditions, instead preferring an academic lifestyle. They embraced the "Russian way of life" that the peasants experienced.

The Northern Society refused to support the new tsar. Instead, they proclaimed their support of Constantine. On December 26th, 1825, about three thousand rebels showed up at Senate Square. They were faced with nine thousand loyal troops. Nicholas I chose to send a war hero, Count Mikhail Miloradovich, to negotiate with the rebels, but he was shot during his speech.

The rebels attempted to take the Winter Palace but were forced to retreat. Nicholas I ordered a cavalry charge on the rebels but was forced to retreat as well. He then ordered his troops to open fire on the rebels, who retreated and tried to regroup on the frozen waters of the Neva River. Nicholas's troops shot cannons at the ice, which caused many rebels to fall into the icy waters. With so many rebel deaths, the revolt came to an end, and the remaining rebels were exiled to Siberia.

The Decembrists failed in their attempts but created a divide between the government and reformers, which would only become bigger and eventually lead to more revolutionary movements.

Nicholas I

Nicholas I was deeply impacted by the Decembrist movement since he could have been killed. As a result, he abandoned many of the progressive reforms initiated by his predecessors and focused on Russian nationalism, autocracy, and the Russian Orthodox Church. It also caused him to become determined to control Russian society and solidified his belief that he needed to be an autocrat who did whatever was necessary to restrain the people.

The government started censoring many areas of public life, such as education and publications. One of Nicholas I's ministers introduced "autocracy, Orthodoxy, and nationality" as the main principles of the government. The Third Section of His Imperial Chancellery (the secret police) was equipped with spies and informers, who were spread throughout the country.

Nicholas I of Russia.

The tsar's unlimited power was emphasized, and the traditions of Russian Orthodoxy became increasingly emphasized. However, these policies led to the repression of the Russian people, foreigners, and non-Russian religions. He also became more aggressive toward the Ottoman Empire. Nicholas I left behind a legacy of being one of the most reactionary leaders in European history.

The Russo-Persian War (1826–1828)

The Russians and Persians had long fought over territories located along the Caspian Sea and in the Transcaucasus. Two Russo-Persian wars had already taken place; the first lasted from 1804 to 1813, while the second occurred between 1826 and 1828. The Persian Shah Fath-Ali hoped to claim Karabakh, Talesh, Shakki, and Shirvan, as he wanted to prevent the Russians from taking over the territories when they annexed the Kingdom of Georgia (which had also been claimed by the Persians). Meanwhile, the Russians wanted to capture more territories, especially along the Kura and Aras Rivers. The First Russo-

Persian War was won by the Russians, who were able to obtain a lot of the territories they were after, including northern Azerbaijan and Dagestan, turning the local territories into vassal states.

Soon after Alexander I died, the Persians decided to invade Russian territories while the Russian government was dealing with the Decembrist Revolt. At first, the Persians managed to secure several victories while the Russian general, Alexei Yermolov, desperately tried to secure reinforcements from St. Petersburg. While the Russians were caught unaware, they were able to prevent the Persians from advancing too far. In 1827, the Russians captured several Persian territories, including Yerevan and Tabriz. The Persians were forced to abandon their war efforts and signed the Treaty of Turkmenchay in 1828, which allowed the Russians to keep Yerevan and the territories leading up to the Aras River. The Persians were also forced to pay about twenty million rubles to the Russians.

Greek Revolution of 1821

Greece had been ruled by the Ottomans since the 15th century. For years, the Greeks tried to overthrow the Ottomans but remained unsuccessful until 1821. In 1814, a secret society called the Society of Friends was formed due to the revolutionary ideas sweeping through Europe. Their aim was to liberate Greece and finally overthrow the Turks. In 1821, a widespread revolution broke out, which the Ottomans struggled to put down. However, the Greeks soon began fighting between themselves, and the Turks called on their vassal states for help, including the Eyalet of Egypt (a part of Egypt controlled by the Ottomans). The revolution began failing as the Turks began winning more territories.

However, Britain, France, and Russia decided to get involved. At the Battle of Navarino in 1827, the Ottoman-Egyptian fleet was destroyed. Russia invaded the Ottoman Empire, and the Turks were forced to grant the Greeks their freedom in the Treaty of Adrianople in 1829.

The Russo-Turkish War (1828–1829)

The Turks didn't take Russian involvement in the Greek Revolution lightly. In retaliation for the Battle of Navarino, the Ottoman sultan, Mahmud II, closed the Dardanelles (an internationally significant waterway in Turkey) to Russian ships, which left both sides poised for war. In the beginning, Emperor Nicholas I commanded the Russian army, while Agha Hussein Pasha led the Ottoman army. The fighting started in the Balkans, namely in modern-day Bulgaria, against three important Ottoman strongholds: Varna, Silistra, and Shumen. The fighting was intense. The Russians took Varna but were forced to retreat due to their ill-equipped soldiers and the diseases that were raging through the ranks. The Russians managed to capture Burgas and Adrianople, which were heavy blows for the Ottoman Empire.

Besides fighting in the Balkans, fighting also took place in the Caucasus. The Russian army was able to win several territories on this front. During the war, thousands of Armenians were forced to move into Russian territory.

Eventually, the Ottoman sultan was forced to negotiate a peace treaty since he faced such a significant loss of territory. On September 14th, 1829, the Treaty of Adrianople was signed. Russia obtained territories east of the Black Sea and the mouth of the Danube. The sultan also gave Russia control of parts of Armenia, and it was allowed to occupy Wallachia and Moldavia. The treaty forced the sultan to recognize Greek independence.

The Russo-Turkish War led to significant territorial gains for the Russian Empire and helped the Greeks finally bring an end to their nearly decade-long war for freedom.

The Polish Uprising (1830–1831)

The Polish Uprising, or November Uprising, saw armed Polish troops rise up against Russia. In 1795, Poland was no longer an autonomous political entity. In 1807, the Duchy of Warsaw was created as a result of Poland's participation in the Napoleonic Wars. When Napoleon was defeated, Poland was divided between Austria, which received territories in the south; Russia, which received hegemony over the Congress Kingdom of Poland; and Prussia, which took control of the Grand Duchy of Poznan. The Congress Kingdom had its own constitution and was only supposed to be indirectly subject to Russia. However, the Russian monarchy frequently disregarded the constitution.

In 1829, Nicholas I claimed the title of "King of Poland." Grand Duke Constantine (the one who didn't want the throne) was the governor of Poland. He disregarded the Polish constitution and abolished several Polish patriotic societies. Constantine replaced

Polish administrators with Russians and allowed serious conflicts to develop within the Polish army. To make matters worse, the Russians planned to use the Polish army to bring an end to the Belgian Revolution and France's July Revolution.

A group of Polish rebels took up arms in 1830 and attacked Constantine's seat of power at Belweder Palace. They managed to take the city's arsenal, and the local Polish government was quickly reorganized. The Polish hoped to gain their complete freedom but soon faced an all-out war against Russia. While the Polish fought hard and found many sympathetic voices, the major powers of the time—Britain and France—didn't come to their aid. In October 1831, the remainder of the Polish army surrendered to Russia.

After the uprising ended, Polish women wore black jewelry to profess their mourning for the loss of their homeland.

Slavophiles vs. Westernizers

Peter the Great implemented several reforms with the hopes of replacing traditionalist and medieval systems with the principles of the Enlightenment. Some of Peter the Great's predecessors, especially Catherine the Great, endorsed his reforms and imposed more changes to Russian politics, economics, education, and culture. Machinery was modernized, the bureaucracy was refined, and Western European tastes and ideals were upheld. This led to the development of a group called the Westernizers, who emphatically believed Russia needed to adhere to Western European values and ideas.

Not everyone was happy about the Westernization of Russia, though. Slavophilia was a movement that opposed the values of Western Europe. They didn't want Russia to embrace democracy, materialism, or atheism; instead, they promoted the values of medieval Russia. Some admitted a few Western values had merit, while others rejected all Western ideas and promoted the absolute power of the tsar and the church. The Slavophiles believed they were protecting Russia's culture and traditions. Rural life was glorified, and Slavophiles endeavored to protect peasant communities against the growing working class. Many Slavophiles adopted traditional Russian aesthetics and rejected Peter the Great's reforms. The Slavophiles also endorsed a militant stance of religious intolerance.

While the 18th century saw the rise of the Russian Enlightenment, the 19th century saw the rejection of many of those ideals, especially under the reign of Nicholas I, whose government upheld many Slavophile ideals.

The Crimean War (1853–1856)

By the 1850s, the Ottoman Empire was in a massive decline, and Nicholas I saw the opportunity to expand Russia's borders. However, Britain and France were concerned a Russian takeover would negatively impact their trade routes and were determined to prevent Nicholas I's power grab. The Crimean War took place in the Crimean Peninsula and was the conflict that made Florence Nightingale, the founder of modern nursing, famous. It was a brutal war that caused the deaths of about 650,000 people.

The Attack on the Malakoff (the main Russian fortification before Sevastopol during the Crimean War).

Tensions rose between Orthodox worshipers and Catholics who wanted access to holy sites ruled by the Turks. After several Orthodox monks were killed in Bethlehem, Nicholas I demanded that the Orthodox worshipers be allowed to access religious sites freely and that he should be made the protector of Orthodox worshipers in the Ottoman Empire. The Turks refused, and

Nicholas invaded the Turkish principalities of Walachia and Moldavia. The Turks declared war on Russia in 1853.

The Russians slaughtered thousands of Ottoman soldiers and sailors. The brutality of the war inflamed Europe to fight Russia. Britain and France joined Turkey and sent their armies and navies to protect the Middle Eastern nation, especially Istanbul. The British and French expected a short engagement but soon found themselves embroiled in a bloody war that dragged on.

Both sides suffered heavy casualties, and the Russian Imperial Army found itself besieged from all sides. When Austria threatened to join the fight against Russia, the Russians were forced to end the war and signed the Treaty of Paris in March 1856. The Russians had to give up the territories they had seized, and their army was never the same again. Tensions between the Turks and Russians continued for years. They even found themselves on opposite sides in World War I.

Chapter 6: Tsar Alexander II's Reforms and Tsar Alexander III's Setback to Autocracy

The Crimean War was a brutal conflict that led to the deaths of thousands of Russian soldiers. It severely diminished the Russian army, which had been a formidable force for decades. When Tsar Alexander II took the throne, he instituted a number of radical reforms that could have changed Russia forever. However, his reforms angered powerful people, and he was assassinated in the streets of St. Petersburg.

His successor, Alexander III, didn't have the same goals of reformation as his father, so Alexander II's reforms were promptly reversed. Alexander III faced many challenges while firmly establishing his autocratic rule but boasted a few notable achievements, such as the construction of the Trans-Siberian Railway.

Tsar Alexander II

Alexander II was born in 1818 and was the oldest son of Tsar Nicholas I and Charlotte of Prussia. During his early years, St. Petersburg was far from the intellectual center that it had once been. Any intellectual innovation or freedom of thought was strongly suppressed, and speaking against the government was a serious offense. Unlike his father, Alexander II wasn't interested in war and shared many of the same notions as his teacher, the liberal poet Vasily Zhukovsky. He was reported to be a kind and gentle young man.

Alexander II of Russia.
Nikolay Lavrov, Public domain, via Wikimedia Commons;
https://commons.wikimedia.org/wiki/File:Alexander_II_of_Russia_by_N.Lavrov_(1868,_Museum_of_Artillery).jpg

Alexander II's father died in 1855, and he ascended to the throne. For the first few months of his reign, he was preoccupied with settling the Crimean War, which had become a costly and humiliating drain on Russia's resources. As soon as the war was concluded, he began enacting a number of reforms. Many of the educated classes supported Alexander II's reforms since they were eager to develop Russia's natural resources and reorganize the government's administration.

Alexander II proved to be a shrewd and cautious man who used his autocracy to bring about practical and progressive reforms. However, not everyone was happy with his reforms, and he became the target of a number of assassination attempts.

Some of his reforms included reorganizing the navy and army. He followed the French model to create a new judicial administration system and penal code. Alexander II simplified the criminal and civil processes, found a way for rural districts to govern themselves with elective assemblies, and abolished capital punishment.

Serf Emancipation of 1861

Alexander II made some changes to the legislation that allowed new freedoms in industry and commerce. As a result, a number of limited liability companies were created. He also wanted to construct a vast network of railways so intellectuals could more easily develop Russia's natural resources and increase the army's ability to protect the country. However, the more reforms he developed, the more he realized that serfdom was a serious problem. Alexander II created a number of committees dedicated to improving the serfs' situation. Emancipation committees were required to follow principles set by the monarch.

The question of solving the problems brought about by serfdom impacted all of Russian life, from the economy to politics. Alexander was presented with the problem of whether or not serfs should be laborers who were economically dependent on their landlords or if they should be allowed to become a class of landowners. Alexander II wanted the serfs to be able to own their own land, and on March 3rd, 1861, the serfs were emancipated.

Sale of Alaskan Territory to the US

For years, Russia had been looking to sell its territory in Alaska. The area was remote and extremely difficult to defend. Selling the territory made more sense than losing the land to Russian enemies. US President Andrew Johnson's secretary of state, William Seward, took the lead in discussions with Russia.

Negotiations for the sale began in March 1867, and while Seward was enthusiastic about the project, the American population didn't agree with his sentiments. Most believed the land was barren and useless. The project was called "Andrew Johnson's Polar Bear Garden" and "Seward's Folly." Much of the animosity may have resulted from Johnson's unpopular term as president.

Despite the unpopularity of the project, about 586,412 square miles of Alaskan territory was sold for $7.2 million, which amounted to a little less than 2 cents per acre.

Russo-Turkish War of 1877–1878

Even though the Crimean War ended and Russia had given back the territory it had taken during the war, there was still lingering animosity between Russia and the Ottoman Empire. In 1877, those tensions turned into an all-out war when the Russians and Turks disagreed over the rights of Orthodox Slavs who lived in the Balkans. The Treaty of Paris stated the Balkan Christians were to be protected by the European powers. When peasants rebelled in Bulgaria in 1876, the Turkish brutally put down the revolts.

This led to anti-Turkish efforts in Serbia. In 1876, several European powers met in Constantinople to come up with a compromise, which the Turks rejected in 1877. To protect the Balkan Slavs, Russia represented the European powers and prepared for war. The Russians launched an offensive in the Balkans and the Caucasus region. They were ultimately successful, and the war was concluded with the Treaty of San Stefano in 1878.

The Russians negotiated independence for Serbia, Romania, and Montenegro while receiving a large portion of Turkish territory for itself. Russia also pressed for the autonomy of Bulgaria, which would be ruled with Russian influence. However, Britain and Austria-Hungary forced Russia to revise the Treaty of San Stefano at the Congress of Berlin a few months later. The revisions angered many parties and caused tensions that would explode in the future.

While the Congress of Berlin allowed many Russian gains, it was still viewed as a defeat. Many Russians felt that Germany had failed to support Russia at the Congress of Berlin. Austria-Hungary was also seen with increasing suspicion, which had started during the Crimean War.

Alexander II's Assassination

Alexander II faced many assassination attempts. He was a progressive leader, but he retained his autocracy and was known for opposing political parties that opposed him, which earned him many enemies. In 1866, Dmitry Karakozov tried to kill the tsar. After Alexander II escaped death, he built a series of churches to commemorate his escape. In 1879, a former student named Alexander Soloviev attempted to shoot the tsar in the Square of the

Guards Staff. The tsar had seen the revolver that Soloviev was carrying and ran away.

That same year, a radical group of revolutionists formed the Narodnaya Volya, or People's Will. The group aimed to create a social revolution and was willing to use terrorism to attain its goal. In 1880, some rebels placed a bomb under the dining room in the Winter Palace. Alexander II was late to dinner and narrowly missed the explosion, but sixty-seven other people were killed or injured.

In 1881, Alexander II signed the Loris-Melikov Constitution, which aimed to create legislative commissions comprised of elected officials. On the day he signed the proclamation, his carriage was traveling along the streets of St. Petersburg when a bomb went off, injuring surrounding civilians. Reports indicate that Alexander survived the initial blast but was met by a suicide bomber who hit him with a grenade. Tsar Alexander II died from his injuries a few hours later. All the assassins were executed. Alexander II's successor, Alexander III, rejected the Loris-Melikov Constitution.

Alexander III

Alexander III was born in 1845 and was the son of Alexander II and Maria of Hesse. Unlike his father, he didn't harbor liberal sentiments and was seen as unrefined and physically powerful. He was his father's second son, and he had little hope of inheriting the throne since his oldest brother, Nicholas, was healthy. Nicholas received the education of a prince, while Alexander was educated as a grand duke, which didn't go much further beyond secondary instruction. When Nicholas died suddenly in 1865, Alexander was thrust into the spotlight and had to study the principles of law and administration. It is believed that Alexander's teacher, Konstantin Pobedonostsev, inspired Alexander's belief that Russian Orthodoxy was a cornerstone of Russian patriotism. Alexander was married to Princess Dagmar of Denmark, who had previously been engaged to his brother Nicholas. Their marriage proved to be a happy one.

Alexander III of Russia.

During the last years of Alexander II's reign, it became clear there was a divide between the monarch and his heir. Alexander II sometimes openly ridiculed Slavophiles, while his son was becoming more of a Slavophile by the day. Another notable difference between the two was that Alexander II had pro-German tendencies, while the tsarevich displayed pro-French sympathies.

When Alexander II was assassinated in 1881, Alexander III was finally able to enact his ideas. During his time as tsarevich, he uncovered rampant corruption within the government and wanted to reform the military. Alexander III also disapproved of many of his father's progressive reforms, believing the reforms had led to the problems Russia was facing. As a result, he reversed much of his father's work as soon as he became king.

The Famine of 1891/92

In 1891, a dry autumn prevented the Russian peasants from planting their fields on time. The delay would prove to be disastrous. The subsequent winter was unusually cold, but almost no snow fell. Snow was supposed to freeze the Volga River and protect seedlings from frost. Unfortunately, the Volga River flooded, and the frost killed the rest of the seedlings. The flood also destroyed fodder that was supposed to feed horses. The next spring was extremely windy, and it carried away topsoil and the remaining seedlings. Then, summer began early and proved to be long and dry. As a result, horses, peasants, and crops began to die. To make matters worse, there were several widespread cholera outbreaks.

The government blamed the famine on a poor harvest and prevented newspapers from reporting what was going on. There was more than enough grain to feed the dying peasants, but the railways weren't able to distribute the grain quickly enough. The government also delayed closing grain exports, and when they finally did, the merchants had a month's warning, which caused them to quickly export what they had. The minister of finance, Ivan Vyshnegradsky, shouldered a lot of the blame, as he had raised taxes so that peasants would sell more grain.

In late 1891, the government urged citizens to form anti-famine organizations. One of the volunteers who formed a committee was the famous writer Leo Tolstoy, who publicly blamed the Russian Orthodox Church and the tsar for mismanaging the situation. He was excommunicated for his criticisms, and the church forbade people from accepting his relief efforts.

Several royals, including the tsar and tsarina, raised a few million rubles for starving peasants. Local governments received about 150 million rubles in relief money, but they were only allowed to lend to peasants who would be able to pay them back. Many starving peasants were forced to eat raw flour and "famine bread," which was made from moss, bark, and husks. In 1892, the government bought about thirty thousand horses to plow the fields. The American government raised about $75 million (about $2 billion in modern currency) to help the Russians; the money was mainly given out in the form of loans.

The famine started along the Volga River and spread as far as the Black Sea and the Urals. By the time the famine came to an end, nearly half a million people had died. This caused lasting anger toward the tsarist government.

May Laws

The May Laws were a program of temporary laws enacted by Alexander III in May 1882 pertaining to the Jews in Russia. When Alexander II was assassinated, the blame was placed on the Russian Jewish population. As a result, anti-Jewish sentiments rose, which led to a number of extremely violent riots. To make matters worse, the government declared the problem had risen because of Alexander II's reforms, which were significantly more progressive than Alexander III's own views.

To come up with a solution to the violence, Jewish representatives met with government officials in 1882. One of the proposed solutions was a mass exodus of the Jewish people from Russia to Central Asia. This was seen as an extreme measure, so a number of "temporary laws" were negotiated. The problem was the rural peasant class viewed the Jewish merchants as rivals and claimed the Jews were disrupting business in rural areas. As a result, the May Laws stated the Jewish population was restricted from settling outside of towns. Real estate sold to Jews outside of towns was revoked, and the Jews were forbidden from trading on certain days. Police were tasked with ensuring the May Laws were followed, which led to the continued harassment of Jews. The laws were finally taken away in 1917.

Franco-Russian Alliance of 1891–1894

In 1875, France faced the prospect of war against Germany. Eventually, Russia and Britain were able to force Germany to back down from starting a war. While France and Germany were experiencing tensions, France engendered friendly relations with Russia. By the end of the 1850s, Russia had received a few large loans from France. In 1892, the Russians and French signed a military convention that stipulated the two countries would support each other in the event of a German attack. By that point, Germany had grown to become a formidable power that was looking to preserve and increase its territory. In 1882, Germany formed the Triple Alliance with Austria-Hungary and Italy.

As the years passed, Russo-German relations began to deteriorate, which only pushed Russia and France closer. In 1894, the Russo-France military alliance was formalized.

The Franco-Russian alliance was mutually beneficial, as France was able to increase its colonial powers with Russia's help, while France helped Russia expand into Manchuria. While Russia was the dominant power in the alliance at first, the tsarist government took out a number of large loans from France, which meant Russia became financially dependent on France.

This alliance would prove to have serious consequences during the First World War, and Russia's financial dependence would cause the alliance to become unpopular in the future.

The Construction of the Trans-Siberian Railway

For years, Russia's railway was left in a deplorable state and eventually became ineffective, which was plainly demonstrated during the devastating famine in 1891. However, Alexander III found a way to fix that. He personally appointed ministers to supervise the construction of a massive railway system. Today, the railway connects western Russia to eastern Russia. It is still the longest railway line in the world, stretching about 5,772 miles long. It starts in Moscow and ends in the city of Vladivostok, which is located by the Sea of Japan.

The building began in 1891 and was finally completed in 1916. While the railway was still being built, adventurers came to see the progress. They eagerly wrote about the sights and adventures they encountered, which only increased the excitement surrounding the project.

Construction of the Trans-Siberian Railway.
https://commons.wikimedia.org/wiki/File:Construction_of_the_Transsiberian_Railway.jpg

The railway made it easier to transport grain from Siberia to Moscow and was used by the military during the Russo-Japanese War. It also allowed peasants to migrate from Russia and Ukraine to Siberia. However, the railway was heavily criticized, as it was alleged that greedy bureaucrats exaggerated the costs of construction to make more money. The project was allegedly poorly planned and not properly supervised. It was also a somewhat fragile system, as it couldn't handle heavy traffic when it was needed during the Russo-Japanese War.

Alexander III's Death and Legacy

Alexander III died in 1894 of nephritis, a terminal kidney illness. He was succeeded by his son, Nicholas II. He left behind a contradictory legacy, as many today remember him as a harsh autocrat who strengthened his rule at the people's expense. Much of his work was left unfinished, and his son was unprepared to take on such an important role in Russian politics.

While there are many who would paint Alexander III in an unflattering light, he managed to keep peaceful relationships with most of his neighbors and stabilize the economy. He was also known as a loving husband and devoted father. Unfortunately, his unwillingness to keep up with the times may have been his greatest weakness. Many claim his son had not been properly equipped with the skills and training he needed to rule Russia.

Alexander III clung to the old way of doing things, especially the autocratic monarchy, at a time when the world was being influenced by modern and radical thoughts. Russia's autocracy bloomed, while the vast majority of its people were uneducated and needed the protection of a strong monarchy. The world was changing quickly, and the Russian monarchy wasn't willing to make compromises or evolve, which eventually led to its violent downfall.

SECTION THREE:
WWI and the Russian
Revolution (1914–1922)

Chapter 7: Tsar Nicholas II and the February Revolution

For decades, the Romanovs ruled under an autocracy. Some of the Russian monarchs were exceptional leaders who brought the Enlightenment to Russia, making it a great country that rivaled some of the most advanced nations in Europe. However, their total autocracy was sometimes brutally enforced, which earned the suspicion and sometimes hatred of their subjects.

Radical new ideas swept Europe, bringing the Russian ruling dynasty's failures to the forefront. Eventually, those revolutionary ideas would become a reality and lead to the downfall of the Russian royal family. In a stunning sequence of events, Russia and the world would be left reeling as a new government took over and Russia's most prominent family faced a firing squad.

Nicholas II

Nicholas II was the oldest son of Alexander III and was born in 1868. One of Alexander III's greatest failures was not adequately preparing his heir for the throne. When Nicholas II took the throne in 1894, he didn't have enough government experience to take on the task set before him. Alexander III believed he would live a long life and was reluctant to make his son take on too many responsibilities within the government. It was suggested that Nicholas II should at least join the Siberian Railway Committee, but Alexander III refused, as he believed his son wasn't ready for such tasks.

A few months before his coronation, Nicholas became engaged to Princess Alix of Hesse-Darmstadt, who converted to Russian Orthodoxy and took the name Alexandra Feodorovna. Nicholas and Alexandra married shortly after Alexander III died, and Alexandra gave Nicholas the confidence he needed to rule. They were a happy couple and had four children: Grand Duchesses Olga, Tatiana, Maria, Anastasia, and Tsarevich Alexei, who was afflicted with hemophilia.

Nicholas II.
https://commons.wikimedia.org/wiki/File:Nicholas_II_of_Russia_painted_by_Earnest_Lipgart.jpg

Nicholas reportedly deeply distrusted his closest advisors but was incapable of ruling without them. While he largely lacked the skills needed to rule Russia, he maintained many of his father's policies and busied himself with the government's administration. While he was fascinated by the notion of a constitutional monarchy like the one practiced in Britain, he did not seek to change the Russian government that much.

Shortly after he inherited the throne, a delegation of peasants approached him with proposals for reforms, including the suggestion that he institute a constitutional monarchy. The reforms would have made life better for his subjects, especially the peasants, but Nicholas angrily rejected their suggestions and claimed he would uphold his absolute power. This was an attitude he shared with many of his predecessors, but it would lead to his downfall.

Nicholas II was coronated on May 26th, 1896, and the next day, a large festival was held in Khodynka in Moscow, as it was large enough to host most of Moscow's citizens. The festival boasted food, free beer, and souvenirs. However, rumors quickly spread there would not be enough food for everyone, which led to a stampede. This led to the death of over one thousand people and came to be known as the Khodynka tragedy. The tragedy was seen as a bad omen, especially since it happened after Nicholas II's coronation, and he found it difficult to gain popularity with his subjects.

The French ambassador's gala had been planned for that night, but Nicholas II wanted to refrain from attending so he could pray for those who died at the festival. He was eventually persuaded to attend since his family believed he risked insulting the French if he didn't attend. As a result, he was viewed as a callous and uncaring monarch, which only exacerbated his unpopularity.

Russo-Japanese War (1904–1905)

At the beginning of the 20th century, Russia was an influential world power with massive territories in Europe and Asia, while Japan was a powerful force in Asia. During this time, there was a drive for European countries to gain more colonial territories. Nicholas II was affected by this attitude and didn't want Russia to be left out. He wanted to expand Russia's borders to include the Liaodong and Korean peninsulas, as these regions would provide Russia with a much-needed warm-water port. The Japanese wanted to limit Russian influence in those areas and instead offered Russia control of Manchuria (located in China). The deal would allow Japan to keep its influence over Korea. Russia refused, and the Japanese decided to go to war. The Russo-Japanese War attracted international attention and set the stage for World War I.

The war was incredibly brutal, and the Russians were accused of looting and burning several villages, as well as raping and killing hundreds of women. Over 150,000 people died on both sides, and 20,000 Chinese civilians also lost their lives. Eventually, the war came to an end in 1905 with the Treaty of Portsmouth, which was overseen by US President Theodore Roosevelt, who later won a Nobel Peace Prize for his efforts. The Russian army sustained many embarrassing losses during the war, and the public blamed Nicholas II for the army's shortcomings. The war ended in a crushing defeat for the Russians and led to serious consequences for the Russian monarchy.

Revolution of 1905

During 1905, social and political unrest spread throughout the Russian Empire. As opposition mounted, the autocracy faced increasing challenges that it could not overcome without giving in to some of the protestors' demands. After a year of near-constant mutinies, unrest, and strikes, Nicholas II was forced to institute a number of reforms to hold onto his power. Unfortunately, the Revolution of 1905 would not be the end of the calls for reform.

Several problems within Russian society caused the revolution. While peasants had finally been emancipated, their freedoms were still severely restricted. They earned very little money and weren't allowed to sell their land. Russian nationalism forced many minorities into lesser positions within the empire, and they weren't allowed to vote or join the army. They also had limited access to schools. Meanwhile, the working class blamed the government for failing to protect them since they weren't allowed to form unions or go on strike. Discipline became less restrictive at Russian universities, with students becoming exposed to radical new ideas from Europe. While these problems had plagued Russia periodically throughout history, they all finally coalesced to form a much larger problem that became fuel for a sustained revolution.

Bloody Sunday

Nicholas II's autocratic government quickly lost popularity and support due to the unpopular war with Japan and increasing corruption within the government. Although political and social parties petitioned for change, they were continuously rejected, which led them to adopt different tactics.

On January 22nd, 1905, an Orthodox priest named Georgy Gapon led a workers' march with the aim of delivering their petitions directly to the tsar. The workers were allegedly warned not to advance past a certain point that was guarded by troops. When the people didn't listen, the troops opened fire, which led to the deaths of many of the protestors. The march turned into a massacre that would come to be known as Bloody Sunday.

The massacre would be the start of a series of strikes, riots, and uprisings that formed the Revolution of 1905. The government claimed that about 96 died and 333 were injured, but those numbers were likely skewed. Some numbers go as high as fifteen thousand deaths. Whatever loyalty the public still held toward the autocratic government quickly died out during the revolution.

The Duma

To bring an end to the revolution, Nicholas II agreed to institute an elected national legislative assembly: the Duma. The Duma was an elected representative body consisting of a number of peasants, workers, and professionals who were supposed to help make decisions on behalf of all of Russia.

Despite his promises, Nicholas II wasn't happy about the Duma and wanted to make sure he would be able to hold onto all of his power. As a result, the Duma was made up of two chambers: one that would be made up of elected officials, while the other would be made up of officials chosen by the tsar. Nicholas II retained his absolute autocracy and gave his part of the Duma the right to veto any decisions made by the elected part. Initially, many hoped the Duma would allow Russia to become a democracy, but Nicholas II crippled the institution before it even began. The people recognized it was an empty gesture. The Duma went through multiple changes, and by 1917, there had been four different versions of the institution.

The first Duma mostly consisted of officials who were angry with the tsar. However, it became clear they wouldn't be consulted on any important matters, and the first Duma was shut down after only two months.

The second Duma lasted for a few months in 1907 but was dissolved when they opposed a series of reforms proposed by one of Nicholas II's ministers. The third Duma consisted of officials who were kinder to the tsar, but the fourth Duma, which was created in 1912, was critical of the tsar and his government. The fourth Duma forced the tsar to abdicate in 1917 and was turned into the Russian Provisional Government.

Russia and WWI

World War I changed the world and weakened several empires. The Russian Empire would not survive the conflict. It wasn't conquered by an enemy power; rather, it crumbled from within. In 1914, Tsar Nicholas II confidently declared war on Austria-Hungary and Germany. At that time, the Russian Empire ruled over a large portion of territory that stretched from Central Europe to the Pacific to the edge of the Arctic and Afghanistan. However, Russia was far behind the rest of Europe when it came to industrialism. Russia's factories and industry weren't fast enough to properly sustain the massive Imperial Russian Army. The Russians entered the war with outdated weapons and limited bullets. Many soldiers had to go into battle without weapons and were forced to pick up guns dropped by dead soldiers.

Nicholas II was also determined to lead his troops in battle, but he didn't have the skills or experience to do so successfully. To make matters worse, Nicholas II entrusted Russia to his wife, Alexandra, who was extremely unpopular with the Russians and increasingly influenced by the controversial mad monk Grigori Rasputin.

As the war dragged on, Russia experienced a series of terrible defeats. Over one million Russian soldiers were killed in the first year alone. The officer corps was severely impacted, which ultimately weakened the entire army. In 1915, the Russian troops were forced to retreat, leading to an influx of refugees fleeing to Russian cities. Inflation soared, food stocks were emptied, and the Russian government was burdened by an increasingly desperate population.

On March 3rd, 1918, Russia signed a treaty with the Central Powers that finally ended Russia's participation in the war. By then, a new government had taken over the country, and the Russian economy was in shambles.

Grigori Rasputin

When Princess Alix visited Russia before her engagement to Nicholas, she made several bad impressions on the Russians, especially on Alexander III and his wife. They initially opposed the match, but once Alexander III's health began to fail, they reluctantly changed their minds.

When Alexandra (Princess Alix) became queen, she didn't improve her standing in the eyes of the Russian population. The people thought she was too German due to her brusque personality. Nonetheless, Nicholas II loved her deeply. When he left for war, he left her in charge. She quickly began making changes in the government, such as firing elected officials, which only turned more people against her.

Grigori Rasputin.
https://commons.wikimedia.org/wiki/File:Rasputin_PA.jpg

To make matters worse, she kept close company with the controversial priest Grigori Rasputin. In 1905, the royal couple approached the priest, who had a reputation as a holy man with prophetic and healing powers. They urged him to help their son,

Tsarevich Alexei, who had hemophilia. Rasputin was repeatedly able to heal the young boy, which increased the royal family's dependency on him. Some contend that he used mystical powers or herbs and drugs to do so, although the more likely scenario is that the doctors' attention stressed Alexei out. Rasputin ordered the doctors away so he could "heal" the boy, which stopped them from giving Alexei aspirin, a blood thinner.

Alexandra heavily depended on Rasputin, and he gained a considerable amount of political and personal influence over her. Rasputin often had public fights with members of the clergy and loudly bragged about his ability to control the tsar and tsarina. Many prominent Russians demanded that he be removed from the court.

As Russia weakened during the war and the population suffered, many people blamed Alexandra and Rasputin. Vicious rumors spread about their relationship, with many claiming they were having an affair, which only served to weaken Nicholas II's already fragile image. Russian nobles murdered Rasputin on December 30th, 1916. By then, the Russian public had lost all respect for the Romanov government.

The February Revolution

During the war, food distribution and transport became more inefficient, which led to food shortages, despite the fact there was more than enough food to feed the population. The Duma was unable to influence the tsar to change, and factory workers began to strike since they needed higher wages to keep up with the rising price of food. On International Women's Day (which began on March 8th, 1917, but was actually February 23rd, 1917, on the Julian calendar), tens of thousands of workers, mothers, and children marched in the streets of Petrograd to demand food. Soldiers were ordered to suppress the march using any means necessary. Many people died, and soldiers eventually stopped fighting and joined the protestors instead.

February Revolution in Petrograd.
https://commons.wikimedia.org/wiki/File:International_Women%27s_Day_-_February_Revolution_-_Petrograd.jpg

Throughout the war, Nicholas II refused to address the problems in his empire and either didn't understand or realize how bad things were going. Finally, the army revolted, and Nicholas II's generals persuaded him to step away from the throne. Nicholas left the throne to his younger brother, Michael, who chose not to take it. This brought a decisive end to the Romanov dynasty.

Aftermath

On March 12th, just days after the February Revolution, the Duma turned into the Russian Provisional Government and called for Nicholas II's abdication. The Romanov government was all but dissolved, and the royal family was deposed and imprisoned. Meanwhile, the provisional government instituted new rights, such as equality before the law, freedom of speech, and the right to form unions and strike. It hoped to prevent a violent revolution. A young lawyer named Alexander Kerensky helped to establish the new program and acted as the minister of war.

During this time, Russia was still involved in World War I, which was extremely unpopular with the Russian public. The war weakened Russia's already failing economy and made food shortages more common. Even though the unpopular tsar and his family were no longer in power, Russia was still in a freefall, with unrest becoming increasingly widespread. Desperate peasants were moved to loot food storages and farms, and riots broke out in almost every major city. The people weren't happy, and the provisional government was struggling to solve the problems.

Meanwhile, Germany wanted to remove Russia from the war and recognized the provisional government was struggling. In order to destabilize Russia, it helped the leader of the Bolsheviks return from exile on a secret train. Almost as soon as he arrived, he began increasing Bolshevik influence, which would lead to more revolutions.

The Execution of the Romanovs

When Alexander III died, Nicholas II became tsar. He was shocked and unprepared. Reportedly, he asked one of his advisors, "What is going to happen to me ... to all of Russia?" A little over two decades later, he and his family were imprisoned by the Bolsheviks, a far-left Marxist group.

The Russian imperial family in 1916 (Alexei is absent from the picture).
https://commons.wikimedia.org/wiki/File:Russian_Imperial_family_in_1916.jpg

Following the October Revolution, Nicholas II finally recognized the danger he and his family were in. He petitioned

France and Britain to take them, but both countries refused, despite the fact that Alexandra was Queen Victoria's granddaughter. This meant they were at the mercy of the Bolshevik government. The family was imprisoned and moved to several different houses. They were harassed by soldiers and forced to live in relative squalor. Despite their docile acceptance of their circumstances, they were still a problem to the Bolsheviks, who feared the royal family would somehow escape and cause problems. Nicholas II and Alexandra both maintained they would be saved. And they were right in a way, as the White Army, which fought against the Bolsheviks, sought to rescue them. They didn't make it in time.

With the White Army approaching, the Bolsheviks knew something had to be done. On July 17th, 1918, the family was told they were going to be moved again. Little did they know that they and their servants were going to be marched to the basement to be executed.

The Romanovs had cleverly sewn jewels, religious icons, and money into their clothes to use in case the family ever escaped. But what should have been a quick execution took twenty minutes. After the initial onslaught, all of the children were still alive due to the number of jewels and other items sewn into their garments. Tatiana, Maria, and Anastasia were wearing pounds of jewels. The executioners shot, stabbed, and beat the family until they were dead. (Although imposters sprang up later on, the Romanov family and their servants all died in the attack.)

The bodies were taken to a mineshaft and drenched in sulfuric acid. However, the mine shaft was not as deep as the ringleader had envisioned. The bodies were moved about until it was finally decided it would be best to bury them. One of the graves was found in 1979, although an investigation didn't take place until 1991. The other grave, which held Alexei and Maria, was found in 2007.

The world was shocked by the murder of the royal family. This act of violence defined the Russian Revolution, not the political victories that Vladimir Lenin and the Bolsheviks had worked so hard to attain.

Chapter 8: The October Revolution and the Russian Civil War

Vladimir Lenin and the Bolsheviks viewed the monarchy as a cancer that impeded Russia's growth and the welfare of Russian workers. They fought hard to bring an end to the autocratic monarchy, but once they did, they found that Russia would be harder to reform than they had imagined. The economy was in a mess, as Russia had fought in the seemingly endless Great War, and the provisional government wasn't willing to give up its power without a fight.

The Bolsheviks quickly gained power and popularity with the people and were able to stage their own revolution, which turned their government into a reality. When Russia finally left World War I, many suspected Russia was on the road to recovery. However, more climactic events would rip through the country until it was plunged into a terrible civil war.

Karl Marx and Communism

Karl Marx was born in 1818 in Prussia. He later attended the University of Bonn, where he was arrested for dueling with another student and drunkenness. He then enrolled at the University of Berlin, where he studied philosophy and law. Marx was deeply influenced by the philosophy of professor G. W. F Hegel. While he was in university, he became involved with the Young Hegelians, which was a movement that opposed many European political establishments. Marx was exposed to many radical ideas that later affected his work as a journalist.

Karl Marx.
https://commons.wikimedia.org/wiki/File:Karl_Marx.png

As a result, he was expelled by several European governments. In 1848, he worked with Friedrich Engels and completed *The Communist Manifesto*. The book introduced many new radical political concepts and claimed that socialism was the result of capitalism's failings. Their theories caused unrest and increased workers' movements, in which Marx participated. Marx's work swept throughout Europe and inspired countless political parties, including the Bolsheviks in Russia.

As the years passed, Marx developed his economic theories and worked as a journalist and revolutionary. In 1864, he helped to create the International Workingmen's Association and later published the first part of *Capital: A Critique of Political Economy*, which was a volume regarding his economic theory. He claimed that capitalism would always self-destruct and lead to communism. While Marx worked hard to finish the book, he never completed his work, as he died in 1883. He had no idea that his work would have such far-reaching consequences and eventually become the basis for Russia's socialist government.

The Rise of the Bolsheviks

The Bolsheviks were a far-left, revolutionary Marxist faction. It was founded by Vladimir Lenin, who split from the Mensheviks, one of the most influential parties of the Russian Socialist Movement. Lenin promoted the split when he wrote a political pamphlet entitled "What Is to Be Done?" The pamphlet was outlawed in Russia, which had strict censorship laws.

Lenin strongly believed a revolution would only occur if it was led by professional leaders who were extremely dedicated to Karl Marx's principles. In 1903, the Russian Social Democratic Labor Party (RSDLP) met at the Second Party Congress. During this time, Lenin and Julius Martov, another prominent member of the party, had a disagreement about the party's membership rules. Lenin aimed to create a group of professional revolutionaries who devoted their full strength to overthrow the tsarist government. The disagreements grew and led to a decisive split within the party.

The Bolsheviks played a small part in the Revolution of 1905 and went on to strengthen their ranks over the years. They eventually created their own official party in 1912, signifying their complete separation from other socialist parties. There were several disagreements within the party as to how Russia should be governed once the party took power, but their political goal remained the same. They wanted to overthrow the tsarist government and bring about complete social change. Many viewed the unequal treatment of the workers as immoral and claimed that social classes had to end. Lenin's works promoted the goal of a group of highly trained revolutionaries overthrowing the government and eventually giving power to a socialist party that would govern more effectively.

When World War I broke out and the tsarist regime floundered, the revolution the Bolsheviks had been waiting for became a reality.

Vladimir Lenin

Vladimir Lenin was born in 1870 to a middle-class family. At the time, his name was Vladimir Ilyich Ulyanov. He was one of six siblings and attended high school, which was impressive for the time. In 1887, Lenin's older brother was executed when it was revealed he had been part of a plot to assassinate Alexander III. This exposed Lenin to radical political ideas that would eventually define his life.

During his childhood, the government clamped down on education. Since Lenin's father was an inspector of schools, the family was targeted by the government, and Lenin's father was threatened with early retirement. This likely contributed to Lenin's aversion to the tsarist regime.

While attending university, Lenin studied law but took part in a student protest that got him expelled. During this period, he began reading more radical literature, including the works of Karl Marx. When he finished university, he gained a law degree. By that time, he had already become a Marxist.

Vladimir Lenin giving a speech.
https://commons.wikimedia.org/wiki/File:Vladimir_Lenin_giving_a_speech.jpg

In the mid-1890s, Vladimir was arrested and exiled to Siberia. A few years later, after his exile ended, he moved to Germany and then Switzerland, where he was able to freely associate with other Marxists. Eventually, he adopted the name Lenin and became the founder of the Bolshevik Party.

Lenin claimed the First World War was a result of capitalism. The German government sent Lenin and several other Russian radicals back to Russia with the aim of destabilizing the government to bring an end to Russia's involvement in the war. Lenin immediately set his sights on overthrowing the Russian Provisional Government, which he claimed was a bourgeois dictatorship.

Leon Trotsky

Lev Davidovic Bronstein, or Leon Trotsky, was born in modern-day Ukraine in 1879. While still in school, he was introduced to Marxism, which would shape the rest of his life. In 1897, he became a founding member of the South Russian Workers' Union. Bronstein was eventually arrested for his political activities and exiled to Siberia. While in exile, he met and fell in love with a co-revolutionary named Alexandra Lvovna Tolstaya (the daughter of Leo Tolstoy). The couple had two children together. In 1902, Bronstein was able to escape from exile, even though it meant he had to leave his family behind. He used the name Leon Trotsky on his forged papers, and he continued to use the name for the rest of his life.

Trotsky went to London, where he met Vladimir Lenin and joined the Socialist Democratic Party. While in London, he met Natalia Ivanovna, whom he married. The couple had two sons.

Leon Trotsky.
https://commons.wikimedia.org/wiki/File:Leon_Trotsky_Sailor.jpg

During those days, the Socialist Democratic Party fought over membership and leadership. Lenin wanted a small group of trained revolutionaries to control a large group of supporters, while Julius Martov wanted a more democratic organization. Trotsky remained neutral and tried to negotiate between the two sides, but many members chose to side with Lenin.

In 1905, Trotsky returned to Russia, where he became heavily involved in the Revolution of 1905. He was once again arrested and exiled. His actions endeared him to the party, and he managed to escape prison once again. Trotsky spent the next ten years in exile in Europe, where he wrote for Russian revolutionary journals.

When the tsarist government was overthrown, he went back to Russia to help solve some of the problems that arose after the revolution. However, he loudly criticized the Russian Provisional Government, which led to his arrest. This led Trotsky to join the Bolshevik Party.

During that time, Petrograd Soviet was the seat of the opposition to the Russian Provisional Government. After Trotsky joined the Bolsheviks, he was made the chairman of the Petrograd Soviet. He would go on to help Lenin and the Bolsheviks overthrow the provisional government. Trotsky also served in the Russian Civil War and became one of Stalin's biggest enemies.

Joseph Stalin

Ioseb Besarionis dze Jughashvili, better known as Joseph Stalin, was born in 1878 in Georgia. He later took on the name Stalin, which means "man of steel." Stalin was the only child of a shoemaker and a laundress. His father was an abusive alcoholic who regularly beat his son. While he was still a child, Stalin contracted smallpox, which left scars on his face for the rest of his life. While attending school, he became a Marxist and was eventually expelled in 1899.

Stalin actively took part in strikes and labor movements, which led him to join the Bolsheviks. During the early years of the party, he took part in bank robberies to raise money for the party. He was arrested multiple times and exiled to Siberia, as were many of his peers.

In 1906, he married Ekaterina Svanidze and fathered a son, Yakov, with whom Stalin was never particularly close. Ekaterina died soon after her son was born. In 1918, Stalin married Nadezhda "Nadya" Alliluyeva, the daughter of a revolutionary. They had two children, a daughter and a son. His daughter, Svetlana Alliluyeva, eventually defected to the United States in 1967. He fathered several illegitimate children, and Nadya eventually committed suicide while she was in her thirties.

Young Joseph Stalin.
https://commons.wikimedia.org/wiki/File:Stalin_1902-1.jpg

While Lenin was in Switzerland, he arranged for Stalin to serve on the first Central Committee of the Bolshevik Party. Stalin was highly ambitious, and during the party's early days, he made sure to side with Lenin during party disputes. When the Bolsheviks became more prominent after the February Revolution, Stalin played a big part in helping them gain power. He eventually became one of the most prominent members of the party.

The Russian Provisional Government

By the time Lenin returned to Russia, the country as a whole was tired of the ravages of war. Lenin promoted the Bolshevik Party under the slogan, "Peace, Land, Bread," which greatly appealed to the war-weary Russians. Meanwhile, the provisional government was struggling to effectively combat all the problems Russia was facing, but several prominent Russians tried to make the provisional government work. However, after the monarchy was removed, there was a power vacuum, and many scrambled to enrich themselves. And despite the fact that most Russians were sick of the war, the provisional government kept Russia fighting on the front lines.

Eventually, Alexander Kerensky was left as the last head of the provisional government. He launched an offensive against the Austrians and Germans in 1917. It was a massive failure and caused an uproar in Russia. More and more soldiers began defecting from the army, and the Bolsheviks spread propaganda within the army, which turned sentiments against the provisional government. Kerensky responded by attempting to send all Bolshevik soldiers to the worst battlefronts, which forced the soldiers to rise against the Russian Provisional Government. These rebellions were known as the July Days. Soldiers and sailors gathered in front of the Tauride Palace in an attempt to overthrow the provisional government. While the rebellion was eventually suppressed, the Russian Provisional Government was on its last legs and wouldn't survive for much longer. It would eventually be overthrown during the October Revolution.

The October Revolution

On October 24th and 25th, 1917 (according to the Julian calendar), Lenin finally made his move against the Russian Provisional Government. He initiated a coup and called for a Soviet government instead. His goal was to replace the bourgeois government with a government controlled by councils consisting of peasants, workers, and soldiers. His party had been gaining popularity after the February Revolution, especially since many Russians wanted to leave the First World War. The coup was almost bloodless, and the Bolsheviks took control of key locations in Petrograd and established a new government.

Workers and soldiers had long been demanding complete change, which provided a good basis for Lenin's long-awaited revolution. He had already set up a volunteer paramilitary force called the Red Guards, which helped him during the coup. He also spent months arranging for workers, soldiers, sailors, and peasants to become effective Red Guards. As soon as the Bolsheviks attained power, they announced Soviet rule with Lenin as their ruler. This was a remarkable feat, and Lenin became the first communist state leader in history.

Bolshevik Government

After the coup, the Bolsheviks set up the Council of People's Commissars, with Lenin as the chairman. Trotsky became the commissar for foreign affairs. The Bolshevik government's first order of business was to bring an end to Russia's involvement in World War I. Trotsky was placed in charge of making peace with the Germans and finding a way out of the war. The Germans, who had a hand in helping many prominent revolutionaries return to Russia, had been hoping for this outcome and were ready with a list of reparations and territory demands.

However, Trotsky didn't want to give in to German demands and advised Lenin to reject them. He suggested they wait for a while to see if the Allies defeated Germany or if Germany was forced to withdraw from the war due to internal conflict. Lenin disagreed, as he wanted to bring a quick end to the war that was proving to be a continuous drain on Russian resources and morale. He wanted to focus on building the new Soviet government instead.

In March 1918, the Bolshevik government signed the Treaty of Brest-Litovsk with Austria-Hungary, Germany, Bulgaria, and the Ottoman Empire. The move cost them a million square miles worth of territory. Trotsky resigned from his post as commissar for foreign affairs.

The Bolsheviks had recently set up the Red Army, and Lenin appointed Trotsky as its leader. Trotsky shined in this role and was given the task of bringing an end to the anti-Bolshevik movement known as the White Movement.

Lenin immediately set about instituting many of the Marxist reforms he had always dreamed about and was on his way to establishing a strong communist government. He also established the Cheka, which was Russia's first secret police. The Cheka was used to silence any opposers within the Bolshevik Party and any political rivals. In response, a political rival shot Lenin in the shoulder and neck in 1918.

The Cheka was given permission to institute a campaign of mass executions. This time came to be known as the Red Terror. Within two months, the Cheka had executed about 100,000 "class enemies." Those who were executed included tsarist supporters, members of the former upper class, and Bolshevik opposers. The events after the October Revolution eventually led to the Russian Civil War.

The Anti-Bolshevik Movement

Ever since the Bolsheviks took power, they were opposed by a number of different factions. However, it wasn't until the Treaty of Brest-Litovsk that anti-Bolshevik factions were moved to take action. The White Army was formed from members of non-Bolshevik socialists, liberals, army generals, former landowners, pro-monarchists, and others who shared a hatred of the Bolsheviks. The White Army controlled large parts of the former Russian Empire and strengthened the army through conscriptions and foreign support.

Many Western Allies were disgusted by the actions of the Bolshevik government and supported the White Army. These Western countries were concerned the Bolsheviks would ally with Germany. The Bolsheviks had also promised to default on massive foreign loans, and the Western Allies were increasingly afraid the revolutionary ideas that had taken hold in Russia would spread. Winston Churchill famously claimed that Bolshevism had to be strangled in its cradle.

To that end, Western Allied countries sent the White Army troops and supplies. The Allies had also given Russia a huge amount of war supplies and were worried those supplies would be given to the Germans, which would prolong the war. As a result, foreign troops were sent to Russia, where they frequently clashed with the Red Army.

The Russian Civil War

The Russian Civil War broke out in 1917, with Trotsky leading the Red Army on behalf of the Bolsheviks. In 1918, the Romanovs were executed, which brought an end to the efforts to restore Nicholas II to the throne. Trotsky proved to be a capable leader who led his army to victory. This was no easy feat, as several

Bolshevik officials, including Lenin, often overturned Trotsky's strategies and efforts. He also had to fight the war on sixteen different fronts, as the White Army came at him from all sides. The war was brutal, and about 300,000 people died. The Cheka continued the Red Terror during this time; according to estimations, it may have killed over a million people.

During the war, Lenin instituted a number of policies that came to be known as war communism. These temporary policies allowed Lenin to strengthen his position and defeat his enemies. Lenin nationalized all manufacturing and industries and took grain from the peasants to feed the Red Army. As a result, industries and manufacturing plummeted, and the grain shortage eventually caused famine. This led to mass poverty and unrest. Many peasants and workers were affected, which caused some to long for the days of the monarchy, but those views couldn't be expressed freely due to the Cheka's reign of terror.

The Red Army managed to win the war in 1920, and the White Army was forced to surrender. Bolshevik rule and the Soviet government were firmly entrenched.

The Russian economy had been ravaged by the war, as infrastructure had been destroyed. A large amount of the skilled and educated population fled Russia, and a disastrous drought caused disease and famine. By that time, the Russian government was near complete ruin.

After the Russian Civil War, a treaty was signed between Ukraine, Belarus, the Transcaucasus, and Russia in 1922. This led to Lenin forming the Union of Soviet Republics (USSR). Lenin was the first head of the USSR, but he wouldn't hold onto the position for long, as he suffered from a series of strokes between 1922 and 1924. During this time, Stalin began gaining power, and it wouldn't be long until the USSR ushered in a new era in Russian history.

SECTION FOUR:
The Journey from Communist Russia to the Russian Republic (1922–2022)

Chapter 9: The Union of Soviet Socialist Republics (USSR)

For years, revolutionaries like Vladimir Lenin worked to bring an end to the tsarist government. When they finally achieved this goal, they were able to build a government based on their Marxist ideals. However, they were forced to contend with serious opposition that threatened their regime. As the first communist state in history, they were left to navigate unprecedented challenges that tested their intelligence and ingenuity.

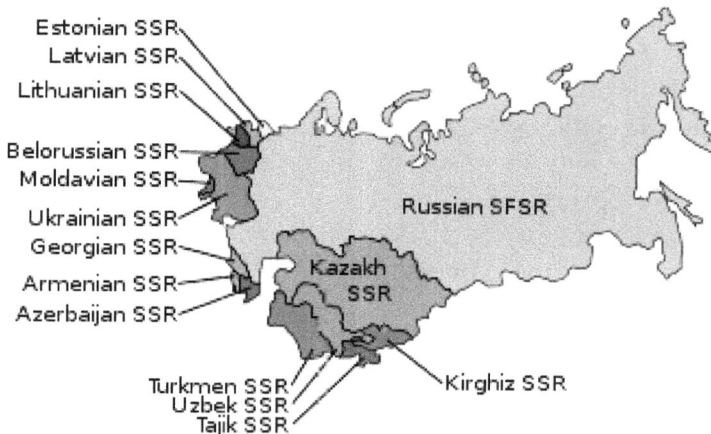

Map of the USSR.

Special:Contributions/Saul ip. Derivative work by Σ, CC BY-SA 3.0 <https://creativecommons.org/licenses/by-sa/3.0>, *via Wikimedia Commons;* https://commons.wikimedia.org/wiki/File:Map_of_USSR_with_SSR_names.svg

After the Russian Civil War, the Bolsheviks' opposition was defeated, but the state was on the brink of collapse. To make matters worse, Lenin's health was failing, and the USSR was rocked by the rise of an ambitious official named Joseph Stalin, who was determined to rise to the top no matter what it took.

Formation of the USSR

On December 29th, 1922, delegates from Russia, Ukraine, Belarus, and the Transcaucasus met and signed the Declaration of the Creation of the USSR. In 1924, Britain formally recognized the USSR, and a Soviet Constitution was approved that legitimized the 1922 meeting. The Bolsheviks could finally get on with creating their new government, and many hoped the brutalities of the past years would be forgotten.

The Bolsheviks, led by Vladimir Lenin, concentrated on restructuring every part of Russia. This included reforming the economy and aimed to provide basic services like electricity to the country. A plan was developed for the construction of twenty regional power stations, hydroelectric power plants, and electric-powered enterprises. This plan would eventually provide the basis for the later five-year plans, which we will touch on in more depth later. Any type of capitalist venture or production was viciously suppressed, as the Bolsheviks wanted to achieve total communism. The policies that had been enacted during the Russian Civil War had led to unrest and desperate poverty. This caused the government to rethink its strategy, and Lenin was forced to come up with the New Economic Policy.

There was little time to enjoy the political victory of the USSR's establishment since there was mounting opposition from within the country as poverty and unrest rose. To make matters worse, tensions rose within the Bolshevik Party, as ministers disagreed about how the new government should be administered and controlled.

Kronstadt Rebellion

Russia had been in a near-constant crisis ever since the outbreak of the First World War. The people had been forced to participate in a terrible war, sending their male relatives off to become soldiers in an army that couldn't even provide them with guns. After that, Russia went through numerous revolutions, rebellions, and uprisings. When the Bolsheviks rose to power, many people hoped that things would improve.

While the Bolsheviks removed Russia from the war, a brand-new war started a few months later that hit a lot closer to home. Once again, the Russian people were subjected to new changes that only worsened their situation since they were forced to adhere to the policies of war communism. Much of the population had been unaware of communism, Karl Marx, and socialist parties before the Bolsheviks took power.

Grain seizures and bans on free trade caused serious distress throughout Russia, as peasants and townspeople suffered greatly. Production fell to shockingly low levels. This caused widespread dissent and strikes, which only made the problem worse. The Bolsheviks struggled to keep the unrest contained, but they were hit by yet another stunning blow before they could achieve their aims. In 1921, the soldiers and sailors stationed at Kronstadt started a massive uprising.

Kronstadt was an island fortress that guarded the key city of Petrograd. The uprising was surprising because the soldiers of Kronstadt had been some of the most loyal Bolshevik supporters during the revolution. Trotsky himself had dubbed them the heroes of the revolution. However, the soldiers and sailors there were moved to action due to the conditions the people faced. When they heard and saw what the country was going through, they fought against the regime they had helped gain power.

The soldiers formed a Provisional Revolutionary Committee and sent the government a list of economic, political, and social demands. The rebels also asserted they wanted soviets without Bolsheviks and established an anti-Bolshevik newspaper. They claimed the Bolsheviks were worse than the tsarist government. However, the rebels also made some good points and urged the Bolsheviks to ease the policies of war communism to bring relief to the people.

The Bolsheviks responded harshly and sent a powerful force to crush the rebellion. Many supporters of the Bolshevik Party were disgusted by the handling of the rebellion, and Lenin quickly realized that things needed to change.

The New Economic Policy

During the Russian Civil War, Lenin introduced a series of temporary policies that came to be known as war communism. Some of these policies requisitioned surplus grain from peasants to feed the Red Army, which caused serious food shortages and famine. The problem was exacerbated by a severe drought that plagued Russia in 1920 and 1921. When the crops failed, there was no surplus grain left to solve the shortage, and thousands suffered. Lenin recognized the need to ease some of his communist policies and introduced the New Economic Policy (NEP) in 1921.

The NEP was a massive departure from many of the ideals that were upheld in the Bolshevik Party, and many officials opposed this move. Essentially, the NEP allowed elements of free trade and capitalism. The policy of grain requisitioning was brought to an end, which brought relief to the peasants. Russian farmers were permitted to buy and sell their goods, leading to the development of a merchant class called "Nepmen."

While many Russians were thrilled by the changes, the NEP caused turmoil within the Bolshevik Party. The Bolshevik government still held control of the most important elements of the economy, such as industries, finance, and banking. Still, many Bolsheviks felt the NEP was a betrayal of their socialist beliefs.

Since farmers were allowed to sell their surplus goods again, they were motivated to produce more, which led to a rise in agricultural production. While the NEP didn't singlehandedly save the Russian economy, it brought much-needed relief to the people and is generally regarded as a success.

Aftermath of Lenin's Death

Between the years of 1922 and 1924, Lenin was afflicted by a series of strokes that severely impacted his health. He struggled to speak and used all his strength to govern. As his life neared its end, he feared what would happen to the government he had helped to create. He was keenly aware of the dangerous forces within his own party. During the last few months of his life, he wrote a few essays about the Communist Party's corruption. He recognized that Stalin was a dangerous individual and suggested that he be removed from his high-ranking office. The essays came to be known as "Lenin's

Testament."

Lenin died in January 1924. His body was moved several times before it was embalmed and displayed in Lenin's Tomb in Red Square, Moscow. Close to a million people lined up in the blistering cold to pay their respects to their former leader. St. Petersburg, which had been renamed Petrograd, was then called Leningrad in Lenin's honor. Despite all the honors that were heaped on his name, his advice about Stalin went largely unheeded.

Lenin's Mausoleum.
Jorge Láscar from Melbourne, Australia, CC BY 2.0
<https://creativecommons.org/licenses/by/2.0>, via Wikimedia Commons;
https://commons.wikimedia.org/wiki/File:Lenin%27s_Mausoleum_(19775699420).jpg

When Lenin suffered his first stroke, there were questions about who would be his successor. Many assumed that Trotsky would take his place since he had a strong record of service, but he had also offended many important officials. Stalin was one of those Trotsky had offended, and he supported the opposition against Trotsky. Stalin had been appointed as the general secretary of the Central Committee, which allowed him to control party member appointments. He used his position to place his allies in strategic positions.

Lenin had supported Trotsky over Stalin, but his rapidly declining health prevented his efforts from being successful. When

Lenin died, Stalin politically outmaneuvered Trotsky and took control of the Communist Party. Stalin became the dictator of the USSR, while Trotsky was slowly pushed out of the government. What Lenin had warned had come to pass.

Joseph Stalin in Power

Stalin was a dictator who ruled through terror and used whatever means necessary to get rid of his opposition. The beginning of his reign seemed promising, as he introduced a series of five-year plans that were supposed to revitalize Russia's economy and turn it into a modern communist powerhouse. When his plans weren't well received, he resorted to exiling, executing, and punishing those who voiced dissent. He implemented policies of forced collectivization that led to widespread poverty and hunger. Stalin employed secret police and created a Gulag system, which was constituted of forced labor camps. Neighbors were encouraged to spy on each other and report any crimes or opposition to the new regime.

Stalin enforced his absolute power and used propaganda to present himself as the perfect leader. He built himself into Soviet culture by renaming cities in his honor, rewriting history books to embellish his achievements, and putting his name in the national anthem. He made sure he was flattered in art, literature, and music. Stalin's regime also controlled the media and exercised extreme censorship.

Leon Trotsky was the only person who seemed to be able to stop Stalin, and he never stopped trying to oppose Stalin's government. By 1928, Trotsky had been pushed out of the government, and his achievements were discredited. He was then banished from the Soviet Union. Although Trotsky couldn't return to his homeland, he continued writing about Stalin's abuses of power. Stalin retaliated by claiming that Trotsky was a traitor and an enemy of his people. Trotsky's allies were persecuted, and Trotsky was assassinated with an ice axe by a member of the secret police in 1940.

The Five-Year Plans

Stalin was an ambitious man who didn't let anything stand between him and the power he craved. When he finally became the leader of the USSR, he revealed his incredibly ambitious plans for the Soviet Union. He introduced a series of five-year plans that were aimed at developing the country's industry and collectivizing agriculture. The first plan began on October 1ª, 1928. Stalin decided the entire economy needed to be reformed to keep pace with Western Europe. He believed that unless Russia caught up with its European neighbor, the country would be crushed by capitalist powers.

The first five-year plan focused on making agriculture more efficient by introducing mechanization and collectivization. New industrial centers were built in uninhabited areas that were rich in natural resources. More emphasis was placed on heavy industries as Russia prepared for a future industrialized war. This shift in focus led to a mass exodus from rural areas to cities, as people went in search of better lives and provided the workforce that the first five-year plan needed to succeed. However, the new labor force was completely unskilled and struggled to operate industrial machinery. Workers also had to endure terrible factory conditions that took a toll on human lives.

Furthermore, the collectivization of agriculture caused famine and unrest. The plan did lead to a significant increase in output, but it also failed terribly in key aspects. Millions had left behind their farms in search of a better life but found themselves trapped in factories and were forced to work in deplorable conditions. Those who had stayed behind were swept up in agricultural collectivization policies that eventually contributed to widespread famine.

Stalin's government placed the blame on kulaks (peasants who had benefited from the NEP and managed to amass a certain amount of wealth). The kulaks were viciously persecuted and were either killed or sent to the Gulag, where they were forced to work on Stalin's projects. Once the kulaks were out of the way, their land was given to the state to support collectivization.

Citizens in non-Russian parts of the Soviet Union also suffered. They were subject to Stalin's policies and soon felt the disastrous effects of the five-year plans. This led to a rift between Russians and non-Russians. To make matters worse, the policies led to a devastating famine in Ukraine called the Holodomor. The Soviet government failed to respond to the disaster, which led to

Ukrainian resentment. Some argue whether this was genocide; sixteen countries believe it was. Up to five million died in Ukraine because of famine.

Despite the failures and suffering caused by the first five-year plan, Stalin continued with his second five-year plan. This allowed the Soviet Union to become one of the major steel-producing countries. There were several successes, such as the improvements made in communications and faster and more reliable railways. However, the second plan failed to live up to projected production levels.

The USSR would continue to use five-year plans until it was dissolved in 1991. Emphasis was put on production, and improvements were continually being made to improve production. For example, childcare was introduced so that mothers could focus on working harder in factories and in the fields. A system of incentives and punishments was also used to motivate people to work harder.

Moscow Trials

During his time as the leader of the USSR, Stalin conducted multiple political purges to rid himself of enemies. This led to numerous show trials, which were perfectly planned to result in Stalin's desired outcome. Political rivals, such as opponents to the Communist Party and Trotskyists, were tried at sham trials that served only to put on a show for the country. The Moscow trials occurred during the Great Purge, lasting from 1937 to 1938. These trials are perfect examples of Stalin's show trials.

The Moscow trials were a series of high-profile trials that put several influential communists on trial for treason. There were even prominent Americans who supported the trials and approved of the verdicts. It was a shocking spectacle designed to display Stalin's power and suppress any possible opposition to his government.

Stalin coerced several high-ranking communists, most of whom had served during the 1917 Revolution and Russian Civil War, into admitting they were traitors to the USSR. Some of these confessions were made after their loved ones were threatened. Most of the trials ended in executions and were transparently rigged. Despite their loyalty to the Russian communist cause, these officials had either supported Trotsky or refused to ally themselves with Stalin, which, in Stalin's eyes, were crimes worthy of death.

Once his rivals were gone, Stalin was able to rewrite history books and claimed many of their achievements as his own. This added to the mythification of his name and turned him into a living legend.

The Great Purge

Stalin worked for years to consolidate his power, and in 1929, he finally became the dictator of the USSR. However, his work was far from over. Many officials within the government began to challenge his authority while the danger of the Nazis in Germany and militarists in Japan were becoming a reality. Some historians claim Stalin initiated the Great Purge to unify the USSR and strengthen the country before those dangers could overpower Russia. However, others claim he wanted to maintain his position as dictator. Whatever his motives were, Stalin launched a violent campaign against his opposition, which included anyone who could possibly challenge his power. This meant members of Lenin's government and those who had supported Trotsky became targets.

Between 1936 and 1938, an estimated 750,000 people were executed. More than a million people were sent to the Gulag. The Moscow trials helped Stalin destroy his enemies' reputations and gave him a legitimate excuse to execute them. The Great Purge also came to be known as the Great Terror and left a lasting mark on the psyche of the Russian population.

The purge started in 1934 with the assassination of Sergei Kirov, a Bolshevik leader. Suddenly, the Bolsheviks found themselves at the mercy of the government they had helped to create.

While the purge started with the persecution of political officials, it soon stretched to include artists, peasants, ethnic minorities, foreigners, intellectuals, writers, and even soldiers. No one was safe. Thirty thousand soldiers of the Red Army were executed after Stalin became convinced they were planning to overthrow him. Stalin's brutality knew no bounds; he even created a law that stated families were liable for crimes committed by a family member. This meant that children from the age of twelve could be executed.

Those who were sent to the Gulag were subject to torture, horrific conditions, and execution, which means the number of people killed during the Great Purge likely exceeded 750,000.

The Great Purge was later condemned by Stalin's successor, but it was too late. Hundreds of thousands of people had died, and the people's spirits were broken. Entire groups of Russian society, such as writers and intellectuals, had been wiped out. It also ensured the people were dependent on the state and, by extension, Stalin.

Russian Society under the USSR

Russian society and culture went through numerous changes under the rule of the USSR. During the first few years after the revolution, artists enjoyed relative freedom, experimenting with various styles to create a unique style that would define Soviet art. Under Lenin, the government promoted art since they wanted it to be accessible to all people. However, the USSR kept a strict watch on intellectuals, including writers and artists. If artists criticized the USSR or seemed to be against the government, they faced exile, harsh punishments, execution, or work bans. The government supported many different trends, which led to an era of experimentation. Films were particularly encouraged since they could influence the illiterate public.

However, things became harder for artists under Stalin's rule. He encouraged the rise of socialist realism and suppressed other trends. Many writers were heavily persecuted during this time as well. It wouldn't be until the 1950s that censorship would be relaxed during the Khrushchev Thaw.

Chapter 10: The Great Patriotic War and the Cold War

When the USSR was formed, it became the first communist state in the world. Communists and socialists around the world had high hopes that it would succeed. However, the flaws in the system quickly became apparent, and the state fell short of the lofty ideals touted by the Bolsheviks. In reality, the road to pure communism was littered with famine, unrest, and violent political purges.

However, these events turned Russia into a major power. By the time the Second World War ended, both Russia and America emerged as prominent countries. They would eventually become locked in a conflict known as the Cold War.

Prelude to World War II

In 1938, France, the United Kingdom, and Italy signed the Munich Agreement with Germany, which gave Czechoslovakian territory to Germany. Since France had made a military pact with Czechoslovakia a few years prior, the Munich Agreement came to be known as the Munich Betrayal.

Germany, which was ruled by Adolf Hitler at the time, had been steadily growing in power and influence, despite the heavy war reparations it was forced to pay after the First World War. A year later, the Soviet Union signed a non-aggression pact with Nazi Germany. Later, it would be revealed at the Nuremberg trials that the Soviet Union and Nazi Germany planned to divide the territories of Poland, Lithuania, Romania, Finland, and Estonia between themselves.

On September 1ˢᵗ, 1939, Germany invaded Poland, which marked the beginning of the Second World War. Stalin launched his own invasion of Poland a few days later. Stalin also invaded and annexed parts of Romania, Estonia, Lithuania, and Latvia. There were some talks about the USSR joining the Axis Powers with Germany, Italy, and Japan. Stalin even went as far as to sign a neutrality pact with Japan, with whom Russia had been competing for interests in the Far East after the collapse of imperial China. However, Stalin wasn't satisfied with Germany's offers, and negotiations soon broke down. He sensed that some Germans were interested in invading the USSR, but he had no idea about Hitler's looming betrayal.

Operation Barbarossa

The non-aggression pact between Germany and the USSR was a blow to the Allied powers, as Russia and Germany had been enemies for years. The pact ensured that neither country would attack the other for at least ten years. Soon after Germany invaded Poland, Britain and France declared war on Germany. After a few months, Germany launched the Blitzkrieg, which means "lightning war." The Blitzkrieg was a surprise attack that consisted of rapid movements to put the enemy off-balance. With this tactic, Germany conquered the Netherlands, Luxembourg, France, and Belgium.

The USSR was busy negotiating an alliance with Germany, but Hitler likely never planned to honor the non-aggression pact with the USSR. He had his eye on expanding eastward and colonizing the USSR, especially Ukraine. This was all part of his Lebensraum ("living space") goal, which aimed to ensure the survival of the German people by allowing them to colonize racially inferior territories. The Nazis believed the Slavic people were inferior to the Aryan race, the false idea that the original speakers of proto-Indo-European languages were superior to everyone else.

Operation Barbarossa lines of attack.
https://commons.wikimedia.org/wiki/File:Operation_Barbarossa_6_lines_of_attack_Why_We_Fight_no._5.jpg

In 1941, Hitler launched Operation Barbarossa, which was the German invasion of the USSR. The operation aimed to advance from the port of Archangel along the Volga River to the port of Astrakhan. Hitler had one of the most impressive invasion forces at his disposal. It consisted of about 80 percent of his Wehrmacht (the Nazis' armed forces). Hitler hoped to quickly subdue the USSR and was buoyed by the success of the Blitzkrieg.

The invasion was especially brutal, as armed SS death squads followed the army and killed civilians, especially Jews. German forces were also ordered to kill any Soviet officers. Many Soviet prisoners of war were executed, which went against international war protocols. The Soviet Army was caught largely unaware, which allowed the Germans to make large territorial gains.

Despite their surprise, the Soviet Army was able to make a strong defense. For some reason, Hitler decided to order his army to press on toward Moscow instead of Ukraine. The Wehrmacht managed to capture Kyiv and besiege Leningrad. Russia's situation looked desperate, especially since the citizens of Leningrad began to starve. Animals disappeared, and there were reports of cannibalism. Around 800,000 people died in the 900-day siege; that was around the same number of British and US deaths in World War II combined. Russia suffered the worst in terms of causalities, with nearly fourteen million deaths by the war's end.

Liberation of the USSR

While Hitler hoped to force Russia to surrender, he was met with stiff resistance. In October, he launched Operation Typhoon, which had the aim of capturing Moscow. However, the Soviets had gathered more troops and equipment. To make matters worse, the Russian roads became muddy and tricky to navigate during the fall months. This was known as Rasputitsa ("quagmire season") and was something the Soviets were used to managing. However, the Wehrmacht was quickly bogged down. While the Germans were delayed, the Soviets prepared to meet them. So, when the Germans finally got to Moscow, they were confronted by a strong Soviet Army.

During the brutal winter months, the German Army was finally forced to retreat. Operation Barbarossa had failed, partially because Hitler had failed to create supply lines that would strengthen his army while they fought in harsh and unfamiliar territory. The resilience of the Russians also played a large role. While the operation had weakened the Soviet Army, the brutal German tactics had made the Soviets determined to fight Germany until the bitter end. Instead of gaining a quick victory over a massive territory, Hitler had made a dangerous enemy.

In 1942, Hitler ordered another offensive against the USSR, which eventually failed. The Battle of Stalingrad, which took place from 1942 to 1943, even managed to turn the tide against Hitler. The siege of Leningrad wouldn't be lifted until early 1944. The Russians proved their resilience was stronger than Germany had anticipated.

The Allied powers eventually managed to overpower Hitler's army. In early 1945, Soviet troops invaded Poland and liberated Auschwitz. They found Nazi concentration camps and exposed the horrors perpetrated by Nazi Germany during the war. They were the first to reach Berlin, where a harsh battle took place between Germans who still believed in the Nazi cause and the Soviet soldiers.

War Against Japan

Although Germany had been soundly defeated, the war wasn't over yet. In August 1945, the USSR declared war on Japan and invaded Japanese-occupied Manchuria (northeastern China). Two days prior, the Americans had dropped a nuclear bomb on Hiroshima with the goal of forcing Japan to surrender. However, the Japanese were deadlocked on what to do next. Some didn't believe the Americans would follow through on their promise to bomb another city. Some didn't even believe the US had bombed the city and wanted to send a fact-finding mission to discover the truth. The Japanese didn't have much time to do this, as the US had placed a deadline on Japan's unconditional surrender. In addition, the Japanese didn't account for the Soviet Army, as they believed the Soviets wouldn't be coordinated enough to attack them until the following year.

The USSR invaded Manchuria with a million troops, vastly outnumbering the Japanese army, which totaled about 700,000 soldiers. The invasion of Manchuria quickly proved to the Japanese that they would not be able to withstand sustained attacks from the Allies, and Emperor Hirohito began reconsidering the terms of his surrender. On August 9th, another atomic bomb was dropped on Nagasaki. About a week later, Emperor Hirohito announced Japan's surrender. On September 2nd, 1945, Japanese representatives signed the Instrument of Surrender, marking Japan's official surrender.

The Effects of the War

As soon as it became apparent that the war was going to end, Allied leaders met in Yalta to discuss what would happen after the war ended. The Germans had conquered many territories, and it was necessary to discuss what would happen to those territories once the Germans were defeated. British Prime Minister Winston Churchill advocated for democratic elections and democratic governments in Europe, especially in Poland. Meanwhile, Joseph Stalin wanted to create governments that were loyal to the USSR that would provide buffer zones in case Germany ever tried to attack the USSR again.

The Yalta Conference ruled that Poland would be ruled by a communist provisional government for a while and that Germany and Berlin would be occupied by America, Britain, the USSR, and France. In August 1945, the Allied powers met again in Potsdam, Germany. By then, US President Franklin D. Roosevelt had died. His successor, President Harry Truman, was suspicious of Stalin and his motives.

During the war, Stalin enacted a scorched-earth defensive policy, destroying anything that might have been used to assist the Germans. This meant parts of Russia needed to rebuild after the war. Stalin participated in many Allied conferences, including the Tehran Conference. He managed to maintain his alliance with Allied countries while expanding the Soviet Empire.

Allied leaders at the 1943 Tehran Conference.
https://commons.wikimedia.org/wiki/File:Allied_leaders_at_the_1943_Tehran_Conference.jpg

The Soviet Union occupied Romania, Bulgaria, Hungary, Poland, and Eastern Germany. During the war, the Soviets helped to set up communist dictatorships in many of the countries they occupied. In 1949, the Soviets set up the Communist German Democratic Republic in the Soviet-German occupation zone.

After the war ended, over a million Soviet soldiers remained stationed in Eastern Europe. In 1946, Winston Churchill said that it was as if an iron curtain had been dropped across the continent.

Many people considered Churchill's words to be the first shot of the Cold War.

First Berlin Crisis of 1948

As the Cold War was brewing, the situation in Berlin worsened. Although Berlin was located in the Soviet occupation zone of Germany, it had also been divided between the other Allies. The western part of the city was controlled by the Allies, while the eastern part was controlled by the Soviets. It soon became apparent that both sides had very different visions for postwar Germany. The Soviets wanted to punish Germany by making the country pay steep reparations and used its industries to help the USSR recover from the war. The Allies wanted to help Germany recover from the war to help prevent the spread of communism.

In 1948, the Allies decided to combine their zones and create the state of Bizonia, a West German state with a stable currency. The Soviets opposed this plan and withdrew from the Allied Control Council, which had been created to coordinate the occupation of the zones. The Allied powers introduced a new currency called the Deutschmark, and the Soviets responded by releasing their own currency, the Ostmark. The Soviets also blocked all access to West Berlin. The blockade ensured the civilians of the western sector of the city were cut off from food, electricity, and other supplies. Two days later, a joint US and British relief operation was carried out. It was the largest air relief operation in history. Over two million tons of supplies were flown into West Berlin over eleven months.

The Soviets had hoped to cause the Allies to abandon West Berlin, but the relief mission prevented this from happening. The blockade was eventually lifted in 1949, but the division between East and West Berlin persisted.

The Cold War

By the end of the Second World War, the United States of America and the Soviet Union emerged as dominant world powers. However, they had diametrically opposed political ideologies. The Americans felt the Soviet policies were a threat that needed to be contained. Many US officials dedicated themselves to containing Soviet expansion, which was already taking place in Eastern Europe. To that end, the Americans decided to use military force to contain communist expansion, which led to a massive increase in defense spending. During this time, the development of atomic bombs was increasing. In 1949, the USSR tested its atomic bomb, which led the US to develop the hydrogen bomb. The nature of these weapons increased the stakes of the Cold War to unprecedented heights.

The two countries became locked in a deadly arms race as they tried to outdo each other. When the first hydrogen bomb was tested in the Marshall Islands, it destroyed an island, resulted in a twenty-five-square-mile fireball, and blew a hole in the ocean floor. To make matters worse, these tests launched nuclear waste into the atmosphere. The Cold War ushered in the age of nuclear weapons, and it became alarmingly apparent what the consequences would be. Although the two engaged in proxy wars against each other, the two never engaged in an all-out war with each other.

Death of Stalin

After the war, Stalin continued his reign of terror, which included purges, exiles, and executions. He introduced the Soviets to the nuclear age and established numerous communist governments. In 1950, he allowed North Korea's communist leader, Kim Il Sung, to invade South Korea, the latter of which was supported by the US. This led to the Korean War.

Stalin may have been responsible for about twenty million deaths during his time in power, so it is no surprise that he became incredibly paranoid during his last years. He died in 1953 from a stroke. His body was embalmed and entombed in Lenin's Mausoleum in Moscow. In 1961, his body was removed and buried near the Kremlin. Stalin was succeeded by Nikita Khrushchev, who began the de-Stalinization process.

Warsaw Pact

In 1955, the US and other members of the North Atlantic Treaty Organization (NATO) decided to allow West Germany to become a part of NATO and remilitarize itself. The USSR viewed this as a direct threat to its power and responded with its own treaty. The Warsaw Pact was signed in Warsaw and included Poland, Albania, the USSR, Romania, East Germany, Bulgaria, Hungary, and Czechoslovakia. The treaty ensured that if any of the countries included in the treaty were attacked, then the other countries would have to defend the attacked country. Essentially, the Warsaw Pact set up a united military power that would be commanded by Marshal Ivan Konev of the USSR.

The Warsaw Pact lasted until 1991, but Albania left the pact after it turned to communist China for help when the Soviet leader, Nikita Khrushchev, deviated from Marxism. As non-communist governments rose in Eastern Europe in 1990, the Warsaw Pact became increasingly ineffective until it was finally dissolved.

Cuban Missile Crisis of 1962

In 1959, revolutionary leader Fidel Castro seized control of Cuba and allied himself with the USSR. In time, Cuba needed the Soviets to provide it with economic and military aid. In 1962, a US spy pilot photographed Soviet missiles in Cuba. US President John F. Kennedy responded by calling a group of advisors who formed the executive committee known as ExComm (Executive Committee of the National Security Council). Both the US and the USSR grappled with the diplomatic crisis, which could have easily ended in outright war.

For years, the Cold War had been stacked in favor of the West since they had nuclear weapons in Turkey and Western Europe. However, Cuba was alarmingly close to US territory, which meant the Soviets would be able to devastate the US more easily with their nuclear missiles.

The US launched the failed Bay of Pigs invasion, which prompted Castro and the USSR to find a way to deter another invasion. The Soviet presence in Cuba was unacceptable to the Americans, so they sent US vessels to block Soviet ships from approaching the island nation. It was a risky move since the Soviets could have breached the blockade, which would have surely led to war. Americans began stockpiling supplies as they feared the worse.

Thankfully, the Soviet ships didn't attempt to break the blockade. The standoff continued for a week while the two global superpowers communicated with each other. Both countries finally came to a deal. Khrushchev promised to remove his missiles from Cuba if the US promised not to invade Cuba and removed their missiles from Turkey. Both sides accepted the deal, and a nuclear war was averted.

Space Race

The Space Race, which was part of the Cold War, became an important area of competition between America and the USSR. Space had been dubbed the next frontier, and both countries were determined to prove their superiority in this new arena. In 1957, the Soviets launched Sputnik (meaning "traveling companion"), which was the first manmade object to be placed in Earth's orbit. The Soviets used an R-7 intercontinental ballistic missile to launch Sputnik, allowing the Russians to make inroads in space exploration. By doing so, the USSR showed off its military might to the rest of the world.

The Americans were surprised and displeased about this turn of events. The US was determined not to allow the USSR to gain too much ground in space exploration.

In 1958, the Americans launched Explorer I, their first satellite, which initiated the Space Race. US President Dwight D. Eisenhower created the National Aeronautics and Space Administration (NASA) that same year. In 1961, the Soviets launched the first man into space, which was another massive achievement. Despite the Soviets' many firsts in space, the Americans are thought to have won the Space Race in 1969 when Neil Armstrong became the first man to walk on the moon.

SALT Treaties and the Anti-Ballistic Missile Treaty

The Strategic Arms Limitation Talks were two conferences attended by the Americans and Soviets that resulted in international treaties. These conferences came to be known as SALT I and SALT II. The first round of negotiations began in 1969 in Helsinki, Finland. The Anti-Ballistic Missile Treaty was created (also referred to as the ABM Treaty). The ABM Treaty was an arms control treaty that aimed to reduce the production of more nuclear weapons and deter both countries from using weapons of mass destruction. The treaty ensured that both nations only had two missile complexes with only one hundred anti-ballistic missiles. The treaty would stay in place for three decades.

The second SALT conference took place from 1972 to 1979 and aimed to reduce the production of strategic nuclear weapons. This treaty banned new missile programs and limited both sides from developing new strategic missiles. The terms of this treaty would only last until 1985. Soon after the treaty was signed, the

Soviets invaded Afghanistan, and the US chose not to ratify the terms of the agreement. However, both sides adhered to the treaty for a few more years.

In the meantime, the USSR was experiencing the de-Stalinization process. A few years after the SALT II treaty was negotiated, the USSR would officially dissolve.

Chapter 11: De-Stalinization to the Republic of Russia

Joseph Stalin was a brutal dictator who left his mark on the USSR. He helped turn his nation into a global superpower, but his methods also caused severe consequences for the Soviets. His successor, Nikita Khrushchev, was determined not to resort to the same methods and began a period of de-Stalinization, during which he worked to undo the cult of personality that had sprung up around Stalin.

While the USSR competed against the United States of America during the Cold War, the Soviet Union was going through several major changes and a period of stagnation. Eventually, the USSR would be dissolved, with the infamous Chernobyl (Chornobyl in Ukrainian) disaster playing a role in the downfall of the communist state. Russia would emerge as an independent republic, but the effects of privatization would lead to a fascinating new class in Russian society known as the oligarchs. This new period in Russian history would be led by two controversial figures: Boris Yeltsin and Vladimir Putin.

Nikita Khrushchev

Khrushchev was born in a small Russian village in 1894. When he was a teenager, he moved to the mining town of Yuzovka, where he worked as a metalworker. He joined the Bolsheviks in 1918 after their triumphant revolution. At the time, many idealistic youths joined the party since they believed communism was the answer to Russia's problems and wanted to be part of the new regime.

Khrushchev later moved to Moscow, where he rose to prominence within the communist government. He eventually became a part of Stalin's inner circle. Khrushchev managed to survive Stalin's paranoia and numerous political purges.

During the Second World War, he fought against Nazi Germany and helped rebuild the country after the war ended. He also earned merit when he suppressed nationalist uprisings in Ukraine. Six months after Stalin died, Khrushchev became the head of the Communist Party, which made him one of the most powerful people in the USSR.

Nikita Khrushchev.

Khrushchev ruled the USSR with other officials under a collective leadership. At the time, Georgi Malenkov served as the premier of the USSR. In 1955, Malenkov was replaced by Nikolai Bulganin, one of Khrushchev's allies. In 1958, Khrushchev himself became the premier of the USSR.

De-Stalinization Policies

While Khrushchev had been one of Stalin's most dependable subordinates, he later criticized Stalin's policies, brutal tactics, egotistical acts, and lackluster leadership. In 1961, he moved Stalin's remains and renamed the city of Stalingrad Volgograd. These words and actions inspired protestors in Poland and Hungary to seek more autonomy. While the Polish were peacefully suppressed, the Hungarian rebellion was met with tanks and soldiers. In 1956, about 2,500 Hungarians were killed, while 13,000 were injured.

Khrushchev continued the de-Stalinization process and worked to undo the mythology around Stalin. He made official pronouncements to the Communist Party of the Soviet Union to remove some of the hyperbolic aspects of Stalin's legacy and blamed Stalin for terrorizing the party. Khrushchev enacted several policies that confirmed the importance of collective leadership, helped rehabilitate some who had been terrorized by Stalin, adopted more flexible foreign policies, and removed the threat of terror from everyday life. Soon, this process picked up the pace, and Stalin's name was removed from places that had been named after him, his writings were taken out of libraries, and his busts, statues, and portraits were all taken down. Intellectuals were given greater freedoms since censorship policies were relaxed.

Meanwhile, Khrushchev worked hard to improve agricultural production. He also weakened the secret police, let many political prisoners go, encouraged foreigners to visit the country, launched the space age, and eased censorship on artists. The Soviet space program has long been considered a great success.

Soviet Space Program

When the USSR launched Sputnik 1, it was the first manmade object to orbit Earth, but it wasn't widely celebrated. In fact, it wasn't announced to the Soviet public until the next day. Meanwhile, foreign countries took notice. Sputnik I had several interactive capabilities. Radio operators all over the world could dial into Sputnik I and listen to it beeping as it orbited Earth. Sputnik I was an amazing achievement that ushered in an interesting new age in human history.

1959 postage stamp depicting Laika.
https://commons.wikimedia.org/wiki/File:Posta_Romana_-_1959_-_Laika_120_B.jpg

Next, the Soviets tried to send animals to space. Laika, the first dog to be sent to space, was a stray taken from the streets of Moscow. She didn't survive the trip. Later, in 1960, the Soviets sent two female dogs, Belka and Strelka, who went to space but returned the next day safely.

The Soviets were the first to send a number of probes to the moon, and in 1966, Luna 9 arrived safely on the moon and took the first close-up pictures of the moon's surface. In 1961, the Soviets sent the first man to space. Yuri Gagarin circled Earth once in a Soviet spacecraft before he safely landed back on Earth. He became an overnight celebrity and was used to promote the space program. In 1963, the Soviets sent the first woman to space. Valentina Tereshkova spent three days in orbit and later became a cosmonaut engineer and influential government official. In 1965, Alexei Leonov became the first person to perform a spacewalk.

Eventually, the Soviets managed to put a rover on the moon. The Lunokhod 1 had eight wheels, four cameras, an X-ray spectrometer, and other fascinating gadgets. It transmitted from the moon's surface for about a year as it analyzed soil samples and sent pictures of the moon's surface back to the space program. After a year, it stopped transmitting. The Soviet space program remained active until the dissolution of the USSR.

Stagnation Era

Khrushchev had lofty plans for the USSR, and in 1961, he claimed the USSR was just twenty years away from achieving full communism. However, his popularity quickly dwindled, as it became clear his policies weren't working as well as they should have. Many people also felt that he mishandled the Cuban Missile Crisis.

In 1964, Khrushchev was deposed by his political rivals. He was succeeded by a collective leadership led by Leonid Brezhnev. The Soviet government focused on initiating several economic reforms that worked at first, which caused the USSR to flourish. However, inefficient Soviet bureaucracy and improper central planning led to a period of stagnation following the peak experienced in the early 1970s.

Several five-year plans were prioritized by economic planners in Moscow, who then came up with targets and quotas to be carried out by Soviet officials at local levels. However, this system had very little flexibility, which would prove to be disastrous. The boom in the Soviet economy that occurred from 1965 to the early 1970s caused the Soviet bureaucracy to grow very quickly. Soon, there were more bureaucrats and clerks than industrial workers. Besides that, the economy was becoming increasingly complex, which made it difficult to control.

The Soviet economy suffered from slow growth. For years, the Soviets had spent massive amounts on the military, and corruption became rampant. While the USSR boasted incredible technical and industrial growth, the agricultural sector became increasingly neglected. This resulted in disastrous consequences, as the USSR eventually wasn't producing enough grain to feed its people. This meant Moscow had to depend on foreign grain imports, which caused a notable trade deficit and impacted the USSR's reputation. The shortage of grain and consumer products caused a downfall in the standard of living. People were forced to wait for hours to buy basic items, while electrical items, cars, clothing, and footwear were rare. Products manufactured in the USSR were notoriously low quality, but products manufactured in the West were nearly impossible to obtain. The stagnation era severely weakened the USSR, leaving it unprepared for future difficulties.

Mikhail Gorbachev

Mikhail Gorbachev was born in 1931 in the North Caucasus region, which belonged to the Soviet Union. His family was poor, and he grew up during Stalin's reign. While he was still in school, he joined the Soviet political youth organization, where he was elected as the leader of his local group and later became a part of the district committee. When Gorbachev was old enough, he joined the Communist Party and went to Moscow State University, where he studied law. During his time at the university, he married a philosophy student named Raisa Titarenko. After he graduated, he began rising in the Communist Party's ranks.

During de-Stalinization under Khrushchev, Gorbachev enthusiastically supported Khrushchev's policies. He occupied several different positions within the government and saw firsthand the problems caused by the stagnation. Due to his upbringing as a peasant, he was also keenly aware of the hardships faced by the people of the Soviet Union. In 1985, he became the general secretary, which essentially made him the leader of the Soviet Union.

Mikhail Gorbachev.

While Gorbachev supported socialist ideals, he believed the Soviet Union needed extensive reformation. He introduced several policies, such as *glasnost* and *perestroika*. Gorbachev also initiated a few democratization policies and formed the Congress of People's Deputies, which would be made up of elected officials. This threatened the one-party state, and his policies angered strict Marxist-Leninist followers.

Perestroika and *Glasnost* Policies

As soon as Gorbachev came to power, he delivered a speech that highlighted the economic problems the Soviet Union was facing. He claimed the economic system was inefficient, making him the first Soviet leader to publicly criticize his own government. He also addressed these issues when he spoke to the Congress of the Communist Party. During this time, he advocated for extensive political and economic reforms or restructuring, which would be called *perestroika*. He also aimed to start a new age of transparency, which would be called *glasnost*.

Gorbachev proved true to his word and began systematically loosening the government's control over businesses, farms, and manufacturers. Individuals were freed from strict price controls, and many central committees within the government had their power curtailed. These policies encouraged businesses to work for profits. Gorbachev also allowed aspects of free-market capitalism into the Soviet Union, which allowed people to open stores, industries, and restaurants. These limited cooperative businesses would later form the basis of the oligarchical system, which is prevalent in modern-day Russia. Unfortunately, Gorbachev's reforms backfired, as the cost of food rose and workers began striking for higher wages. To make matters worse, he faced backlash from within the Communist Party, as many felt he was betraying communist ideals. More liberal parties accused him of not making enough changes.

Besides reforming the economy, Gorbachev also worked on restructuring the political system. In 1988, he set plans in motion to hold the first democratic elections in Russia since 1917. This allowed many officials to campaign for a place in the new Congress of People's Deputies. Thanks to *glasnost*, many censorship rules were lifted, which allowed the press to honestly report the campaigns. In 1990, Gorbachev became the first president of the USSR. He also withdrew Soviet troops from Afghanistan and began engaging with Western leaders, most notably US President Ronald Reagan.

While Gorbachev had held high hopes for the restructuring of the Soviet government, his policies ultimately failed and led to the swift end of the Soviet Union.

Chernobyl Disaster

After the Second World War, the USSR began heavily investing in nuclear power and weapons, which is evidenced by the events of the Cold War. In 1977, Soviet scientists installed nuclear reactors at a power plant in Chernobyl (Chornobyl), Ukraine. A few years later, in 1986, workers conducted a test to see if the reactor would be cooled if the plant somehow lost power. Unfortunately, the workers disregarded several safety protocols, which caused a power surge. The workers tried to shut down the reactor, but it was too late, as another power surge set off a series of explosions that exposed the nuclear core and released radioactive materials into the environment. Firefighters tried to kill the fires and contain the contamination. Chernobyl and Pripyat (a nearby city that housed the people who worked at the plant) were only evacuated about thirty-six hours after the explosion.

The Soviet government attempted to cover up the disaster, but the radiation had spread as far as Sweden, which forced the Soviet government to make an announcement about the disaster. The disaster released 30 percent of Chernobyl's uranium into the atmosphere, and the Soviets had to evacuate 335,000 people from a 19-mile radius around the reactor. This area came to be known as the exclusion zone. About twenty-eight people died in the accident, while one hundred were injured.

The disaster contributed to the end of the Soviet Union and kicked off the global anti-nuclear movement.

Fall of the Berlin Wall

In 1961, the communist government of East Germany built a massive wall to separate East and West Berlin. The official purpose of the wall was to keep Western fascists from entering East Berlin, but the truth was that many people were defecting from East Berlin to West Berlin. The wall kept the people contained. Before the wall, citizens were allowed to move freely between the two sides of the city, but the wall put a stop to that. Few people were allowed to cross the wall. The wall separated families and prevented refugees from fleeing East Germany.

In 1989, a spokesperson for East Berlin's Communist Party announced that people were free to cross the border. About two million people from East Berlin visited the western part of the city, resulting in a massive street party. Soon, people grabbed hammers and picks to tear down pieces of the wall. Cranes and bulldozers began removing sections of the Berlin Wall until it finally came down. In 1990, East and West Germany were reunified.

Dissolution of the USSR

Gorbachev aimed to improve the Soviet Union's relationship with the rest of the world, as he hoped this could help the Soviet economy. He bowed out of the arms race, despite the fact US President Ronald Reagan had initiated a massive military buildup. He also reduced Soviet troops in Eastern Europe and withdrew his troops from the controversial war in Afghanistan. In 1989, a revolution took place in Poland, where non-communist trade unionists successfully negotiated for free elections. This sparked more revolutions in Eastern Europe. Czechoslovakia overthrew its communist government, and countries within the Soviet Union began declaring their independence from Russia.

Gorbachev's efforts to bring an end to the Cold War earned him the Nobel Peace Prize in 1990. In 1991, Gorbachev was placed under house arrest by members of the Communist Party. The coup seemed successful, and a state of emergency was declared.

The military attempted to take Moscow, but Russian citizens formed barricades and human chains to stop the tanks and protect the Russian Parliament. Boris Yeltsin, who was the chair of Parliament, supported the civilians' efforts. In the end, the coup failed. Yeltsin famously stood on top of a tank in front of Parliament to stop the military from advancing. In December, Belarus broke away from the USSR. Eight other countries followed, with many more having already broken away, such as Ukraine and Armenia. Yeltsin took control of the KGB (the USSR's security agency) and Parliament, and on December 25th,

1991, Gorbachev resigned as president. The USSR had officially fallen.

Boris Yeltsin

Boris Yeltsin was born in 1931 in the Ural Mountains. His family was poor, as his peasant grandparents had been uprooted during Stalin's rule. His father had been sent to the Gulag. In 1949, Yeltsin attended the Urals Polytechnic Institute. He became a civil engineer and married Naina Iosifovna Girina. In 1961, he joined the Communist Party and quickly rose within the government. Yeltsin was summoned to Moscow by Gorbachev and fought against corruption within the government. However, in 1987, he lost his position after he clashed with Gorbachev. In 1990, Yeltsin became the chair of the Russian Parliament and left the Communist Party. In 1991, he was elected as the Russian president.

Boris Yeltsin.

Yeltsin immediately began dismantling the Soviet Union and the Communist Party. He took away many price controls and privatized major state assets. Yeltsin also adopted many free-market principles, allowing the stock exchange, private banks, and commodities exchanges to come into existence. This led to increased inflation and a high cost of living. A select few oligarchs were able to take control of privatized state assets and became incredibly wealthy in a short amount of time. Unfortunately, corruption, crime, and decreased industrial output became rampant. Yeltsin allowed Western culture into Russia, supported the freedom of the press, agreed to nuclear arms reductions, and withdrew soldiers from Eastern Europe.

In 1999, Yeltsin surprised the world when he resigned from his post and asked for forgiveness for his past mistakes. He then gave power to his successor, Vladimir Putin.

First and Second Chechen Wars

The First Chechen War was a war of independence fought by the Chechen Republic of Ichkeria against Russia. It took place from 1994 to 1996. The war was in response to the Russian attempt to secretly overthrow the Ichkerian government. While the Russians had the advantage in regard to firepower, military technology, weapons, and soldiers, they found the Chechen guerillas difficult to defeat. The Russian military was demoralized since it was not making much progress, and the Russian public firmly opposed the war. Yeltsin's government was forced to declare a ceasefire in 1996, which resulted in a peace treaty in 1997.

The Second Chechen War took place from 1999 to 2009. In 1999, Islamic soldiers took over Russia's Dagestan region and declared it to be an independent state. By 2009, the Russians had largely brought an end to the fighting. The Russians left Chechnya, and the local police were tasked with dealing with any minor insurgencies. The exiled leader of the separatist government eventually called for an end to the resistance, bringing the conflict to a stop.

Vladimir Putin

Vladimir Putin was born in 1952 in Leningrad (now St. Petersburg). He attended Leningrad State University, where he studied law. After he graduated, he became a foreign intelligence officer for the KGB. In 1991, he retired from the KGB, and in 1994, he became the first deputy chairman of St. Petersburg. In 1996, he moved to Moscow and moved up within the government. Putin gained a reputation for being able to get things done. In 1998, he became the director of the FSB (the Federal Security Service, the KGB's successor). Finally, in 1999, Putin was chosen as Yeltsin's successor and became president. Putin proved to be a levelheaded leader who launched a successful operation against the rebels in Chechnya.

Putin helped the economy recover, a feat that was aided by the rise of oil prices. He encouraged economic growth, which improved his popularity with the Russian government. In 2008, he was forced to step down from his position due to a constitutional provision. He chose Dmitry Medvedev as his successor, and he was appointed as prime minister. Although Medvedev held the position of president, Putin was still the one calling the shots. In 2012, Putin was reelected as president, and he made Medvedev his prime minister. While Putin faced a lot of opposition, he managed to stifle protest movements and had opposition leaders put in prison.

Vladimir Putin.

During Putin's third term as president, Russia annexed Crimea and later sponsored a war in eastern Ukraine. These actions led to international sanctions that caused a financial crisis in Russia. During his fourth term as president, he ordered a military buildup on the border of Ukraine and then accused the Ukraine government of persecuting its Russian-speaking minority (although history might tell a different tale later on, at the moment, it is believed these are false accusations). Putin ordered an invasion of Ukraine in 2022, which led to increased sanctions and international condemnation. Many have called for Putin to be prosecuted on charges of war crimes.

Chapter 12: Russian Arts, Literature, and Science

During Russia's long and storied history, its art and culture went through several significant changes. The climactic events that took place in the country's history provided inspiration for some of the most influential literature and music in the world. At various periods in Russia's history, the country housed cities that became intellectual hubs, attracting scholars from all over the world. This led to major advancements in subjects like science and mathematics.

This chapter explores the lives and achievements of some of Russia's most talented and influential musicians, writers, and scientists. These individuals provide a unique view into the different time periods in which they lived.

The Great Russian Musicians

- **Tchaikovsky**

Pyotr Ilyich Tchaikovsky was born in 1840 in Kamsko-Votkinsk, Russia. He was the second of six children, and his father was the manager of a metalworking company. Early in his childhood, Tchaikovsky displayed an interest in music and wrote his first song at four years old. In 1845, he began taking piano lessons and studied the works of Chopin and Friedrich Kalkbrenner. At the time, music wasn't taught in Russian schools, so Tchaikovsky's parents arranged a career in civil service. In 1850, he attended the Imperial School of Jurisprudence in St. Petersburg. He was a popular student who got good grades. Around this time, he formed intense emotional bonds with several of his peers.

Pyotr Ilyich Tchaikovsky, c. 1870.
https://commons.wikimedia.org/wiki/File:Pyotr_Tchaikovsky_%D1%81._1870.jpg

As a teenager, Tchaikovsky's father invited a professional teacher to give Tchaikovsky lessons. He was heavily influenced by Italian singing teacher Luigi Piccioli, which led to a passion for Italian music. In 1861, he traveled to Germany, France, and England. He later attended the newly founded Russian Musical Society. In 1865, Johann Strauss the Younger conducted Tchaikovsky's Characteristic Dances in Pavlovsk. This would be the first time his work was played in public. While working as a teacher for the Russian Musical Society (later the Moscow Conservatory), he produced his first opera, *The Voyevoda*, and his first symphony, Symphony No. 1 in G Minor.

In time, his music became increasingly popular throughout Russia and the world. Tchaikovsky became known for his colorful orchestration and impressive harmonies. He eventually wrote seven symphonies, three ballets, five suites, three piano concertos, a violin concerto, eleven overtures, four cantatas, three string quartets, a string sextet, twenty choral works, and over one hundred songs. According to tradition, he died in 1893 from complications arising from cholera. However, some speculate that he committed suicide.

While Tchaikovsky experienced major criticism during his lifetime, he became a national icon in the Soviet Union. He experienced a lot of criticism because Russians didn't see it as being "national" enough and too European. Although Russia denies that Tchaikovsky was gay, his biographers all agree that he was but that he kept it private for most of his life. Tchaikovsky's letters are definite proof of his sexual orientation, as he wrote about being enamored with his servant and his nephew.

- **Rachmaninoff**

Sergei Rachmaninoff was born in 1873 on his grandparents' estate in the Novgorod district. His father was an army officer, and it was assumed Rachmaninoff would also join the army, but his father lost the family fortune and abandoned his family. Rachmaninoff's cousin, Alexander Siloti, who was a pianist and conductor, noticed the boy's talents and arranged for him to study music in Moscow. Rachmaninoff was tutored by Nikolai Zverev and later attended the Moscow Conservatory.

After Rachmaninoff graduated from the conservatory, he won a gold medal for his opera *Aleko*, which was based on one of Pushkin's poems. His two compositions, Prelude in C-sharp Minor and Piano Concerto No. 2 in C Minor, launched him into stardom. The young musician suffered from bouts of self-doubt and depression but was helped by the psychiatrist Nikolai Dahl, who reportedly helped Rachmaninoff regain his confidence. In 1905, Rachmaninoff worked at the Bolshoi Theatre and saw firsthand the events of the 1905 Revolution.

Later, he moved with his family to Dresden, where he wrote three major scores. He conducted several musical tours in the United States, which were successful. Rachmaninoff was invited to work at the Boston Symphony but declined in favor of returning to Russia.

After the Russian Revolution, Rachmaninoff went into self-imposed exile and spent time between the US and Switzerland. His alienation from his home country had a severe negative impact on his creative ability. He lived a rather isolated life from then on and wrote a few more pieces before his death in 1943.

- **Rimsky-Korsakov**

Nikolai Rimsky-Korsakov was born near Novgorod in 1844 to an aristocratic family. He showed an affinity for music at an early age but was sent to study at the Russian Imperial Naval College in St. Petersburg, after which he joined the Russian Navy. While Rimsky-Korsakov was in the navy, he completed his first symphony, which made him the first Russian to compose one. He completed two more works before he resigned from the navy in 1873. Rimsky-Korsakov worked with a group of composers who often collaborated and edited each other's work. The group came to be known as "The Five."

Rimsky-Korsakov was largely self-taught but became a professor of composition and orchestration at the St. Petersburg Conservatory. He produced many orchestral works and influenced later composers. In 1905, Rimsky-Korsakov was fired from the conservatory due to his political views but was eventually reinstated once a few of his colleagues resigned in protest. His opera *The Golden Cockerel* harshly criticized imperial Russia and was banned. He died in 1908 and was interred in St. Petersburg.

- **Stravinsky**

Igor Stravinsky was born in 1882 near St. Petersburg. His father worked as a bass singer at the Mariinsky Theatre in St. Petersburg. Later, Stravinsky studied law but switched to composition. Rimsky-Korsakov was the head of the Russian Conservatory at the time and offered to give Stravinsky private lessons, which Stravinsky eagerly accepted.

During the First World War, Stravinsky moved to Switzerland and later to Paris, where he wrote ballets and other compositions. He loved exploring different aspects of art and literature. Stravinsky notably worked with Sergei Diaghilev, Pablo Picasso, Jean Cocteau, and George Balanchine.

Igor Stravinsky.

Stravinsky was known for his innovative ballets that revolutionized the genre. His musical works ranged from opera to jazz, and he experimented with many different classical forms of music. Stravinsky was an accomplished pianist and conductor. He also worked as a writer and complied the *Poetics of Music*. Stravinsky moved to the US in 1939. He became a naturalized US citizen and remained there until he died in 1971.

- **Shostakovich**

Dmitri Shostakovich was born in 1906 in St. Petersburg. Shostakovich displayed remarkable musical talent after he began taking piano lessons at the age of nine. In 1918, he wrote a funeral march and was admitted to the Petrograd Conservatory a year later. Shostakovich made his musical debut in 1926 with the Leningrad Philharmonic Orchestra, which performed his first symphony. It was well received, and the crowd demanded an encore.

Shostakovich was reportedly an obsessive man who was obsessed with cleanliness and regularly sent himself mail to check that the postal service was still working. His peers said he was vulnerable and receptive, which likely increased the quality of his music.

He achieved fame in the Soviet Union, but some of his work, particularly his opera *Lady Macbeth of Mtsensk*, was condemned by the government. He suffered from state censure, and his work was occasionally checked by the state.

His work was often characterized by distinct contrasts, neoclassical influences, and elements of the grotesque. During the Second World War, he composed Symphony No. 7, which was written during the siege of Leningrad. The composition would come to be known as his most famous wartime composition.

Shostakovich loved using different musical techniques, making his work varied and interesting. The composer was greatly influenced by Stravinsky's works. He also wrote a lot of music for films and the theater. Scholars continue to debate his work, especially the nature of his work and his feelings toward the Soviet government. He is widely regarded as a musical genius. Shostakovich died of heart failure in 1975 in Moscow.

Famous Russian Writers

- ### Leo Tolstoy

Leo Tolstoy was born in 1828 on his family's estate in the Tula Province of Russia. He was the youngest of four and was raised by his father's cousin when his mother died. During his childhood, he lost several close family members but always remembered his childhood fondly.

Tolstoy was educated at home by French and German tutors. In 1843, he attended the University of Kazan, where he studied Oriental languages. He wasn't a successful student and was forced to transfer to a law program. He partied excessively and eventually left university without a degree.

In 1847, Tolstoy returned to his parent's estate, where he attempted to become a farmer, but his work was interrupted by his frequent social visits to Moscow and Tula. During this time, he began keeping a journal, which would help develop his writing skills.

Leo Tolstoy.
https://commons.wikimedia.org/wiki/File:Leo_Tolstoy,_portrait.jpg

He later joined the army, and in 1855, he fought in the Crimean War. During his time in the army, Tolstoy began working on a story called *Childhood*. It would become his first published work. He then began working on a book called *The Cossacks*, which detailed daily life in the army. It was finished after he left the military.

When Tolstoy returned to Russia, he found his works had made an impact on Russian literary circles. He refused to ally himself with any particular school of thought and declared himself an anarchist. He went to Paris for a while but eventually returned to Russia. In 1862, he married Sophia Andreyevna Bers. In the 1860s, Tolstoy spent his time creating one of his great works, *War and Peace*. It was well received, and in 1873, he began working on *Anna Karenina*, which also achieved critical and public acclaim.

Later in life, Tolstoy suffered from depression caused by a spiritual crisis. He attempted to find the answers he sought in the

Russian Orthodox Church but wasn't satisfied with what he found. He then decided to develop his own beliefs, which caused the Russian Orthodox Church to oust him from the church. During the last years of his life, he regarded himself as a religious leader and was influenced by the teachings of Mahatma Gandhi. Tolstoy eventually died in 1910.

- **Alexander Pushkin**

Alexander Pushkin was born in 1799 and later became Russia's most famous poet. He was born into a prestigious noble family; many of his ancestors had played influential roles in Russian history. He became a student at the Lyceum of Tsarskoe Selo and became enamored with French poetry and Russian neoclassicism. He graduated in 1817 and became involved in partying and politics.

Pushkin's early poems often commented on autocracy's limits and would later be used by the Decembrists, a military organization that challenged Tsar Nicholas I. He was known for breaking poetry traditions, and his mock epic, *Ruslan and Ludmila*, was a massive success. However, his political views got him exiled to southern Russia. During this time, he traveled extensively, writing lyrics and poems.

Alexander Pushkin.
https://commons.wikimedia.org/wiki/File:AleksandrPushkin.jpg

Pushkin later invented a new stanza in his poem *Eugene Onegin*. He was eventually released from his exile but was subject to government censure.

His life was defined by romantic and political scandals that put a strain on his position in the royal court. In 1831, he married Natalia Goncharova. She was a famous beauty who enjoyed a good position at court. Nicholas I was infatuated with Natalia. A French royalist, Georges-Charles de Heeckeren d'Anthès, also pursued her, which caused Pushkin to challenge him to a duel. Pushkin lost the duel and died from his injuries about two days later.

Pushkin left a lasting legacy on Russian literature, and the Russian public mourned his passing.

- **Fyodor Dostoyevsky**

Fyodor Dostoevsky was born in 1821 and was the second of seven children. His father was a retired military surgeon who worked at the Mariinsky Hospital for the Poor in Moscow, which was located in one of the worst areas in the city. Dostoevsky grew up among the poor and developed a deep compassion for them, which would become evident in his later works.

As a child, Dostoevsky loved spending time with the patients in his father's hospital since they would regale him with their stories. In 1837, he was sent to the Military Engineering Academy in St. Petersburg. Dostoevsky suffered from epilepsy from the age of nine; some of his characters are also afflicted with the condition.

In 1844, Dostoevsky began writing fiction after he left the army. His first short novel, *Poor Folk*, was met with great acclaim. In 1849, he was arrested for being part of a liberal intellectual group. He was sentenced to death, which was later commuted to four years of exile with hard labor in a Siberian labor camp.

When Dostoevsky returned to St. Petersburg, he began a successful literary journal with his brother. His wife and brother died in quick succession, which plunged him into a deep depression. He began gambling and accumulated massive debts. Many claim that his best-known novel, *Crime and Punishment*, was completed in a hurry because he needed an advance from his publisher.

Dostoevsky has been accredited with founding existentialism and showed an acute understating of human psychology. He also managed to capture Russia's political, social, and spiritual state on paper while making his work compelling. He is known as one of the greatest writers of all time and influenced many other famous writers, such as Ernest Hemingway. He died in 1881 after suffering from multiple pulmonary hemorrhages.

- **Maxim Gorky**

Aleksey Peshkov was born in 1868 in Novgorod. He later adopted the pseudonym Maxim Gorky. His father was a shipping agent who died when Gorky was five. He was then sent to live with his grandparents. He went to school until he was eight years old before he was sent out to earn his living. He worked as an errand boy, a dishwasher, and an assistant. Gorky was introduced to reading at a young age, and it soon became his passion.

Gorky was frequently beaten by his employers and treated terribly by his grandfather. These experiences made him intimately aware of the problems faced by the Russian working class. He claimed his childhood experiences were often bitter, which was why he chose the word *gorky* (meaning "bitter") as his pseudonym. He attempted suicide as a young man but survived and became a tramp.

Maxim Gorky.
https://commons.wikimedia.org/wiki/File:Maxim_Gorky_LOC_Restored_edit1.jpg

In 1895, his story "Chelkash" was published and met with critical acclaim, launching his career. His works were compared to Leo Tolstoy and Anton Chekhov. Gorky wrote a series of novels and plays that weren't as well received as his previous work. He later became a Marxist and supported the Social Democratic Party.

When the Bolsheviks began rising to prominence, he found himself at odds with Lenin but gave much of his earnings to the party, which became one of the Bolsheviks' main sources of income. In 1906, he left Russia and lived in Italy. While Gorky agreed with some of the Bolsheviks' policies, he opposed their seizure of power in 1917. He tried to help exiled and imprisoned writers but was opposed by Lenin, who exiled him in 1921.

During his last few years, he produced some of his greatest works. Gorky died suddenly in 1936 while receiving medical treatment. Many speculated that he was covertly killed by Stalin since he was openly critical of Stalin's government. The theory has some merit, as Stalin famously didn't take criticism well.

- **Nikolai Gogol**

Nikolai Gogol was born in 1809 in Ukraine, which at the time was part of the Russian Empire. His works later became some of the most beloved pieces of Russian literature. He has been called the first Russian realist, as he often used comic realism and satire to great effect. His work influenced other Russian writers, namely Ivan Turgenev, Leo Tolstoy, and Fyodor Dostoyevsky.

Gogol was born into a noble family, and his father died when he was still a teenager. His mother raised him as a Christian, which would later influence many of his decisions. In 1828, Gogol moved to St. Petersburg, where he became friends with Pushkin, who greatly supported his career. Many of his witty lines later became popular Russian sayings. His work was well received, and he worked as a history professor at St. Petersburg University.

His play, *The Inspector General* (also known as *The Government Inspector*), was a biting satire of Russian bureaucracy. It caused so much controversy that Gogol decided to spend the next twelve years abroad. He found ways past political censorship by using fantastical and supernatural elements to soften anything that offended the government. His work later inspired other Soviet writers to use the same methods.

Gogol died in 1852 after burning the manuscript of his last book since he was unable to reconcile his Christian beliefs to his writings. He died a few days later after taking to his bed and refusing to take any food.

- **Anton Chekhov**

Anton Chekhov was born in 1860 in Taganrog, Russia. He attended a local school for Greek boys. In 1879, he moved to Moscow, where he enrolled at a university and studied medicine. His father had been unable to work for years at that point, so Chekhov became the family's breadwinner. He worked for a time as a journalist and comic writer, which he used to support his family and pay for medical school. In 1888, Chekhov was already a popular writer with the general public. Eventually, he strayed away from his comedic writing and began focusing on serious writing that studied misery and despair.

Anton Chekhov in 1904.
https://commons.wikimedia.org/wiki/File:Anton_Chekhov_1904.JPG

Chekhov's works became renowned for exposing human nature, while his plays and short stories often lacked clean solutions. His work created a unique atmosphere and was often described as haunting. He was able to describe Russian life simply without relying on literary devices.

Chekhov remained popular in Russia for most of his life but only received international attention after the First World War. Anton Chekhov died in 1904 after a long battle with tuberculosis.

- **Aleksandr Solzhenitsyn**

Aleksandr Solzhenitsyn was born in Russia in 1918 to a family who opposed the Soviet anti-religious campaign and clung to their Russian Orthodox faith. As a child, he became an atheist and Marxist-Leninist. He served as a captain in the Soviet Army during the Second World War. However, he was sentenced to eight years in the Gulag for criticizing Joseph Stalin in one of his private letters.

Due to his time in the camps, he became an Eastern Orthodox Christian. After Solzhenitsyn was released from the Gulag, he began writing novels about his experiences and the Soviet Union's repression. His first novel was published in 1862 with Nikita Khrushchev's approval; it provided a detailed account of Stalin's oppression. In 1963, Solzhenitsyn published a book called *Matryona's Place*, which would be the last book he published in the Soviet Union.

Once Khrushchev was removed from power, the Soviet government discouraged Solzhenitsyn from writing any more novels. He kept working but published his books in other countries. His works angered the Soviet government. In 1974, he lost his Soviet citizenship and was flown to West Germany. Two years later, he moved to the United States, where he continued writing. During this time, he harshly criticized communism and tried to raise awareness about the repression caused by the Soviet Union. He regained his citizenship after the USSR was dissolved and lived in Russia until he died in 2008.

Influential Russian Scientists

- **Dimitri Mendeleev**

Dmitri Mendeleev was born in 1834 in Siberia. His father was a school principal and a teacher. Mendeleev was raised as an Orthodox Christian and encouraged to search for scientific and divine truths. He had seventeen siblings, fourteen of whom survived childhood. Mendeleev was the youngest.

In 1850, he entered the Main Pedagogical Institute in St. Petersburg. In 1861, he published a textbook on organic chemistry, which won him the Demidov Prize from the Petersburg Academy of Sciences. In 1864, he became a professor at the Saint Petersburg Technological Institute, and a year later, he taught at Saint Petersburg State University. Mendeleev managed to turn St. Petersburg into an internationally recognized center focused on chemistry research.

Dimitri Mendeleev.

In 1863, there were about fifty-six known chemical elements, but chemists were discovering new elements almost every year. This caused a dilemma, with chemists trying to organize these elements differently. Mendeleev's textbook, the *Principles of Chemistry*, became one of the most influential textbooks of his time. While working on the textbook, he tried to arrange the elements according to their chemical properties. He soon noticed patterns, which led him to create the periodic table of elements. Mendeleev later published his periodic table in a journal and even predicted a few new elements.

Today, Mendeleev is known as the "Father of the Periodic Table." Although his periodic table was by no means finished, it left room for discoveries and improvements. Mendeleev died in 1907 of the flu.

- **Mikhail Lomonosov**

Mikhail Lomonosov was born in 1711 in the village of Denisovka, which would later be renamed in his honor. He was born to a poor family and eventually made his way to Moscow on foot. Lomonosov had a boundless curiosity and thirst for knowledge that wasn't being satisfied in his rural village, which made him decide to seek education elsewhere. He was able to gain admission into the Slavic Greek Latin Academy, where he made rapid progress.

In 1734, he was sent to St. Petersburg, where he distinguished himself and was sent to complete his education in a foreign country. He went to the University of Marburg in Hesse, Germany, which was one of the most important universities in Europe. There, he studied under the influential German Enlightenment philosopher Christian Wolff. During this time, he also began writing poetry.

When Lomonosov returned to Russia, he quickly rose to prominence and was made a professor of chemistry at St. Petersburg State University. He helped found Moscow State University and eventually became the secretary of state. He made many scientific discoveries and greatly improved Russian education.

Lomonosov was also the first person to ever record the freezing of mercury. In 1745, he published a comprehensive catalog of over three thousand minerals, and a few years later, he was able to explain the formation of icebergs.

He had many varied interests, which included the ancient art of mosaics. He even set up a glass factory that produced the first non-Italian stained-glass mosaics. Lomonosov made about forty great mosaics. He also reformed the Russian literary language and wrote extensively about literary theories. Lomonosov was deeply interested in poetry, and his work is considered the best of his generation.

Lomonosov died in St. Petersburg in 1765 and left behind a legacy as a gifted polymath and writer who revolutionized Russian literature, science, and education. Due to his efforts, he is one of the most well-known and influential scientists and writers in Russian history.

- **Ivan Pavlov**

Ivan Pavlov was born in Russia in 1849. His father was a priest, so Ivan was educated at a church school and theological seminary. However, he was introduced to the works of I. M. Sechenov and Charles Darwin, which led him to pursue a scientific career instead. He studied chemistry and physiology at St. Petersburg University. He later went on to study under Rudolf Heidenhain and Carl Ludwig, who were some of the most renowned physiologists of the time.

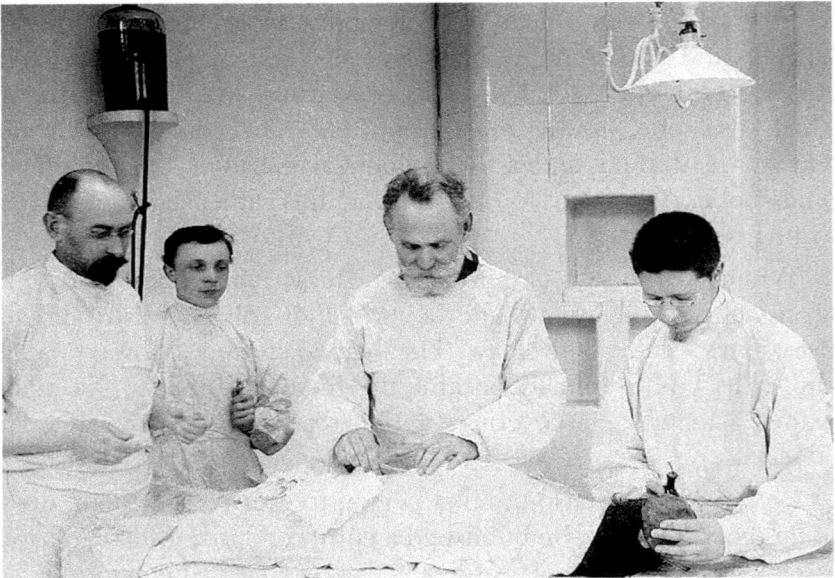

Ivan Pavlov in his laboratory.

Pavlov studied human digestion extensively and gained a deep understanding of gastric secretions and the role of the mind and body in the digestive process. In 1897, he published a book called *Lectures on the Work of the Digestive Glands*. His work earned him a Nobel Prize for Physiology in 1904. He also received an honorary doctorate from Cambridge University and the Order of the Legion of Honor.

Pavlov is best known for his research on conditioned reflexes. He was able to prove that dogs instinctively salivated at the prospect of food. Later, he realized the dogs began salivating at the mere sight of a person in a lab coat since those people usually brought the dogs food. They learned the lab coat usually resulted in food, which triggered an unconditioned response. From then on, Pavlov began to study conditioning. He discovered that certain stimuli could cause dogs to associate those stimuli with food, triggering a conditioned response. Pavlov also found out how to break that response.

While he tested his theories on animals, the principles could also be applied to humans. Pavlov believed that certain behaviors in people with psychological problems were conditioned responses that could be unlearned. His theories would later be confirmed.

Pavlov continued working in his lab until he died in 1936 in Leningrad after contracting double pneumonia. His lab was turned into a museum, and a monument was erected in his honor.

Conclusion

Russia is the largest country in the world and has a long and varied history. While this book doesn't contain every event from Russia's history, it includes some of the most important periods, incidents, and individuals.

The first section of this book dealt with the early Slavic kingdoms, the Mongol invasion, and Russia's time as part of the Golden Horde. These events left a lasting mark on Russia. At one point in Russia's history, the Slavs were ruled by Viking princes who built a powerful state. The Mongols wreaked havoc on Russia, but eventually, Russian princes were able to overthrow their Mongol overlords to build a strong ruling dynasty.

The second section of this book explored the Christianization of the Rus' and the rise of the Russian Empire, which all started with the Grand Duchy of Moscow. Eventually, the Rurikid dynasty was replaced by the Romanovs after a long period of political and economic strife. The Romanovs held onto power for a little over three centuries. During that time, several influential leaders took the throne, including Peter the Great and Catherine the Great. While they held on to their absolute autocracy, they managed to reform and modernize the country. Their efforts helped build the mighty Russian Empire, which was divided between Slavophiles and Westernizers. Both sides thought they knew what was best for Russia. Imperial Russia managed to defeat Napoleon but was severely weakened by the Crimean War. As the ideas of revolution became prevalent in Russia, Tsar Alexander II tried to reform his country to meet some of the demands made by revolutionists. Unfortunately, that work was undone by his successor, Tsar Alexander III, who was a firm Slavophile.

In the third section, the events of World War I and the Russian Revolution were discussed. The Romanovs were overthrown, and the monarchy was substituted with the world's first communist government under Lenin, who formed the USSR.

Finally, this book looked at the rule of Stalin, Russia's involvement in World War II, and the start of the Cold War. During this period, Russia belonged to the Soviet Union and boasted an impressive collection of nuclear weapons and a flourishing space program. However, the USSR went through a period of stagnation, which severely weakened it. The USSR wouldn't survive for much longer. When it was dissolved, its state assets were privatized.

Russian history is full of interesting events and fascinating figures who either made Russia better or worse. Comprehensive knowledge of Russian history will contribute to an expanded understanding of world history and current events. Russia is certainly making news in the headlines as of this writing, and it is likely that trend will continue in the future.

Part 2: The Romanovs

An Enthralling Overview of the House of Romanov

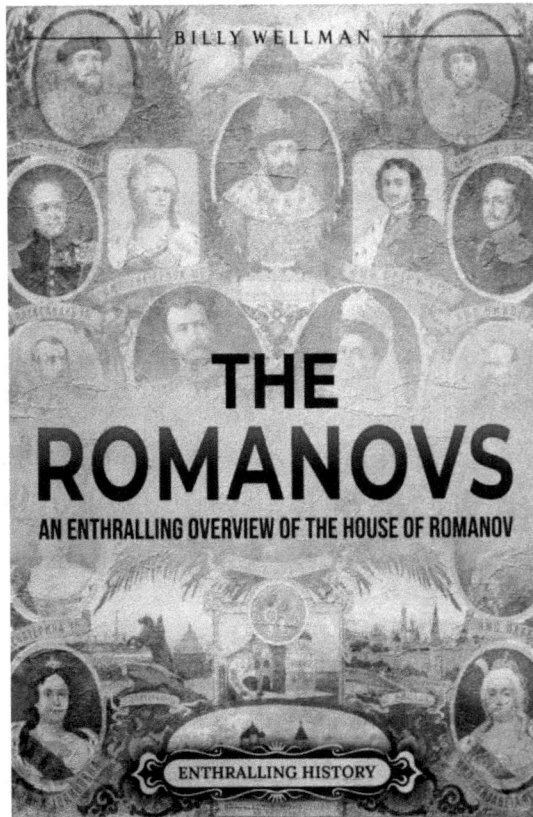

Introduction

When it comes to listing the most iconic or infamous dynasties throughout world history, several names instantly come to mind. Powerful families have always challenged each other for dominance in different parts of the world—something that largely characterized the social and political landscapes of ancient, medieval, and early modern times. These families often emerged from the uncertain and chaotic political turmoil of their respective regions and time periods as superior rulers, forming dynasties, some of which would last for centuries. For example, in the competitive societies of ancient China and Japan, dynasties temporarily rose to power and united their dominions, defining entire eras and playing important roles in the establishment of distinct cultural, social, and political characteristics. The Meiji Restoration period of 19th-century Japan under the Meiji dynasty is rather notable, while the Ming and Qing dynasties dominated China beginning in the early 14th century.

Unlike medieval Asia, where a single dynasty often overpowered the others to enjoy a period of solitary rule, powerful European dynasties often existed simultaneously in different countries, something that can only be attributed to the cultural and ethnic diversity present in the continent. Some of these European family names, like the Habsburgs and the Bourbons, are recognizable even to the most casual of history enthusiasts. Thriving in competition with each other and remaining at the top for centuries, the European dynasties are well known for their roles in history and have been a subject of fascination because of the complexities that characterized them.

However, when it comes to the famous dynasties of Europe, perhaps none are as intriguing as the Romanov dynasty, a family that ruled Russia for around three hundred years. Their renown stems from the fact that Russia itself, as a sovereign nation-state, has had an interesting journey, with the country undergoing the most substantial and long-lasting transformations of any European superpower. The different state-like formations in Russia struggled for centuries to find their true identity, plagued by their difficult, remote geographical location at the meeting point of European and Asian cultures and constantly bothered by either external threats or domestic instabilities.

Although the Rurikid dynasty can be considered the most powerful in Russian history (after all, the legendary Rurik was the one to organize the primitive settlements in the area as a Russian proto-state, and his descendants generally ruled the different provinces in the centuries that followed), the socio-political structures in place would make it rather difficult for a single family to emerge on top of the hierarchy and keep their position of power. Instead, the history of medieval Russia is filled with instances of dominant rulers who would leave their mark due to their explosive, charismatic personalities, although there was a plethora of forgettable ones. The combination of all the above-mentioned facts makes the Romanov dynasty stand out even more, as it is truly fascinating how a single family maintained its firm rule over so many of its subjects in such a chaotic place.

Thus, this book will explore the history of the Romanovs—Russia's greatest dynasty—from its relatively humble beginnings to the height of its power to its rather brutal end. First, the book will dive deep into the background before the emergence of the Romanovs. The first chapters will be concerned with the final days of the Rurikids and the Time of Troubles, a period in Russian history where uncertainty and chaos reigned. We will then talk about the first Romanovs, who slowly managed to unify the vast and unruly Russian provinces and provide a basis for a little over three centuries of firm rule. Next, the book will explore the consolidation of the dynasty under the enlightened despotism of Catherine the Great, as well as the challenges the Romanovs had to face during the early 19th century against Napoleon.

The middle part of the book discusses the rest of the Romanov rulers. We cover their most notable contributions to Russia and the rest of Europe up until the start of World War I. Finally, the book will talk about the rather difficult parts of the Romanov rule in the early 20th century, including the country's involvement in the Great War, the Bolshevik Revolution, and the tragic end of the Russian monarchy.

Chapter 1: Before the Romanovs

Before we discuss the Romanov dynasty, we should first briefly look at the two hundred years or so before the Romanovs came to power. As a matter of fact, the 14th and 15th centuries were vital for Russia since "Russia," as the state we know today, would form during this period. Therefore, it is only logical to go over those social and political developments in the 1300s and 1400s that stimulated the unification of many different principalities and explain how they affected the course of Russian history. This first chapter of the book will be concerned with covering the very interesting period immediately before the first true Russian state, discussing the emergence of Moscow (also known as Muscovy) as a new center for Russian civilization and the immense implications it had on the geopolitical climate.

Briefly on Medieval Russia

It is important to mention that Russia, as a unified state, was still a new phenomenon in the mid-16th century. Throughout history, the rulers of Russia, known as the grand princes, faced a lot of difficulties because of the decentralization of power that was innate in the political landscape, which was diverse and thinly stretched out. Many larger and smaller provinces were ruled by individual princes, who, in theory, were loyal to the grand prince but, in practice, acted as independently as they desired. They were in all aspects "Russian," as they spoke the same language, pursued the same culture and religion, and came from the same descendants. But the complex power politics that characterized the dynamic relationships between them made it so they never lived in harmony, coexisting instead as rivals, ready to rise to the top as soon as they saw the opportunity. This had been the case for hundreds of years, ever since the legendary Rurik had come down from Scandinavia to unite the primitive settlements in the Russian territories under his rule. His descendants—the Rurikids—had since ruled the Russian people, with some of them certainly finding better success than others.

The lands ruled by the Rurikid princes and their subordinates were referred to by other Europeans as "the lands of the Rus" for about five hundred or so years after the death of Rurik, although "Russia" as a unified state would take much longer to emerge. Challenged by the interests of individual princes and constant foreign threats, including the nearly two-and-a-half centuries of Mongol occupation, the Russian rulers had to struggle for their own survival before they could try uniting their subordinates and forming a strong state. Because of the difficult circumstances, Russia eventually fell behind to Europe. Russia was influenced by several different ideologies and struggled to find its own identity for centuries, something that would later be heavily addressed by the likes of Peter the Great.

These circumstances also influenced another phenomenon, which would repeat itself throughout not only the medieval times but also during the reign of the Romanovs: in order to have at least some hope of effectively resisting the challenges that presented themselves over and over again, the Russian people needed a strong leader, someone capable of uniting the rival princes and reforming the country from top to bottom. In different centuries, several individuals scratched the surface of this, emerging as powerful leaders who led the Russian people for a short period of greatness, only for the country to experience a rapid period of decline after their death. This was perhaps the biggest problem medieval Russia faced. Although some kings and princes managed to briefly lead the Russians to stability, they were rarely able to organize a strong basis for their successors to continue on the same trajectory.

The Grand Duchy of Muscovy

Russia existed in this state of struggle for several centuries, all while different princes from different provinces temporarily rose to the top and replaced each other. From the fall of Kievan Rus', the "first" strong Russian state, to the rise of the Mongols in the 13th century, several different Russian principalities challenged each other for dominance. The city of Kiev (also spelled as Kyiv), once the most prosperous in all of Eastern Europe after Constantinople itself, was ravaged not only by the Mongol horde but also by Russians who were eager to see the Rus' fall. The title of the grand prince was assumed by the ruler of Vladimir, a city in the far northeastern province of Vladimir-Suzdal, and the center of Russian civilization shifted from the lands near the Dnieper River all the way to the Volga River and its surrounding principalities. During the Mongol occupation, Vladimir-Suzdal remained the most important Russian principality, becoming a favorite of the khanate but, nevertheless, failing to spread its influence to the rest of the Russian lands.

Novgorod was another powerful principality in Russia. It was located in the northwestern part of the country and controlled a vast territory in northern Russia, including parts of the Baltic Sea. Due to Novgorod's great geographical location, it had always been one of the richest and most prosperous principalities, but unlike its rivals, it was hardly ever interested in dominating the rest of the Russian lands. In a way, Novgorodians always had a sense of superiority, opting to limit their involvement in Russian politics unless absolutely necessary or unless it would grant them direct benefits. From the 12th to the 15th century, Novgorod existed as a separate republic, the first of its kind in Russia. It was effectively ruled by a democratic city council.

Vladimir-Suzdal and Novgorod were only two of the big Russian principalities. The others, like the central cities of Chernigov (today's Chernihiv) and Smolensk, Ryazan in the east, or Polotsk at the Polish-Lithuanian border in the west, were also important actors in Russian politics, but none of them managed to gain a significant edge over the others. Eventually, a rather unlikely contestant claimed the title of the most powerful Russian province.

In an interesting turn of events, by the early 14th century, a small, relatively unimportant town by the name of Moscow, located at the southern border of Vladimir-Suzdal, started almost exponentially growing its power by gaining control over its bordering territories. Daniil (Daniel) Nevsky, the ruler of Moscow in the early 14th century and the youngest son of the powerful ex-ruler of Vladimir-Suzdal Alexander Nevsky, seized the neighboring territory of Kolomna, allowing him to control the important point where the Moskva River joined with the Volga. His son, Yuri, continued his efforts, quickly imprisoning the prince of Mozhaysk in the west in 1303 and almost doubling his possessions. Still, compared to other principalities, the territory held by Yuri of Moscow was insignificant; however, a good enough base had been established to challenge Moscow's much-larger neighbors for dominance.

It is important to highlight that by this time, the Mongols were still reigning freely in Russia. To assume the title of grand prince, the candidate must pay a visit to the khan and ask for a *yarlyk*—a blessing from the Mongol ruler to become the grand prince of the Russian principalities. He also had to pledge his allegiance to the horde. After imprisoning the prince of Mozhaysk, Prince Yuri visited the khan to try and gain the *yarlyk*, arguing that he had a legitimate claim since he was a descendant of Alexander Nevsky. However, the khan instead gave the *yarlyk* to Mikhail of Tver, the ruler of a neighboring province who had promised the khan more concessions and a larger amount of yearly tribute.

This complicated the relationship between Yuri and Mikhail, and Moscow and Tver soon became fierce rivals. Fortunately for Yuri, Mikhail proved to be an unsuccessful ruler. He not only failed to live up to the khan's expectations but also angered the Orthodox Russians when he tried to install his preferred candidate as the new head of the church in Vladimir. The rightful Metropolitan Peter, the one who had been installed from Constantinople (the Russian Church was not independent by then), had no reason to support Mikhail of Tver, who had effectively tried to reduce his legitimacy by challenging his position. Metropolitan Peter instead forged a close relationship with Yuri of Moscow. His successor, Metropolitan Theognostus, was influenced by his predecessor and later transferred the official seat of the metropolitan of Russia to the city of Moscow, greatly increasing the city's importance in the eyes of the Russian people and starting the chain of events that would eventually lead to Moscow's rise to prominence.

In the following years, Yuri of Moscow managed to wrestle the title of grand prince away from Mikhail of Tver by personally visiting the city of Sarai on the Lower Volga—the seat of the khan of the Golden Horde—and forging close relations with the new khan, Uzbeg. He even managed to marry the khan's sister, Konchaka. After gaining the backing of the horde, Yuri officially managed to secure the khan's *yarlyk*, earning him the title of grand prince. It was pivotal, as Yuri was now not only the prince of Moscow but also the grand prince of Vladimir-Suzdal, the de-facto capital of medieval Russia, earning him much-needed fame and status.

For the rest of the 14th century, the principality of Muscovy tried to expand its influence over the bordering territories, although it was constantly challenged by Tver. However, after gaining the horde's favor, Muscovy was in a much more advantageous position. The Muscovite rulers forged alliances with different principalities, and these agreements would come in handy. The city of Moscow started to grow in importance, especially thanks to the seat of the metropolitan being transferred to it. Eventually, after the fall of Constantinople in 1453, Moscow would famously claim the title of "Third Rome," further stressing its status not only in Russia but also in all of the Christian world.

Ivan Kalita, the younger brother of Yuri who gained the nickname Kalita ("moneybag") because of his generous nature, would further consolidate and expand the power held by Muscovy. Ivan Kalita acquired new territories in the Transvolga, bringing Muscovy closer to the Asian trade routes, which ensured the flow of new riches into his realm. Crucially, during his reign, the title of grand prince started to be taken more seriously by the princes.

Thanks to Ivan Kalita's territorial acquisitions, he was in charge of a very large piece of land and had the ambition to consider himself not only the grand prince of Vladimir-Suzdal but also of all of Russia. This distinction would soon start to take shape, as the grand prince would begin to be the only person allowed to have direct contact with the khan. Before, any prince could approach the ruler of the horde in cases of necessity.

As Muscovy's influence grew, so did the number of its enemies. At the time of Ivan Kalita's death in 1340, almost all of the eastern Russian principalities had been virtually united, having sworn loyalty to the grand prince in Vladimir. This consolidation of power in the east, in turn, caused the western principalities to fall prey to the neighboring Kingdom of Lithuania, whose Grand Prince Olgerd managed to gain control of most of western Russia by the 1350s and even seized Kiev in 1361. Olgerd saw Muscovy as his direct rival and a threat to Catholic Lithuania, so he journeyed out to capture the city on three different occasions but was ultimately unsuccessful.

In 1375, Olgerd sought help from Prince Mikhail Aleksandrovich of Tver, who had secretly negotiated the *yarlyk* with the khan in Sarai. Together, the two marched against the city of Vladimir, with Mikhail claiming to be the new grand prince, but both of them were eventually driven back by Grand Prince Dmitry Donskoy of Moscow and Vladimir-Suzdal. Dmitry's army consisted mostly of troops from the regions that had been acquired during Muscovy's expansion, further stressing the fact these principalities were loyal to the grand prince.

After learning the Mongols had negotiated with Mikhail of Tver behind Grand Prince Dmitry's back, the relationship between the Golden Horde and Muscovy started to slowly deteriorate. Technically, the Muscovite rulers still needed *yarlyks* from Sarai to be named grand prince, but as we already mentioned, the position had largely become independent from the Mongols and gained much more prominence after Moscow's rise. In addition, the Golden Horde was facing countless internal issues, with different clans, descendants of the great Genghis Khan, squabbling with each over the control of the empire's vast lands.

By the late 1370s, the Mongols would regularly attack and raid the lands ruled by Muscovy, something that caused doubts in the minds of Muscovite officials on whether or not the Mongol rule was beneficial for the country's future. Crucially, in 1380, in another attempt to undermine the growing power of Moscow, the Mongol leader, Mamai Khan, led a force of about 200,000 men against Prince Dmitry, the latter of whom was supported by the prince of Ryazan and the Lithuanians. Grand Prince Dmitry met the enemy at Kulikovo near the River Don with about 150,000 soldiers and was able to decisively defeat the Mongols. This legendary victory earned Dmitry his nickname "Donskoy" ("of the Don"). The Battle of Kulikovo would be the first sign of Russian resistance against Mongol rule. The Mongols would eventually be driven out of Russia about one hundred years later.

Ivan the Great

Despite the success at Kulikovo, the Mongol rulers were adamant about keeping their influence over the leaders of Russia and proceeded to retaliate by quickly mustering up new armies to attack Muscovy while Dmitry Donskoy was recovering from his losses. In the early 1380s, Mongol cavalry raids devastated the countryside of the Lower Volga, with Russian settlements falling prey to the invaders and causing an economic recession that slowed down Muscovite expansion. However, these incursions did not break Muscovy's unity, and Dmitry Donskoy's son and successor, Vasily I, managed to hold onto the expanded territories. Instead of answering the Mongols with more aggression, Vasily I adopted a peaceful approach, visiting Sarai and asking the new khan for his forgiveness and blessing. He knew that despite all the success Muscovy had had over the past decades that it was still too early to engage in an all-out war for liberation. In addition, Vasily I consolidated the power Moscow held over the neighboring princes and further contributed to forming the basis of what would later become Russia, knowing that liberation from Mongol rule was close at hand. The Russians just needed to patiently wait for the opportunity to strike.

The Muscovite ruler that would eventually lead the Russians to independence was Vasily I's grandson, Ivan III, now known as "the Great" for his efforts. Ascending to the throne in 1462, Ivan III found himself in the middle of a complex political climate. Among the latest geopolitical developments was the fall of Constantinople to the Ottomans in 1453, which amplified the symbolic role of Moscow as the "Third Rome" and the new torchbearer for all of Christianity. In addition, his father, Vasily II, had struggled with neighboring Prince Yuri of Galich for dominance over the Russian lands, as well as with the Lithuanians, who had increased their influence over the western Russian principalities. Crucially, however, the most interesting occurrence was undoubtedly the further weakening of the Mongol Empire and its division into multiple rivaling realms. There was the Crimean Khanate, which occupied the northern coast of the Black Sea, and there was the Kazan Khanate in the east. This split complicated the power dynamics of the region and especially affected the Russian rulers, who were confused as to which khanate was more legitimate. It was apparent that the Mongols, in one way or another, were losing their control of Russia.

Ivan the Great realized that he needed to act. He first started to consolidate his power by forging close ties with the boyar nobility, who were the main landowners and catalysts in the Muscovite armies. He implemented new etiquette rules to boost the significance of the title of grand prince and made sure that all the lesser princes strictly followed them. Ivan was the first ruler to adopt the title of tsar, which was adopted from the Roman word Caesar.

A very impactful decision Ivan III made was to wage a campaign against Novgorod in 1471, during which he managed to finally subjugate the rich city and its lands after centuries of being free. Being in control of Novgorod had, in the past, proven to be crucial for gaining any sort of military or economic advantage for Russian rulers, and Ivan III was no exception. He installed a Muscovite governor in the city and limited its freedom and local governance before eventually incorporating it into the territories of Muscovy. Ivan also defeated the long-standing rival principalities of Tver and Ryazan, taking firm control over their lands and leading Muscovy to the most dominant position it had ever enjoyed.

Then came the main objective of liberation from the Mongols. Recognizing the hostile relationship between the different khanates, Ivan the Great assembled his army, with different principalities contributing troops from their lands, and forged an alliance with the Crimean Khanate to make a stand against Sarai and the remainder of the Golden Horde. In 1480, the Great Horde's Ahmed Khan campaigned against Moscow with the same objective as many of his ancestors: to "punish" the overly-confident Russians and reassert Mongol dominance.

In October, the two armies met at the Ugra River, where Ivan had assumed a defensive position. He knew the Mongols, with their famous cavalry, were more favored to win an open battle, so he decided to stall, waiting for winter to arrive, which would force the enemy to retreat. In what has come to be known as the Great Stand at Ugra, the two sides engaged in combat multiple times, with Ahmed Khan and his mighty army trying unsuccessfully to cross the river. After failing time and time again, winter rolled around, and just as Ivan had hoped, the weather forced the Mongols back without them having made any progress.

The Great Stand was a crucial victory for Ivan and Muscovy and is considered to be the end of Mongol rule over Russia. After the invaders went back to Sarai, Ivan never paid them the yearly tribute, and the title of *yarlyk* would never again be bestowed to future rulers. The Great Horde (what was left of the Golden Horde) would soon see its complete demise due to internal squabbles. Ahmed Khan was assassinated by his rivals, and the Great Horde would then be conquered by the Crimean Khanate in the 16th century. Russia was now finally free from the Mongols.

Although the liberation from the Mongols is considered to be Ivan III's greatest achievement, he contributed much to the formation of a stable, unified Russian state. We have already briefly mentioned the domestic policies that allowed him to centralize more power. With Moscow's increased importance as the new center of Christianity, Ivan the Great's reign is considered to be a sort of a renaissance for the Russian Orthodox Church, which was greatly reformed and modernized. The church, for the first time in a long while, transformed from an institution associated strictly with the highest classes to something universal. Monasticism became a noble pursuit, and Orthodoxy occupied a central part in the lives of the Russian people. Respect for religion became infused in the collective minds of the Russians and was arguably one of the first true Russian national identities. New churches were built, and the clergy developed a good relationship with the grand prince, who never hesitated to aid them.

Ivan the Great also shined when it came to foreign policy, becoming the first Russian ruler to forge diplomatic ties with many different European and Middle Eastern states, like the Holy Roman Empire, the Ottoman Empire, and Persia. He also stabilized the situation in the western Russian principalities by making peace with the Livonian Order on the Baltic coast, which he considered a future corridor into the Western world. This concept would be further developed by Peter I when he constructed the first Baltic Russian port of St. Petersburg. In the late 1590s, Ivan III turned his attention to the ever-growing Lithuanian threat in the west, defeating the Lithuanian princes in several encounters and forcing them to renounce their claims on the bordering Russian lands. By the early 16th century, Ivan had successfully undermined Lithuania's position and reached a peace deal.

All in all, Ivan the Great, the first tsar, was undoubtedly one of the most influential leaders of Muscovy. He quickly consolidated his status and power after becoming the grand prince, expanded the realms in his possession, liberated the country from the tyrannical rule of the Mongols, and reformed Moscow's institutions to achieve a period of domestic stability and economic growth. During his reign, Muscovy emerged as a dominant player in the region and experienced great progress toward the formation of the first unified Russian state.

Chapter 2: The Last of the Rurikids

Before the Romanovs took over the rule of Russia and became one of the most famous dynasties in world history, the nation experienced a period of slow decline that eventually resulted in the final days of the Rurikid dynasty. The highs of Ivan the Great would only last for so long before the country descended once again into chaos. After the death of Tsar Ivan IV (Ivan the Terrible, as he has come to be infamously known in history due to a number of atrocities he committed during his reign), Russia found itself in a period of turmoil, despair, and uncertainty. This short but impactful era, fittingly named the "Time of Troubles," was a pivotal point in Russian history and marked the end of both the Rurikids and medieval Russia, acting as a "gateway" to early modern times.

The first Romanovs rose to prominence during the Time of Troubles, so it is natural that the focus of this chapter is on discussing those circumstances in detail to better understand the emergence of the new Russian dynasty.

Succession Difficulties

Despite Ivan the Terrible's rather appropriate nickname, he was, in fact, one of the better kings Russia had seen in a long time when he ascended the throne in 1547. He became tsar after a brief succession crisis that emerged in Muscovy during the final years of

Ivan the Great's reign and persisted for decades after his death in 1505. Different sons of Ivan III claimed legitimacy over the Muscovite throne for about forty years, an occurrence caused by the fact the king had children from both of his marriages. The heir to the throne, Ivan the Young, who was the only son of Ivan the Great and his first wife, Maria of Tver, tragically passed in 1490, leaving the old king with a difficult problem of succession. The next decades saw the struggle for succession break out between Vasily, the eldest son of Ivan the Great and his second wife, Sophia Palaiologina, and Dmitry, the son of Ivan the Young. Eventually, the former came out on top and was crowned Vasily III in the first decade of the 16th century.

Vasily III's reign was focused on consolidating the grand prince's power, which had noticeably dwindled away, with some lesser princes being unwilling to bend the knee to the new ruler. However, Muscovy's succession crisis did not stop there, as the new king had no heirs. After obtaining a blessing from Metropolitan Daniel, he divorced his wife Solomonia, forcing her to become a nun, and instead married Yelena (also known as Elena) Glinskaya, who finally bore him a son, Ivan. Three years later, in 1533, Vasily III unexpectedly passed away, making Ivan (now Ivan IV) the grand prince of Muscovy at only three years old, which meant Yelena became a regent before her son came of age.

Throughout her time as the regent, Yelena tried her best to protect the throne from various competitors, who tried to take advantage of the fact the Crown was weak. Among the contenders were Vasily III's brothers, who all believed they had legitimate claims to the throne since they were the sons of Ivan the Great. For the next thirteen years, the brothers instigated numerous rebellions to try and take over the city of Moscow and claimed the title of grand prince on numerous occasions. They might have succeeded in undermining Queen Yelena and the rest of the royal supporters, but they lacked public backing and unity—something that eventually resulted in none of them coming out on top.

Different lesser princes also challenged the young Ivan, but, to the surprise of many, the Crown persevered. Ivan IV finally came of age and was fit to rule in 1547. The fact he had retained control over the throne signaled the strong foundation that had been built by Ivan the Great, but it by no means meant Ivan IV's reign would be free of troubles.

Ivan the Terrible

A painting of Ivan the Terrible by Viktor Mikhailovich Vasnetsov.
https://commons.wikimedia.org/wiki/File:Ivan_the_Terrible_(cropped).JPG

Thus, Ivan the Terrible became the new tsar in 1547. Although he was still very young (he was only seventeen years old), he immediately got to work. Ivan was relatively inexperienced compared to his grandfather but did enjoy support from some of the most influential figures in Russia at the time. One of those people was Metropolitan Makary, and the first reforms the new tsar passed concerned nearly all aspects of Russia's religious life. The first three years of Ivan's reign would see two ecclesiastical councils, each led by the metropolitan, that would eventually produce a hundred-chapter statute book by the name of *Stoglav*, which carefully described and regulated religious matters. Among the new reforms was the crucial implementation of a new Russian Orthodox calendar with dates to commemorate the saints, which, in turn, resulted in the creation of new rest days. The *Stoglav* also touched upon the details regarding worship at religious sites and increased the number of lands the church possessed, a change that was a clear indication that the church had royal support.

In 1551, a new legislative code was introduced in one of the ecclesiastic councils. This new piece of legislation, by the name of Sudebnik, proposed new laws regarding court proceedings and serf and land ownership. New forms of punishment for crimes were also added, greatly expanding the already existing legislation. All in all, Ivan IV's first few years as tsar saw not only an amplification of the Russian Orthodox Church's importance but also legislative expansion to modernize Muscovy.

Throughout the 1550s, Ivan IV tried to centralize the monarchy's power, following in the footsteps of his grandfather. In Moscow, he assembled his own advisory council, which was made up of his most trusted allies. The council informally assisted Ivan in all major decisions. In the provinces, Ivan reduced the power held by the local governors by giving them limited access to local law-making and instead granting them new responsibilities of dealing with crime and corruption. Ivan and his *Izbrannaya Rada* ("chosen council") handpicked administrative representatives from Moscow and placed them in positions of power in the capitals of principalities. These individuals reported directly to the council and worked on implementing the changes the local populations desired the most while being reliant on Moscow in terms of protection. The principalities were also assigned fixed yearly tax rates based on their economic status.

The reform that produced perhaps the best results for Ivan IV's realm was the long-overdue modernization of the military. New laws not only regulated the number of soldiers each landowner had to provide the Crown during wartime but also resulted in the creation of elite military contingents that would be given estates in Moscow and were expected to be ready for service at all times. The army became more disciplined, thanks to the yearly training sessions in Moscow that assured the men's readiness for combat. These changes proved more than effective, as Ivan IV was able to finally put an end to the Kazan Khanate's raids and gradually conquered the territories held by the Mongol realm. In the end, the tsar gained control of virtually all of the Volga River by 1556.

Unfortunately for Ivan IV, the successful early campaigns against the Mongols in the east would not be followed up by similar triumphs elsewhere. Instead of focusing his army to the south to take over the lands held by the Crimean Khanate and gain access to the northern coast of the Black Sea, the ambitious tsar turned his attention to the Baltic, a region whose importance had been greatly amplified by Ivan the Great. When Ivan IV restarted the war against the Livonians in 1558, Muscovy did not have direct access to the Baltic Sea. Although the Livonian Order quickly disintegrated after being repeatedly targeted by bigger powers over the next decades, the war for the Baltic would last for another twenty-four years and would take up much of Muscovy's necessary resources.

By the late 1570s, Ivan IV was constantly at war against the kingdoms of Sweden, Lithuania, and Poland, and despite making initial progress, he was feeling the toll of the war due to domestic and external pressure. The military reform was not enough for Muscovy to put up a fight on multiple fronts against multiple enemies, and in 1582 and 1583, Ivan IV was forced to sign peace treaties, making significant territorial concessions to his enemies.

As the war effort proved increasingly difficult to maintain, Ivan's reign entered a period of decline, and the decisions taken by the tsar would eventually earn him his infamous nickname, "the Terrible." Throughout the 1560s, his actions increased the tsar's power even more and, in many cases, can only be classified as purely authoritarian. In 1564, for example, all Russian territories were divided into *zemshchina* (the state lands) and *oprichnina* (lands in possession of the tsar). The Crown's possessions increased quite dramatically due to this change. The servants of the *oprichnina* were then recruited as a special police force and would basically do anything the tsar desired. These individuals, called *oprichniki*, were used by Tsar Ivan IV to spy on his subjects and enforce his ruthlessness upon them if he suspected anything malicious of them. Although the *oprichniki* apprehended many landowners, boyars, and officeholders, the institution proved to be fatal for the well-being of the tsar, who became increasingly paranoid.

This paranoia and constant search for conspiracies against his rule started because of the unfruitful military campaigns in the Baltic. One by one, Ivan IV started arresting, exiling, or outright murdering those who had been with him since the beginning of his reign. For example, Ivan IV arrested members of his chosen council after they talked him into signing a peace deal with the

Livonians in 1560. By 1564, the tsar had grown so arrogant and paranoid that he regarded the victory of his friend, Prince Kurbsky, against the Polish as a threat to the throne. Ivan also suffered a couple of psychological traumas. The passing of his wife, Anastasia, and his closest friend, Metropolitan Makary, induced more stress. Ivan's fears of a conspiratorial boyar rebellion against his rule made him leave Moscow and threaten abdication in time of war in the mid-1560s. During all this time, the *oprichniki* continued to ruthlessly arrest any suspicious person, and it was clear the tsar's personal police force served not to enforce laws but to personally complete the tasks given to them by Ivan.

The unlawfulness and chaos reached their peak when the tsar's cousin, Prince Vladimir, admitted the existence of a boyar conspiracy to overthrow Ivan after being arrested and tortured by the *oprichniki*. This had a detrimental effect on the tsar, who had his cousin murdered in 1569, making an example out of him and signaling that anyone who dared to oppose him would meet the same fate. Then, he ordered the *oprichniki* to ravage the streets of Novgorod, which he suspected of harboring an anti-crown conspiracy.

But all these measures were not enough to reinstitute stability. Aside from being busy with the war in the north and west, Ivan the Terrible was also under constant threat from the south, where the Crimean Khanate frequently crossed the border and raided the Muscovite territories. By the 1580s, when Ivan was forced to admit defeat and sign peace treaties, his country had already entered a period of social, political, and economic decline. With all the resources directed to the army and the power stripped away from the local governments, Ivan was unable to keep the population in his vast territories content, as thousands had become impoverished. All of these factors had a negative impact on the tsar's mental and physical health, culminating in an accident in 1581 when he struck his own son in the head with a staff during an argument, shattering his skull and murdering him. Ivan spent the rest of his days being less and less involved in the country's politics before dying in March 1584. A promising reformer turned into a paranoid authoritarian, but history still remembers Ivan the Terrible as one of the final impactful tsars from the Rurikid dynasty.

The Time of Troubles

As one would expect, the death of Ivan the Terrible brought yet another catastrophic and chaotic period to Russia. Historians now fittingly call this period the Time of Troubles, and there is no clear consensus on when exactly it started or ended. However, one thing is clear: the effects of the Time of Troubles would be felt by the Russians for decades after the end of the period. The social and political consequences it produced require a rather in-depth analysis, as it brought about the emergence of the Romanov dynasty as the ruling family of Russia.

We shall start the analysis of the Time of Troubles right after Ivan the Terrible's death because the strength of the Russian state, which had been built up by the previous couple of generations, would start to dwindle quickly by the end of the 16th century. The person who succeeded Ivan the Terrible was his son Fyodor (also spelled as Feodor), who was a king with a rather different personality than his "terrible" father.

Fyodor had not really been interested in politics, preferring instead to spend his time reading religious texts and composing church music. Because of this, the institution that would be in charge of Russian affairs was the regency council, which was organized by the tsar and consisted of several major princes, his uncle, and, most importantly, a man by the name of Boris Godunov, the brother-in-law of the new tsar. One of the most important, as well as the earliest decisions, of the council was to exile Ivan the Terrible's youngest son, Dmitry, to Uglich as a precaution to avoid potential succession struggles. As we will see, this decision later proved to be very costly for Russia.

As for Boris Godunov, he quickly became the tsar's most trusted advisor and friend. By the late 1500s, Boris Godunov had made his name known, as he was a skilled diplomat and influential political figure, having gained the trust of the boyar council to engage in diplomatic matters with other countries. He personally traveled to the patriarch of Constantinople to ask for the independence of the Russian Church, which was still formally dependent on the Greek Orthodox Church, despite the latter's recent weakening due to the Ottoman destruction of Byzantium. Godunov's request was accepted, and in 1589, the metropolitan of

Moscow, Iov (also known as Job), was elected as the first patriarch of the now-independent Russian Orthodox Church.

In addition to Godunov's diplomatic achievements, he also led the country to success on the battlefield throughout the 1590s, managing to reclaim some of the northern territories from Sweden and making an effort to end the Crimean Khanate's raids in the south. Then, he completed a peace deal with Poland to secure Russia's western flank before shifting his focus to internal affairs and leading the charge for new reforms to address peasant migration and fix some of the landowners' economic concerns. All in all, by the time Tsar Fyodor's reign came to an end in 1598, Boris Godunov had clearly become the most important person in all of Russia, sometimes being referred to as the "lord protector" in foreign records.

Tsar Fyodor had no heirs, leaving the country without a new tsar after his passing, which was a very difficult situation for any monarchy during medieval times. Fyodor would be the final Rurikid king to rule Russia after nearly seven hundred years of his family being on top. His death prompted Patriarch Iov to call a great council to discuss the succession. Boris Godunov would be the one to eventually earn the assembly's nomination to become the new tsar in February of 1598.

At first, Godunov declined the offer, but after seeing the overwhelming support from the assembly, he accepted. However, despite his illustrious status throughout all of Russia and Europe and his vast list of diplomatic and military achievements, a part of the Russian boyar nobility was reluctant to show their support. They feared Godunov would slowly try to reduce their influence in the country, so they challenged him, nominating their own candidate. Still, despite their best efforts, Boris Godunov was crowned as the new tsar of Russia in September 1598, swiftly dealing with the opposing boyars and starting a new era in Russian history.

Boris Godunov was an exceptional political figure, but even his might would not be enough to end the Time of Troubles. The series of unfortunate events started with historically disastrous harvests in Russia from 1601 to 1603, with thousands of lower-class people starving and being forced into poverty. The situation was so desperate that the Crown was forced to release the royal reserves and distribute food to the starving on a daily basis. However, this caused even more problems, as the poor flooded to the big cities to receive their portions but were still unable to get any food. In turn, they created bands and started assaulting others throughout the cities for supplies. Urban crime rates reached such high levels that city policemen were unable to deal with the newly formed bands, causing a special part of the army to be assembled and slaughter the criminals outside Moscow in late 1603.

The difficulties did not end there. Amidst the chaos caused by famine and crime, a person emerged who suddenly gained a lot of traction among the commoners, as they were desperate for someone to lead them out of their misery since Tsar Boris was not able to. This person would claim to be Prince Dmitry—the exiled son of Ivan IV—who had supposedly returned after the Crown's failed attempt to murder him in Uglich. In reality, the "Pretender Prince" or "False Dmitry," as many historians would later call him, was not Prince Dmitry. It was instead a former monk by the name of Grigory Otrepyev who had taken advantage of the Russian people's misery and decided to sweep in as the "hero" they needed. Since nobody had time to question the legitimacy of his claims, the starving people rallied around him. By 1604, False Dmitry went even as far as to visit Poland and Sweden to ask the local nobility for military and financial help. He promised that he had the potential to organize a full-blown rebellion and weaken Russia, which had emerged as the dominant actor in the region and had overshadowed their power thanks to the efforts of Boris Godunov. Thus, in the autumn of 1604, he managed to gain military support from a couple of smaller Polish nobles, assembling an army of about four thousand men, while the Swedish promised him gold to carry out his goals.

False Dmitry marched his men from Lviv to Moscow, being joined on his way by the upset populations of different villages, as well as many Cossacks who dwelt in Ukraine. The Cossacks were very interesting people. They were ethnically Russian but lived the horse-reliant nomadic lifestyle of the Mongols. As great warriors, they valued their freedom and wanted to exclude themselves from Russia to form their own separate state; joining False Dmitry was a logical move. After greatly bolstering his numbers, the Pretender

Prince was able to overcome whatever resistance Boris Godunov was able to put up.

The morale of the Russian soldiers under the tsar was pretty low, as the famine had greatly affected their lives. After their defeat in January against False Dmitry's forces, they were completely routed, and the Pretender Prince secured free passage to Moscow. If that wasn't enough, Boris Godunov would pass away in April 1605, leaving the kingdom in the hands of his young son, who had neither the experience nor the ability to rule during such tough times. By the summer of the same year, he would be overthrown by the boyar nobles, who had held a grudge against Godunov for a long time, and False Dmitry was able to march into the streets of Moscow uncontested. Then, he summoned Queen Maria, the exiled mother of the actual Prince Dmitry, and forced her to publicly admit he was her real son. In July 1605, Grigory Otrepyev, the Pretender Prince, crowned himself as the new tsar of Russia.

Against all odds, Otrepyev had managed to become tsar. This was only the beginning of the Time of Troubles, as the new tsar found it increasingly difficult to maintain his position of power, something that stemmed from the fact he had only risen to power as an attractive figure during a time of turmoil. In reality, he did not know how to rule a realm, let alone such a vast kingdom experiencing difficult times. He never behaved like a royal, and those of noble descent quickly realized what had happened. To them, it was apparent False Dmitry was unfit to rule, even for a short period of time, as all he would do was throw feasts and spend his time with several different women. His rather lavish lifestyle was not meant for tsars, nor was it suited for an Orthodox monarch.

Otrepyev tried to make it up to the boyars by giving them back some of the privileges Ivan III and Ivan IV had taken away from them, but the boyars were no fools. Many of them knew that Otrepyev was an illegitimate king and only regarded him as a placeholder until a suitable replacement could be found or until the social problems could be better addressed. Because of this, none of them showed any real support toward the new tsar, despite his apparent display of gratitude toward them and despite the fact they had helped him overthrow Godunov's son.

Many other factors also contributed to the rapid end of False Dmitry's reign. For example, the Cossacks, whose help had been crucial for him to succeed in the rebellion, refused to answer his rule and demanded he step down from the position of tsar. After he refused, the Cossacks proceeded to ravage the Russian countryside and continued to be a thorn in the side of the Crown for years to come. The Russian people also quickly realized the fraudulent nature of the new tsar, as he failed to implement any sort of solutions to the problems they had faced for many years. They also disliked the fact False Dmitry was very friendly toward Poland, a historical rival of Russia. After all, his rebellion had largely succeeded due to the financial and military support from the lesser Polish nobility, and the tsar would be influenced by Western traditions and customs.

False Dmitry married Marina Mniszech, who was of Polish descent. She refused to have a wedding according to the Orthodox standards, as was the norm in Russia back then. Instead, she insisted the two get married according to Catholic tradition in the Kremlin cathedral in Moscow, a move that was considered to be utterly disrespectful toward the Russian Church and toward the people who had entrusted their support to False Dmitry.

In short, if the new tsar was not of royal descent, was incapable of ruling over his subjects, behaved incompetently, and acted disrespectfully, why should he remain in power?

The boyar nobility overthrew the Pretender Prince with relative ease. The boyars were upset with how things were going, and when the situation worsened at the beginning of the 17th century, the boyars instigated a rebellion and marched against the tsar. Led by Vasily Shuisky, the boyars took the Kremlin by storm but could not personally get to Otrepyev, as the latter attempted suicide and jumped out of a high window. His body was found by the citizens of Moscow and was mutilated to death before being burned. The ashes were shot out of a cannon. The reign of False Dmitry lasted for not even a year and saw one of the most gruesome endings to any tsar in the history of Russia.

The Struggle for Moscow

The Time of Troubles did not end with the boyar rebellion and the removal of False Dmitry. Vasily Shuisky replaced Otrepyev as the new tsar after being elected by a small group of rebels and Muscovites. People all around the country were content that the Pretender Prince was gone. Unlike Otrepyev, Shuisky was of noble descent and was much more competent than his predecessor when it came to almost every aspect of ruling. His reign lasted for the next four years, from 1606 to 1610, and Russia would sigh a breath of relief, at least compared to the previous decade.

One of the first things Shuisky—now Tsar Vasily IV of Russia—did was give the boyars even more rights to balance out their power in relation to the tsar. Shuisky understood he would need every bit of support he could for his reign to be at least somewhat longer than that of his predecessor, and he thought the boyars could provide that support. However, the main problem lay in the fact that not all of the Russian provinces were prepared to accept the newly elected tsar. The different principalities had largely operated on their own; Moscow did not effectively have control over them since the early 1600s. Technically, they still answered to the central government, but as Tsar Vasily's reign entered its first few months, many provinces rose up.

The tsar proceeded to deal with these rebellions one by one and was able to suppress most of them thanks to the rebels' lack of a competent army. Shuisky enjoyed the support of the nobles, who bolstered his ranks with professional troops. Eventually, however, Shuisky would face his biggest challenge in the form of a completely new insurrection in early 1607, which was led by a rather interesting figure by the name of Ivan Bolotnikov.

A slave-turned-Cossack before being captured by the Mongols, Bolotnikov had lived through a lifetime of struggle for freedom, something that inspired many from the Russian lower classes. He finally managed to escape from captivity to Poland, where he started gathering supporters for another rebellion against Tsar Vasily. Much like Otrepyev, he realized that it was the perfect time to seize the seat of the tsar for himself. Unlike False Dmitry, Bolotnikov did not rally the people around him just because of his "legitimate" claim over the throne. Instead, he was an inspirational figure for thousands of peasants, as he said that he was fighting for them.

Thus, with a force of about ten thousand peasants, Cossacks, and enemies of the tsar, he tried to wrestle the title away from Vasily Shuisky, marching toward Moscow in early 1607. However, as his movement grew in numbers, the fighters' spirit slowly diminished, and Tsar Vasily Shuisky was able to defeat the rebels in a head-to-head battle in the autumn of the same year.

Ironically, Bolotnikov's defeat sparked yet another rebellion—a sign that thousands were still upset with how things had unfolded. In one of the final insurrections of the Time of Troubles, another Prince Dmitry emerged. This man claimed to have been the son of Ivan IV and was thus a rightful heir to the throne. He had supposedly escaped murder both in Uglich and then in Moscow in 1606. Obviously, in the early 1600s, there was no effective way of spreading information, and a part of the angry mob quickly decided to side with the Second False Dmitry.

What made the matter even more absurd is the fact that the Polish wife of the First False Dmitry, Marina Mniszech, claimed the new man was her husband who had gone into hiding to escape the wrath of the boyars but had now returned to rescue the people of Russia once again. The new pretender gathered up his supporters in a small town named Tushino and organized a false government. Nicknamed "the thief" by Tsar Vasily's supporters, the new False Dmitry would challenge the tsar's rule in Tushino and its surroundings for the next two years, but he did not dare to march on Moscow.

Throughout the Second False Dmitry's rise as the leader of the new rebellion, Tsar Vasily Shuisky had been rather busy fighting off rebels in different parts of his kingdom and had exhausted his military. Thus, he approached the king of Sweden with a request to grant him a force of six thousand men in return for giving up claims of the contested lands of Livonia. The Swedish king granted him the men, which Tsar Vasily planned to use to crush the Second False Dmitry.

However, the news of the Swedish force under the Russian tsar was seen as a direct threat to the Polish king, Sigismund III, who decided to break the peace agreement between the two nations and declared war on Russia in 1609. Tsar Vasily Shuisky was put in a very difficult position, as he was not only losing support in the different Russian provinces but also had to deal with the rebellion of False Dmitry and the incoming Polish incursion.

Fortunately for the tsar, the Polish invasion shifted attention away from False Dmitry's rebellion. Supposedly, many of the Second False Dmitry's supporters dropped him, realizing the Polish threat was more severe. They united, in a weird way, for the defense of their country after trying to destroy their tsar for quite some time. As for the Second False Dmitry, he met a very gruesome death, being killed during an all-out brawl that broke out in his camp not long after Poland's declaration of war.

The Polish took the city of Smolensk in late 1609. Smolensk was a very important city, as it was perceived as a sort of gateway to Russia from the west. Its control was crucial for the kingdom's stability. The loss of Smolensk further weakened Vasily Shuisky's position, and he was eventually forced to abdicate since he was seen as unable to defend the country from a foreign invasion.

The popular assembly, which made the tsar abdicate and take monastic vows, tried to search for suitable alternatives, briefly giving the right to rule to a council of seven boyars. Amidst the crisis, the boyar council decided it would be best to invite a foreigner to become the new ruler of Russia, something that had happened many times in different European kingdoms in the medieval era. They chose Prince Wladyslaw of Poland, the eldest son of Sigismund III, to come to Moscow and become the new tsar.

However, Sigismund III did not approve of this. He was not amused by the thought of his son becoming the new tsar of Russia, as he had always desired to rule over Moscow himself. So, instead of stopping at Smolensk and being content with holding the territories that had historically been contested by Poland, he decided to march to Moscow. When the Russian people heard about Sigismund's advances toward the heart of the kingdom, they quickly realized they needed to settle their internal squabbles to unite against a common enemy. This was true for the vast majority of the population, including those who lived in the provinces. Soon enough, the Russians acknowledged the threat a potential unwanted foreign invader posed to Russia's integrity and banded together to avoid such a catastrophe, which was a rather uncharacteristic move if we consider the rest of medieval Russian history.

The people started organizing themselves into militia groups, which were all based in different provincial capitals. Since the kingdom was still without a king, local mobilization was needed at every possible location to fend off not only the Polish in the west but also the Swedish, who targeted Novgorod in the north, trying to capitalize on the chaos themselves. The militia groups gathered whatever resources they could find and quickly gained a lot of traction, even to the point that Patriarch Hermogenes gave them his blessing and endorsed their creation. Although they were not able to drive out the Polish from Moscow and its outskirts in 1611, the second national levy, which was assembled a couple of months later in Nizhny Novgorod, was able to reclaim the capital and give the Russians much-needed hope.

The Time of Troubles, though, was still not over, but it had entered its final stage.

Chapter 3: The First Romanovs

The first decade of the 17th century was perhaps the most difficult in medieval Russian history. The process that had started after the death of Ivan IV—searching for a suitable king to rule Russia— spiraled into years of uncertainty and chaos. Many claimed the title of tsar, but none were able to gain enough influence. As we observed, by the end of the 1610s, a foreign threat would unite the squabbling Russian people together to defend their country, and for the first time in a while, the future looked somewhat promising.

This chapter will explore the final stage of the Time of Troubles and talk about how domestic political maneuvering caused the Romanov dynasty to rise to the top.

The National Assembly's Decision

Thanks to the efforts of the national levies that had assembled in different Russian provinces to drive out the Polish from the capital, the situation had somewhat stabilized, at least compared to the chaos beforehand. However, after regaining control of Moscow, the Russian people were confronted with a very important question: who should be the next tsar? After the events of the past decade, it would be difficult to find someone with a legitimate claim to the throne. So, the matter was devoted to the newly formed Zemsky Sobor, a rather diverse group of about five hundred men from different provinces and social strata. Everyone was curious to see who would be nominated to ascend the throne.

The national assembly prioritized finding a person from a higher class, one accustomed to formal traditions and customs and who had a decent education and demonstrated personality traits that would be suitable for a monarch. The assembly started looking for a tsar when it first convened in June 1613 and nominated a couple of worthy candidates. Finally, after much consideration, it chose to elect a sixteen-year-old named Mikhail Romanov as the next tsar of Russia—a decision that would change the course of Russian history forever.

Young Mikhail was the son of Filaret Romanov, the Patriarch of Russia. When his son was elected as tsar, he was being held as a prisoner in Poland. Filaret had been promoted to the position of patriarch during the reigns of the False Dmitrys but had been part of a powerful boyar family before he was forced to take monastic vows under Boris Godunov. In the final decades of the 16th century, he served in the army and engaged in diplomatic relations with important states like the Holy Roman Empire, thus earning himself quite a reputation in Russia. In fact, during Boris Godunov's election, he was also considered a potential candidate but was overlooked, something that eventually resulted in Godunov forcing him and his wife to take monastic vows.

In short, Patriarch Filaret Romanov was a very important figure in Russian politics from the end of the 16th century, and the fact he was also the first cousin once removed of the last Rurikid, Tsar Fyodor, gave his son, Mikhail, a much better claim to the throne than others who were considered at the assembly.

Mikhail would officially be crowned as tsar in July 1613 on his seventeenth birthday. Although a new tsar was a significant step toward stabilization, the inexperienced Mikhail had a lot of immediate problems to address. The most important of these problems was, of course, the threat of foreigners to Russian lands. By the time of Mikhail's election, both Sweden and Poland had taken over vast chunks of land in the north and in the west, lands that needed to be liberated. Russia could not field an army that could compete in head-to-head combat against these European powers, as years of instability had completely destroyed the military.

The coronation of Mikhail Romanov.

So, Mikhail decided to make peace with the two nations, and he was ready to compromise in return for more stability in his realm. In 1617, with the help of England as a mediator, Mikhail signed the Peace of Stolbovo, ending the war with Sweden. According to the terms of the treaty, he regained control of Russia's northern territories in Novgorod but was forced to give up claims in the Gulf of Finland. Still, it was a favorable agreement for the new tsar. This was followed by the Truce of Deulino with Poland in December of 1618, in which Russia ceded control of most of its western lands and surrendered Smolensk to the enemy.

The situation with Poland was much tenser than with Sweden, as King Sigismund refused to acknowledge the legitimacy of the newly elected tsar and still claimed the throne of Muscovy for himself. Although the terms of the truce between the two sides favored Poland because of the territorial gains, they also established a fifteen-year armistice, which was time the weaker Russia could use to build up its defenses and reemerge as a dominant actor in the region.

These diplomatic achievements went a long way in helping stabilize the situation domestically, as the Russian countryside was finally free from constant raids. The next important development would be the return of the tsar's father, Filaret, from Poland in 1619. Upon his arrival in Moscow, Filaret would not only regain the role of patriarch but also assume the title of Velikiy Gosudar ("great sovereign"), which was previously exclusively held only by the tsar. Filaret would essentially take over the control of the country after returning to Moscow, while Tsar Mikhail would follow the lead of his father until Filaret's death in 1633. Despite the fact that Filaret's assumption of power was highly unusual, it has to be said the reforms he implemented during his time were very effective, utilizing peacetime in a manner that would have long-term benefits for Russia.

Filaret was a person of strong character and had proven himself to the rest of the high-ranking boyars, securing the support the previous tsars had so desperately lacked. Among the new policies was, for example, the increase of funding for the agricultural sector. Agriculture had been the most important aspect of Russia's economy for all of its history, and boosting production was a great decision. In addition, a large portion of the Crown's lands, those that had been claimed by Ivan the Terrible as his own personal possession, were distributed to the servicemen. The reason behind this move was the fact that under the new owners, these lands would be given more attention and become much more profitable, increasing the wealth of not only the individual families that dwelt on them but also the state. New taxes ensured the investment the Crown had made into agriculture paid off dividends in the long term.

The state also forged favorable relations with several European nations, most importantly England, which loaned the Crown a considerable amount, which was much-needed support for a fairly empty royal treasury. The administrative sector was also a high priority. Filaret's and Mikhail's decisions were often supervised by the national assembly, which remained an important institution after the tsar's election. The balance between the monarch and the assembly was crucial for the successful implementation of new reforms, with the two often struggling to assume a more dominant role in decision-making.

Pre-Petrine Romanovs

Filaret passed away in 1633, a year after Russia and Poland had once again gone to war. Tsar Mikhail pushed for peace, as he believed the country was still not ready for an all-out conflict. Thanks to the diplomatic efforts of his father, the Holy Roman Empire brokered a peace agreement between the two sides in 1634. According to the terms of the "Eternal Peace," Poland remained in control of the western Russian lands, but King Wladyslaw officially gave up his claim to the Russian throne. This meant Mikhail's claim to the throne became even more legitimate, and his first years as the "true" king were given a much-needed boost. After the death of his father, who had undoubtedly overshadowed the inexperienced tsar since his return to Moscow, Tsar Mikhail ruled for about another ten years before passing away in 1645. Although the rule of the first Romanov tsar had unfolded under strange circumstances, Mikhail's reign was relatively successful and promised a prosperous future.

Mikhail would be succeeded by his sixteen-year-old son, Alexis. Tsar Alexis would become known as Tishayshiy ("the quietest" or "the most gentle"), as he was seen as being very intelligent, kind, and even-tempered. The new tsar, who was quite inexperienced and not really interested in politics, heavily relied on his court to rule. Boris Morozov, the tsar's mentor who was of noble descent, quickly assumed influence.

However, the first years of Tsar Alexis's rule proved to be very difficult, as the state, which was effectively under the orders of Morozov, tried to increase taxes after a universal census of 1646 determined the economic situation of the Russian population. Raised taxes and lowered salaries caused mass unrest, and corruption skyrocketed throughout the country. Two years later, in June 1648, people took to the streets in the capital, protesting the decisions of the Crown and forcing Tsar Alexis to completely change the ruling elite around him, including Morozov.

Prince Nikita Odoyevsky assumed most of the responsibilities previously held by Morozov, but unlike his predecessor, he was a more honorable and intelligent man. He greatly contributed to the legislative reform that came a year later, in 1649. The new legal code, the Sobornoye Ulozheniye, was drawn up. It touched upon the most important aspects of life for everyday citizens. It was much more favorable toward the middle class, which, as it was considered in the 17th century, was the backbone of the economy. The code reduced the power held by the clergy and the boyar nobility, limiting the former from acquiring more lands, while the latter was restricted when it came to peasant ownership. Middle-class merchants saw great benefits, as Archangel (Arkhangelsk), the city located in the northernmost part of the kingdom on the coast of the White Sea, was named the city where all foreign trade was to be concentrated—something most of them had wanted for a long time. The Sobornoye Ulozheniye was printed and distributed on a previously unseen scale; about two thousand copies were spread throughout the country to make sure everyone was familiar with the new laws. Although few could read, word spread quickly.

Despite these changes, the following decade was very unfortunate for Tsar Alexis. Multiple revolts occurred across the country, with Pskov and Novgorod protesting the new trade regulations, forcing the royal army to march to Pskov to resolve the issue with the help of the national assembly, which convened at the tsar's request. Four years later, in 1654, Russia suffered great losses due to the plague, which completely destroyed the Russian economy, as the workers were physically incapable of fulfilling their duties. This was also followed by mass inflation, as foreign trade deteriorated. The efforts to replace domestic currency with copper coins instead of silver proved to be catastrophic. After years of economic and social crises, the Crown was forced to stop issuing copper coins and release its silver reserves in 1663 since the decision had prompted many to rise up once again in protest.

Crises also erupted in the Russian Orthodox Church, which experienced a period of instability and chaos. The first main concern was a Russian Orthodox schism. Some prominent members of the church proposed new changes to the old rites and liturgical books to correct some of the "inaccuracies." They were, of course, opposed by those who believed that changing ancient, sacred texts and traditions were heresy, and they were prepared to stand by their claims even if it meant being excluded from the church. The ecclesiastical council that convened in 1654 addressed these issues and determined that new amendments would be added to the old texts, something that was confirmed a year later by the Greek Church as well as by the Great Moscow Synod in 1666. This did not undermine the protestors' spirit, as they chose to form their own sects despite the acceptance of new texts, causing them to be actively persecuted. They were sometimes referred to as the "Old Believers."

The second issue that concerned the Russian Church was caused by Metropolitan Nikon of Novgorod, who was elected as the patriarch of Russia in 1652. Tsar Alexis placed great trust in him and valued his advice very much, even granting him the title of "Great Sovereign" and making him as powerful as Patriarch Filaret had been about thirty years earlier. However, Patriarch Nikon was eventually blinded by the power entrusted to him by the tsar. He wished to establish the church's dominance over the state, causing him to be confronted by Tsar Alexis. Nikon would leave Moscow in 1658, feeling insulted and infuriated, although he refused to resign his see (Latin for "seat").

Over the next few years, the clergy was not sure whether to follow the patriarch since he had essentially become an enemy of the state. On different occasions, religious officials debated his status as a patriarch but could not reach a consensus that would please both their majority and the Crown. The matter would finally be resolved at the Great Moscow Synod in 1666, which was attended by representatives from Constantinople, Jerusalem, Alexandria, and Antioch, as well as powerful Russian nobles and members of the ruling class. The council decided to strip Nikon of his title and exiled him to the Ferapontov Monastery.

If economic, social, and religious problems were not enough, Tsar Alexis also had to endure a serious armed Cossack insurrection. The Cossacks, as mentioned previously, largely enjoyed their autonomy and were not exactly loyal to the tsar, at least to the same degree the different principalities were. Throughout the 17th century, they slowly migrated from their original territories of the Don River toward the east, contesting the Persians who held the lands near the Caspian Sea. Under an influential leader by the name of Stepan (Stenka) Razin, who had gained notoriety after his campaigns against Persia in 1668 and 1669, the Cossacks rose up against Moscow in 1670, demanding more equality and rights as second-class citizens. Razin's insurrection quickly gained traction among the peasants and lower classes and spread to include not only those living in the Volga Basin but also those who were generally against the tsar's rule. His army, which counted about ten thousand men, pillaged towns and villages on its way to Moscow, which was their final objective. Throughout the rebellion, Razin inspired thousands to rise up against the tsar and the cruel boyar nobles, who had mistreated their subjects for centuries.

In 1671, Tsar Alexis was able to muster up enough troops to crush the rebellion, thanks to help from thousands of foreign mercenaries whom he had hired to temporarily serve and defeat the Cossacks. The tsar was able to deal with the Cossacks in the most merciless of ways since they had been brutal when plundering and raiding the Russian settlements.

After his death in 1676, Tsar Alexis was succeeded by his son Fyodor, who was the eldest surviving son from the tsar's first wife. Tsar Fyodor III ruled for six years and was greatly influenced by the powerful individuals who surrounded him due to his poor health. Prince Vasily Golitsyn and boyars Ivan Yazykov and Alexei Likhachev basically took over the rule of the country, influencing the most important decisions and closely monitoring day-to-day affairs. In addition to some administrative reforms, which were aimed at taking care of the Crown's fiscal problems, they also took part in spreading some Western customs among the Russian nobility, such as the study of Latin and Catholicism. Under Tsar Fyodor, a new Greco-Latin-Slavonic academy was founded in Moscow, which was a great advancement in the field of education, providing poor children with much-needed access to high-quality teaching.

Unfortunately, Fyodor's reign was short-lived, and the tsar died without any heirs. He was succeeded by his brothers Ivan V and Peter, who ruled jointly. This marked the beginning of a new age in Russian history. The pre-Petrine period of Romanov Russia, a period that was instrumental for its political and social consequences and for successfully rallying the country from the devastating Time of Troubles, had ended. The pre-Petrine period certainly had its highs and lows, but as history would show, what was to come would be far more glorious.

Chapter 4: Peter the Great

Peter the Great is one of the most famous figures in Russian history. He is well known for his reforms, which influenced all aspects of Russian life, and is often considered to have been the person who modernized "old-fashioned" Russia, implementing a new European lifestyle and greatly contributing to Russia's struggle of finding an identity. He was undoubtedly one of the best Romanov rulers, so it is only fitting to devote a whole chapter to his reign.

Accession and Early Years

Peter ascended the throne of Muscovy under unnatural conditions. Due to the untimely death of childless Tsar Fyodor, who was Peter's older half-brother, the country spiraled into yet another succession crisis, but this time, the dispute was settled relatively easily compared to other instances in Russian history.

The point of contention was between the family of Tsar Alexis's first wife's side of the family (the Miloslavskys) and his second wife's side of the family (the Naryshkins). Peter, being the son of Tsar Alexis from his second wife, was supported by the Naryshkins, whereas his older half-brother, Ivan, was favored, naturally, by the Miloslavskys.

At first, the Naryshkins seized power, and the Zemsky Sobor—the great advisory assembly that had greatly transformed since Ivan IV had first called it in the 16th century—declared Peter as tsar. However, this did not last for long, as the Miloslavskys instigated a revolt to undermine the Naryshkins' power, attacking the Kremlin and killing a number of their rivals. Eventually, on May 26th, 1682, a day after the revolt, the two sides agreed to a compromise. Ivan and Peter were to co-rule, as senior and junior tsars, respectively. The great council also advised that before the two tsars could gain enough experience, real power should be held by Ivan's sister, Sophia, who thus became a regent queen (she was a pretty successful one too).

Queen Sophia contributed quite a bit to Russia's prosperous future, especially on the diplomatic and administrative fronts. In 1686, for example, she signed a treaty with Poland that gave Russia full possession of Kiev (spelled as Kyiv today). This resulted in the Crown deciding to pursue a policy of expansion in the south to gain better access to the Black Sea since it was a corridor to the rest of the world. The time was right since the situation in the Baltic was very tense. Prince Vasily Golitsyn, who acted as chief minister during Sophia's reign, aided the queen in many of her reforms.

Meanwhile, the junior tsar, Peter, lived in Preobrazhenskoe on the outskirts of Moscow, where he received his education. He became increasingly keen on warfare and military campaigns, something that influenced his reign once he became tsar. Since he spent his time outside of the Kremlin, he got to meet a lot of interesting people in his youth who would later become his most trusted friends, such as a Swiss man named Franz Lefort, who eventually was appointed as Peter's admiral and general. Perhaps no other person had more impact on young Peter than his teacher, Franz Timmerman, who was of Dutch origin. He taught the young tsar geometry and arithmetic. Timmerman was also the first one to take Peter to the port of Archangel, where Peter saw English and Dutch merchant ships for the first time. The city amazed him and made him fall in love with the sea and shipbuilding.

All these interactions with Westerners made Peter quite different from his predecessors, who, he believed, were devoid of the traits possessed by Europeans. Since adolescence, Peter regarded Europe as a symbol of freedom, knowledge, and progress, while Muscovy, corrupt as it was, stood for ignorance and the past. Peter learned how to speak several foreign languages, including German and Dutch, and regularly traveled to other countries to experience firsthand what it meant to be a European.

All in all, young Peter had many passions and interests and possessed a worldview from the very beginning, which would make him different from almost every other Russian tsar before him.

A painting of Peter the Great.
https://commons.wikimedia.org/wiki/File;Jean-Marc_Nattier,_Pierre_Ier_(1717)_-002.jpg

Peter married Eudoxia Lopukhina in January 1689 and was of age to start thinking about a potential heir, a matter that was still up in the air due to the rushed nature of the joint tsardom. Suspecting that Prince Golistyn and regent Queen Sophia were planning to conspire against him, Peter fled Preobrazhenskoe while his family, the Naryshkins, moved against the queen and her supporters. They managed to emerge victorious, exiling Golitsyn and forcing Sophia to take vows and join a convent outside Moscow. Under such circumstances, Peter and Ivan were able to rule without Sophia's interference in 1689. Still, Peter decided not to be fully involved with ruling the country and returned to his dwelling in Preobrazhenskoe. However, in seven years, Ivan tragically passed away due to ill health, meaning that Peter was now the sole tsar of Russia.

Military Reform

Peter the Great was, as his title might suggest, a great reformer, transforming every aspect of Russian life during his reign. Once he became the sole tsar in 1696, he was confronted with a long list of problems that required immediate attention. To the surprise of many, the young tsar was able to address everything, something that stemmed from his resilient and confident personality.

One of the most important matters was the question of the Russian military, which had become rather weak after decades of domestic troubles and foreign wars. It was apparent that it needed a top-to-bottom change, especially since Peter was at war from the day of his accession to the throne. The army was in rough shape at the time of his accession due to the ineffectiveness of old regiments that had become corrupt and pseudo-privileged. For example, the streltsy—the standing army that counted about twenty-two thousand men—were very old-fashioned and ill-equipped but still regularly paid and enjoyed their position as the tsar's "palace guard." The feudal cavalry, which was one of the oldest-standing regiments in Russia, was inefficient to maintain since it was composed of landowners who did not owe the king full-time service. Also, since the 1630s, some Western officers had been put in charge of special foreign units, which constituted the bulk of the army but were, in turn, very expensive.

Peter started to reorganize the army in late 1699, first touching upon the matters of conscription and volunteers. Volunteers were offered more pay and food to increase their motivation to join the army, and their numbers increased as the years passed, especially since Peter made a name for himself with his successful campaigns. In addition, according to new laws, landowners, the gentry, and the clergy were each to provide a foot soldier for a fixed number of households (for example, the clergy was supposed to raise one soldier for every twenty-five peasant households). The new recruits were not allowed to be serfs to ensure that crop production continued at the same rate, and they were also supposed to serve for life.

These new recruits were organized into different foot and cavalry regiments and underwent intense training to make sure they were always fit for battle. Peter also started retraining Russian officers to meet Western standards, something that increased the effectiveness of the army and laid the foundations for a more professional military tradition. Thousands of European muskets and handguns were purchased by Peter when he visited England in 1698, and their designs were copied and approved for manufacture in the coming years. New cannons were added to the army and the Russian fortresses to bolster defenses, and the personnel was retrained to man the new equipment. Even new uniforms, which were modeled after German ones, were commissioned.

All in all, the size and effectiveness of the military grew greatly during Peter's reign, and some estimates suggest that about 300,000 people served throughout his rule in the army, with well over 250,000 active personnel at its greatest extent. What made the army special was not only its sheer numbers but also the fact that Peter made sure they stayed up to date with new advancements in technology and strategy and were actively retrained every year.

One major aspect that also saw colossal improvements during Tsar Peter's reign was the Russian Navy. Peter's great love of shipbuilding would play a big part since Russia had never had a competent enough navy to challenge its rivals. Russian rulers of the past had never truly considered constructing a large naval force since it would require a lot of time and resources. Because of this, the tsardom lacked good shipbuilders, and the ships that were anchored in Russian ports were privately owned and of foreign origin. However, Peter realized that without a strong navy, Russia would be unable to take control of the Baltic and the Black Seas, which were the only two marine corridors available to Russia to access the rest of the world.

Several measures were taken to build up the fleet. Peter had gained quite a lot of knowledge from his travels and invited several experienced European shipbuilders to come and share their expertise. He commissioned the building of galleys and barges in the town of Voronezh. But to further increase the navy's size, he also ordered the landowners and the church to supply one ship per eight thousand households, just as he had done when it came to recruiting soldiers. As a result, the number of Russian ships grew almost exponentially during the first fifteen years of his reign. By 1725, records show the Russian Baltic fleet had become the largest in the region, counting about twenty-eight thousand active seamen, thirty-four large warships, fifteen frigates, and many galleys. This also meant the Crown spent heavily on maintenance; the navy cost more than a million rubles in 1724, compared to about eighty thousand rubles at the start of the 18th century.

To make sure the reforms Peter had implemented in the first few years of his reign stayed effective and that the army's and navy's progress would not be thwarted, the tsar also established several institutions that inspected the military. The Department of Military Affairs, the War Chancery, and the War College were all set up by 1719 to monitor the army's developments and make sure that problems were addressed quickly and competently. The naval academy of St. Petersburg, on the other hand, employed a lot of foreign marine officers and trained Russian sailors. In addition, many aspiring soldiers and sailors from Russia were sent to Europe to gain firsthand experience in their relevant fields and bring back valuable knowledge they could share with their compatriots. All in all, the advancements in the military remain one of the most effective measures taken by Peter the Great.

Russia at War

It is now logical to discuss how these military advancements shaped the wars Russia experienced during Peter the Great's reign. At the time of his accession, Russia had two main rivals: Sweden in the north, with whom the country had a history of conflict, and the Ottoman Empire to the south, which had reached the peak of its strength and had spread its influence to dominate the Black Sea. Gaining a significant advantage over these powers would bring great economic benefits and respect since the other European nations were watching the situation unfold. Since Peter wished Russia to become a true member of the European family, a decisive military victory was necessary.

Although Russia and the Ottomans had not gone to war with each other, they had warily eyed each other for a couple of decades by the time Peter became tsar. Neither one had a good enough justification to engage in an all-out conflict with the other, so it is unsurprising that Peter declared war on the Ottomans when an instance presented itself. The continuous raids of the Crimean Tatars on the southern Russian lands prompted Peter to launch a campaign against the Turkish fortress of Azov in 1695/1696. What is interesting is the fact that Tsar Peter would serve in the army as a bombardier sergeant, something that can only be attributed to his keenness regarding warfare and his personality.

The first attempts to successfully march against the Ottomans failed, as the inexperienced and still somewhat unprofessional Russian forces faced supply issues. However, this did not stop Peter from changing the army's command and making another attempt to capture the fortress. Peter increased the size of his army and commissioned the immediate construction of a navy in Voronezh, literally transporting ships overland from the heart of the kingdom to the south so the shipbuilders had a model to work with. He personally mobilized his forces and oversaw the construction of the fleet, which was the first navy he built during his reign, and set out to capture Azov once again.

By the end of July 1696, the Russians had managed to take Azov from the Ottomans, with Peter now serving as one of the galley captains. The victory at Azov was very important for securing a passage to the Black Sea and would prove to be useful in the future against the Ottomans. In fact, Peter's efforts against the Ottomans prompted him to start implementing many of the military reforms we discussed above in a quick manner.

What followed the Azov campaign was another of Peter's very intriguing decisions, as he decided to travel to different European countries to unite the Christian nations against the Ottoman Empire, which controlled most of southeastern Europe by the end of the 17th century. On paper, it was a diplomatic mission called the Grand Embassy to the West, but Peter also wanted to learn about Western traditions and technology and gather up military specialists to employ them in Russia. What made this one-and-a-half-year period so interesting was the fact Peter decided to disguise himself as Peter Mikhailovich. He refused to travel as the tsar, perhaps doing so to gain as many authentic experiences as possible.

From March 1697 to September 1698, Peter went from country to country. For example, he stayed in the Netherlands, where he studied shipbuilding in great detail from the best shipwrights in Amsterdam and also attended Leyden University in his free time to learn more about medicine, another one of his many hobbies. Then, Peter went to England, where he visited the dockyards in

Portsmouth and Deptford, pursuing his passions and making contacts that would come in handy in the future.

As for the "official" purpose of his travels, the diplomatic aspect of the Grand Embassy was not as successful. The Ottoman problem had largely been resolved by the Europeans by the time of Peter's visit, and the Treaty of Karlowitz, which would be signed by Poland, Austria, Venice, and the Ottoman Empire in 1699, marked the end of Ottoman expansion into Europe. Although Peter was able to meet with several European leaders, these meetings never produced anything of actual political value. Thus, disappointed, Peter was forced to sign a thirty-year truce with the Ottoman Empire in June 1700.

In the first decade of the 1700s, Peter turned his attention to the north, where multiple European nations had allied together to end Swedish dominance in the region. Denmark, Brandenburg-Prussia, and Poland-Lithuania had all joined an anti-Swedish coalition and were more than glad to let Russia participate. Sweden had been facing some domestic problems, as the nobility was unsure about the newly assumed leadership of fourteen-year-old Charles XII. Peter declared war on Sweden in 1700 after having secured Russia's southern flank with the Turks with their thirty-year truce. He marched on the pivotal fortress in Narva on the Baltic with forty thousand troops.

However, despite Peter's seemingly advantageous position, the young Charles XII landed nearby with a force of eleven thousand men and routed Peter's army in October. The Swedish victory stemmed from their previous triumph against the Danes at Copenhagen, which raised their spirits and allowed them to pull off a small military miracle. The siege of Narva was abandoned, and the Russians suffered up to ten thousand casualties.

Narva was a disaster for Peter the Great, and the tsar took the following years to regroup. With Denmark defeated, Poland remained his only ally, so keeping the Polish king, Augustus II, on his side was crucial in achieving success against Sweden. Peter was very lucky the Swedish decided not to chase him after their victory at Narva, as they instead focused on slowly defeating the Poles.

While Charles was busy fighting Russia's allies, Peter launched another offensive in October 1702, this time successfully taking the fortress of Nöteborg, which he renamed Shlisselburg (Schlüsselburg in German) ("key fortress"). This was followed by several crucial victories on the Baltic coast, with the divided Russian army managing to take control of the poorly garrisoned cities one by one. By the end of 1703, it looked as if Peter had gained an advantage over the enemy, and for the next three years, the Russian army acquired even more territories in the region. However, King Charles of Sweden was able to retaliate quickly in 1706, defeating the Polish and forcing them to abandon the coalition. Peter was now left alone against an impending Swedish invasion, and with a long list of domestic problems as a result of the constant warfare and heavy taxation to finance the wars, he was put in a difficult situation.

Charles XII invaded in late 1707 with a large army of no more than forty thousand men. However, Peter was prepared. Anticipating the Swedish offensive, he retreated from the newly captured Baltic coast and razed everything to the ground on his way out. Moscow's fortifications had been upgraded, and Russia was ready to fight, for the first time in a long time, a defensive war. The Swedes were perhaps too confident due to their victory at Narva, as they thought the Russian army was inferior to them and believed they could swiftly defeat any resistance. At first, their belief was proven true. In July of 1708, Charles was able to confront and defeat the Russian forces at Golovchin with ten thousand fewer men (the Swedish had about thirteen thousand men, while the Russians had more than twenty-five thousand men). However, the Russians were able to put up a much better fight, inflicting many casualties and slowing down the Swedish king's advance. The Battle of Golovchin was a clear indication that Peter's military reforms had borne fruit, but it would not mark the demise of the Swedes.

Charles hoped his numbers would be reinforced by another force of twelve thousand under commander Adam Ludwig Lewenhaupt, but he had misjudged his ability to wage a prolonged war on foreign soil, especially considering the harsh conditions the armies had to endure. In fact, Lewenhaupt's army was intercepted and heavily defeated by Tsar Peter, so only half of the original force reached King Charles. And this half was demoralized and without sufficient supplies.

The scarcity of food and a harsh winter caused Charles to change his strategy. Instead of continuing toward Moscow, which he knew would be heavily defended, he marched south to Ukraine, where an anti-tsarist revolt was already ripe. Hoping to utilize the unpredictable Cossacks as allies, Charles spent the winter in Ukraine. However, Peter quickly reacted by reinforcing the southern provinces and sending General Alexander Menshikov to crush the Cossack uprising. Unfortunately for the Swedish king, the winter in Ukraine turned out to be the worst in a very long time, making the situation even worse for the invaders. In addition, the Cossacks were unwilling to offer their help due to their recent defeat by the Russians. So, in the spring of 1709, Charles XII and his forces, weakened by the winter and still experiencing serious supply issues, laid siege to the city of Poltava, northeast of the Dnieper River. This would turn out to be a fatal mistake.

Peter the Great arrived with his relief force in June. He was unable to assess the strength of the Swedes, so he offered to negotiate with Charles. The latter, however, refused and launched an attack in early July against Peter's army, which was about twice as large and much more fit for battle. After a four-hour battle, forty thousand Russians relatively easily defeated around twenty-two thousand Swedes in the Battle of Poltava, with both Charles and Peter narrowly escaping death in the midst of the flying bullets. The defeated Swedes were chased and routed two days later at the Dnieper. It was a decisive victory for Peter the Great and marked a turning point in the war.

Poltava put Tsar Peter and Russia back on the radar for other European powers. The word of his victory spread fast throughout other kingdoms, and it had the effect the tsar had desired for so long. It was also relieving for the people at home, as they had been upset with the new laws and expensive wars but came to rally for their victorious leader. As for the war with Sweden, it was clear that Russia had assumed a more favorable position, and Peter even convinced Denmark to reenter the war in 1710 after regaining Poland as an ally by supporting George Ludwig of Hanover to take power in a coup (the same man would become King George I of Britain). All of these developments earned Russia a much-deserved place in European politics.

With the confidence Peter had gained from his success against Sweden and with the relations between Russia and Turkey deteriorating since the peace agreement of 1700, it is not surprising that Peter went to war with the Ottomans again in March 1711, although it was actually the sultan who declared war, doing so six months earlier. Peter's strategy involved attacking the Turkish Balkan holdings, which was a predominantly Christian area. Although the Russians achieved some success at the beginning, attacking the provinces of Wallachia and Moldavia and prompting the Slavic peoples to rise up against the Ottomans, poor supply networks and overextension brought an early end to the war. Peter was forced to negotiate an unfavorable peace treaty, ceding back control of the fortress of Azov and much of the northern Black Sea coast in July 1711 with the Treaty of the Pruth.

Peter the Great would return to Russia for a short while after the peace agreement to marry his second wife, Catherine, in 1712 before embarking on yet another military campaign. This time, the Russians landed on the Finnish coast in May 1714, thanks to their newly formed Baltic fleet, and took the fight to the Swedish. Peter had managed to hold onto the territories he had gained after the initial Baltic conquests, but since Sweden had refused to surrender after Poltava, he felt compelled to launch another offensive.

Two years later, Peter planned to launch a full-scale invasion of the Swedish mainland from Copenhagen with about fifty thousand troops but wisely called it off at the last minute, believing he was overreaching by relying on his allies to support him. For the next two years, Russia and Sweden entered a stand-off and even tried to negotiate a peace agreement. However, the terms presented by the Swedish in 1718 were so disliked by the tsar that he elected to withdraw from the talks, knowing he had an advantageous position, as he had heavily weakened the enemy and was still in control of the Baltic.

The Great Northern War—as the conflict has come to be known—finally ended in September 1721 with the Treaty of Nystad. The Swedes had failed to push back the Russians from Finland time and time again, and the Russian Baltic fleet had only grown in size and matured in experience. The Russian galleys were the masters of the Baltic, maneuvering in the tides thanks to their mobile and quick nature. This constant warfare and the threat of further invasion caused Sweden to reopen negotiations in November 1720, and this time, they made concessions Peter found favorable.

Russia gained total control of all the Baltic lands that were formerly led by Sweden, including Estonia and Livonia, as well as the part of Finland Russia had occupied since 1714. The Swedes, on the other hand, only settled for a payment of 1.5 million rubles and some trade rights in the ceded territories.

Peter the Great's Social, Administrative, and Economic Reforms

Let's now close out the chapter with what Peter the Great is perhaps best known for: his social, administrative, and economic reforms. It is worth noting that Peter was active in the process of heavily reforming Russia while he was busy with his military campaigns against Turkey and Sweden. Peter was not one of those kings who is only known for one particular thing, like success in war, for example. He had the ability to find solutions to many problems at once and introduced measures to effectively help Russia develop and Westernize, making him a great reformer.

Peter the Great was able to give the Russian economy new life, completely reimagining it and allowing the country to stay economically competitive with the rest of the European powers. During Peter's reign, Russia experienced a sort of industrial boom. It was not on the scale of what Europeans were able to achieve during the Industrial Revolution decades later, but it was enough to significantly increase the production of local goods and materials and encourage their export. Eighty-six new factories specializing in the production of textiles, iron, copper, sulfur, gunpowder, and weapons were built during his time as tsar. There was a tenfold increase in iron production, which Russia had in great abundance, thanks to its large size and diverse terrain. Metallurgy, on the whole, was greatly improved, mainly to meet the army's increased demands.

In the early 18th century, Russia controlled a large part of the economy, which, as a result, limited thousands of people from accumulating wealth. One of Peter's personal goals was to transfer the means of production to the hands of individuals, encouraging the creation of an "entrepreneur" class that would go into the business of manufacturing and would privately train laborers. Although Peter would not reach his goal, as most non-serf Russians relied on their serfs for income, the industrial reforms transformed the Russian economy, especially foreign exports. By 1726, about half of Russia's exports came from locally manufactured goods, and new factories and workplaces employed thousands of Russians who had suffered from unemployment before Peter's reign.

Peter believed existing administrative institutions also needed massive changes to make them more European and, therefore, more efficient and productive. Upon his accession to the throne, the power dynamics between the local institutions, as well as their exact roles and areas of governance, were unclear, so these problems had to be addressed too. Peter introduced changes that affected all aspects of the administration at once.

First, he established the Russian Senate to replace the Boyar Duma, a rather old institution that had lost its purpose and power when the Romanovs assumed power. Composed of nine (later, ten) members, the Senate acted as a governing body, overseeing the different provinces and tax collection. It was the country's highest legislative court, a function that was taken away in 1721. Attending Senate meetings was mandatory, and members missing any of the sessions would be at first fined and then risk imprisonment. This measure proved extremely effective, especially considering that only a third of the boyars actually showed up to the Duma meetings and wasted their time arguing over useless topics. Five hundred men were also given a new title (*fiskaly*) and they had the responsibility of being the eyes and ears of the Senate, rooting out corruption and fraud and making sure each officeholder fully completed their duties.

The creation of the Senate was followed up with the introduction of eleven new colleges, a system copied from Sweden. The colleges specialized in different aspects of social, political, and economic life and acted like modern ministries. The colleges of foreign affairs, war, and admiralty were the three most important ones and were created before 1718. The rest dealt with industry, commerce, finance, justice, provincial governments, and land ownership. Each institution had its own clear duties and objectives, as well as similar establishments and structures to each other, which made it easy for Peter and the Senate to regulate. The colleges were an improvement to the existing *prikazy*, which had mixed functions and goals.

Peter also tried to rethink the administrative division of Russia, something that meant more decentralization of power in the hopes of raising the effectiveness of governance. In December 1708, the Russian lands were redivided, this time into eight *gubernii* (governorships), which were, in turn, divided into fifty smaller provinces nine years later. The number of *gubernii* would eventually increase to twelve in 1718, and the system would last way beyond the reign of Peter. The main functions of these new administrative units were tax collection and recruitment, just like in other European countries. Peter personally appointed the governors for these territories, and they would directly report to the court. Peter also made sure that Ukraine, where the Cossacks were still largely autonomous, was under the firm control of the central government and introduced forced conscription and Russian laws. However, in the newly acquired Baltic territories, more autonomy was permitted.

To reach his goal of Westernizing Russian society, Peter knew he had to start with the members of the higher classes, as they held much more power than commoners. He forced them to look European by stripping them of their old, traditional Russian clothing and giving them Western attire. Peter even made the men shave their beards, which he believed were a symbol of the past and would be laughed at in Europe. The boyars were given new Western titles, like count and baron, and were forced to learn and live by Western etiquette. However, instead of weakening the boyars' influence, Peter made them more involved in politics, granting them different offices and making them army officials. He also introduced a new "table of ranks," a social mobility system that could allow someone to rise up to a higher hierarchy if they carried out their duties well.

Perhaps Peter's harshest reforms were those concerning the church, which the tsar thought enjoyed far more privileges than what was considered "modern" in Europe. The role of the church in 18th-century Russia was undeniable, but Peter was more concerned with the patriarch's status in relation to the monarch, as the two were often considered equals, with the former having just as much say in political decisions, thanks to his popularity from his supporters.

Peter made sure to push a radical church reform after the death of Patriarch Adrian in 1700, greatly reducing the number of lands and power held by the Russian Orthodox Church and forcing the institution to retrain and reeducate the majority of its clergy. The clergy was also deprived of tax privileges, and their spending was heavily reduced. To avoid joining the church as a means of dodging military service, he banned all men under the age of thirty from becoming priests. Finally, concluding his harsh changes, he set up a special spiritual *kollegiya* ("college" or "committee"), later renamed the Holy Synod, which made the church another one of the administrative units used for governance. By regulating legislation for religious officials, Peter asserted his dominance over the Russian Orthodox Church, making everyone realize the tsar was the most important figure in the country. The way in which he transformed the church remained for about two hundred more years.

Last but not least, perhaps nothing symbolizes the rule of Peter the Great as much as the construction of Russia's new capital, St. Petersburg, a clear symbol of the tsar's persistent nature and enthusiasm to bring the country closer to Europe. Built on the newly captured coast of the Baltic in flood-prone swamps, which made the construction extremely difficult, St. Petersburg was perceived by many as a dangerous and unnecessary project. Peter was motivated by his love for the sea and wished to leave Moscow—a city that symbolized Russia's old and backward ways—for something new, something that would be closer to Europe.

The workers faced many problems during its construction, and they were regularly forcibly transported to work under terrible conditions. Nevertheless, St. Petersburg quickly became the new center of Russia, thanks to the promotion and personal efforts of Tsar Peter. It would be the first Russian city that had a real urban plan, with buildings and streets modeled after what Peter had seen in Amsterdam and London. Peter would almost force Europeanness on its residents by requiring them to speak foreign languages and attend regular balls and parades. St. Petersburg meant a modern, Petrine Russia, and it remains one of Peter the Great's most remarkable achievements.

Peter's Legacy

It's not possible to include every single achievement and important occurrence of Peter the Great's reign simply due to the fact that so many events and laws require going into great detail to fully talk about their short- and long-term implications for Russia. However, it is undeniable that Peter the Great is one of the most widely known Russian monarchs of all time. He was arguably the most influential Romanov to ever ascend the throne of Russia.

Thanks to his efforts, Russia was able to reenter European politics and reemerge as an influential and powerful actor on the world stage. Peter's military, social, administrative, and economic reforms established a strong base for the country's future, and his transformation of Russian society and lifestyle, however radical and harsh it may have been at first perceived, prepared the country for its long and tumultuous future. Peter the Great had a long-lasting impact on his country and put great pressure on whoever would succeed him.

Chapter 5: The Age of Enlightened Despotism

Peter the Great singlehandedly started the process of Russia's transformation from a backward country to a modern, powerful empire of European standards. The next Romanovs would build upon those foundations to place Russia in an even more dominating position. This chapter will cover the Romanov dynasty right after Tsar Peter, mainly focusing on Queen Catherine II, the enlightened despot who is often credited with giving Russia a soul.

After Peter the Great

Peter the Great died in 1725; he was still relatively young, dying at the age of fifty-two. Historians believe that his persistent personality and always being fixated on overachieving on multiple fronts at once played a big role in his eventual demise. Peter also had a severe drinking problem, which, combined with the never-ending stress of running a country, greatly weakened his health. Since his health was slowly deteriorating, he issued a decree in 1722 that gave him the power to name the heir to the throne. Despite this, the matter of succession upon his death was still undecided. Peter had fourteen children throughout his two marriages, but most of them had died during infancy or at an early age, leaving Russia without a clear heir.

Thus, his widow, Catherine, was declared the first empress of Russia by a group of officials once Peter passed away. Catherine I would rule for the next two years. Although she had been a good wife to Peter, she had no real experience with politics and was not the person Russia needed, especially after such an influential period with Tsar Peter.

Peter's close friend, Alexander Menshikov, took over as the main decision-maker during Empress Catherine's reign and, despite being under constant pressure, was able to maintain the empress's authority over her subjects. After Catherine passed away in 1727, Menshikov and other powerful officials declared that eleven-year-old Peter would become the new tsar. He was the son of Peter the Great's son Tsarevich Alexis, who had died in 1718 after trying to rise up against his father's rule. However, in an unfortunate turn of events, Peter II died of smallpox before he could truly become tsar in 1730.

What followed next was a desperate attempt by the Supreme Privy Council, which played an advisory role during the succession crisis, to find the next suitable ruler. After some searching, the council chose Anna, Duchess of Courland, who was the daughter of Ivan V (the co-ruler of Peter once upon a time). Special terms were proposed to her that would divert the real power into the council's hands; the government would be something along the lines of a constitutional monarchy.

Although Anna accepted these conditions and arrived in Moscow as the new empress in early 1730, she proceeded to tear them up and dissolve the Supreme Privy Council, assuming more power than originally intended. However, much like Catherine, she was not interested in politics and instead formed a German advisory council led by her lover, Ernst Johann Biron, which took over the day-to-day tasks. Before her death in 1740, Russia took part in the War of the Polish Succession, where it managed to successfully support a pro-Russian king. Russia also fought in the Russo-Turkish War, where it defeated the Ottomans but gained very little.

Before Anna died, she named her successor: her niece's son, Ivan. She also said that Biron should act as regent before young Ivan came of age. However, soon after her death, anti-German sentiment became more widespread. Biron was ousted, and the empress's niece, Anna Leopoldovna, assumed power. This complicated matters even more, and the two sides, the former Empress Anna's German clique and Regent Anna's Russian supporters, clashed for power. A new contender emerged from the chaos. Her name was Elizabeth, the daughter of Peter the Great, whose safety was threatened by Anna Leopoldovna (at least, that was what many of her supporters argued). With the support of the French ambassador in Moscow and members of the court, Elizabeth successfully instigated a coup against Anna Leopoldovna and declared herself the new empress in 1741.

Elizabeth cared a bit more about politics and governance than her two predecessors, but she was mostly concerned with her love for lavish attire and was careful about who she surrounded herself with, making it very difficult for her to retain her popularity. Still, she would rule for the next twenty years, and her reign saw the introduction of several new important aspects. For example, the first academy of arts and the first university were both founded during Elizabeth I's rule. The Senate—an institution created by her father—also reemerged after being pushed aside by unofficial councils and advisory assemblies. Russia also succeeded geopolitically, winning wars against Sweden and Prussia during the Seven Years' War. It formed new relationships with Britain, Austria, and France and continued to gain prestige as one of the most powerful empires in the world.

Complications arose over Empress Elizabeth's successor. Upon becoming empress, she had no children, so she chose a presumptive heir: Peter, the son of Anna (the eldest daughter of Peter the Great) and Duke Charles Frederick of Holstein-Gottorp. Anna had been married to Duke Charles for many years now and had given birth to their son in Kiel. Young Peter, who was named heir presumptive, was thus more German than Russian and only arrived in Moscow in the autumn of 1742.

Interestingly, Charles XII of Sweden—Peter the Great's archnemesis—was also young Peter's great-uncle from his father's side. Upon his arrival in Moscow, he was proclaimed by the Swedish parliament as the presumptive heir to the Swedish throne. The parliament was not aware at that time that Peter had already converted to Orthodoxy in Moscow and was the heir presumptive to the throne of Russia. Thus, young Peter, who was still underage, had to renounce his claims to Sweden, even though those claims were very legitimate).

In 1745, Empress Elizabeth married Peter to her second cousin, Princess Sophie Friederike Augusta of Anhalt-Zerbst-Dornburg. Sophie arrived in Moscow, converted to Orthodoxy, and changed her name to Catherine. She eventually gave birth to two children: Paul, the future heir, and Anna.

Under these strange circumstances, Peter became the emperor of Russia after the death of his aunt, Empress Elizabeth, in 1762. Emperor Peter, now Peter III, was not really favored by the Russian nobility, as they did not really consider him Russian because of his German origins. In fact, one of the first decisions he made was to accept peace with Prussia in the Seven Years' War due to his personal fondness for Germany. For many years, Russia had pursued an anti-Prussian policy, and this decision greatly angered the Russian elite. Peter III even went as far as to make allies with the Prussians and ordered his twelve-thousand-strong army that occupied Berlin to march against the Austrians, his former allies.

Then, amidst all this chaos, he planned an invasion of Denmark to take back some of the lost lands of his duchy (remember that he was still the duke of Holstein-Gottorp). Peter even transferred about forty thousand troops to the Danish border in the town of Kolberg with the intention of starting a war with the Danish. However, before he could advance further with his plans, he was overthrown by his wife Catherine, which started a new era in Russian history.

Catherine the Great Becomes Empress

Catherine the Great, the enlightened despot, is another one of the most influential Russian rulers. Born as Sophie Friederike Augusta, Catherine was another German-born Russian monarch. Technically, Catherine was never meant to ascend the Russian throne and become empress, but the situation that developed after her marriage forced her to "save" Russia from her husband, whose foreign policy decisions were under great scrutiny from his contemporaries.

Unlike her husband, Catherine started adapting to Russian customs and ways of living upon her arrival in Russia. She enthusiastically learned the Russian language since, as she believed, a future queen must be well-spoken. In the early days of her marriage, Catherine became aware of Peter's dull and arrogant personality and started hating her husband, whom she thought was undeserving of being tsar. To entertain herself, she began reading books in French, something that would eventually become her passion. The writings of Voltaire and other contemporary French philosophers from the Age of the Enlightenment made the biggest impression on her.

As she drifted further and further away from Peter, whose presence she found unbearable, she started to get more and more involved with members of the court, often taking them as her lovers to answer the adulteries her husband committed. She became increasingly interested in politics and governance, and as the public's distrust of Peter grew, those with whom she had become acquainted through her openly lavish sex life started considering her as a potential replacement for Peter III.

The conspiracy against Peter would grow as the months passed, as he continued to make decisions that many believed went against Russian national interests. In comparison, Catherine seemed much wiser and cooler, somebody who actually cared for her and her country's future and who had enough knowledge, interest, and competence to become the next ruler of the country. Thus, in the summer of 1762, with the help of her lover, Grigory Orlov, Catherine was able to overthrow her husband and become the new empress of Russia.

Orlov, as well as many of Catherine's other lovers, would be involved in her court during the early years of her reign, with some of them having more influence than others. One useful thing that emerged from these connections was the fact that all of them were of noble descent, allowing them to forge a close relationship with the empress early on. It was an informal alliance, as the ruling elite favored Catherine, and Catherine favored the ruling elite. This relationship would be greatly reflected in some of the domestic policies she introduced.

Enlightened Despot

Catherine's rule is perhaps just as all-encompassing as that of Peter the Great, as developments were made in all fields of Russian life, and both foreign and domestic situations got significant attention. Domestically, Empress Catherine had two main goals: to build upon and further advance the administrative and political foundations from the days of Peter the Great and to introduce a new educational reform that would begin the long process of properly reeducating all of Russia. Heavily influenced by the Western knowledge she had gathered in her early years after arriving in Moscow, Catherine wished to be the one who would start a sort of Russian Enlightenment. She believed the country desperately needed it.

Portrait of Catherine the Great.
https://commons.wikimedia.org/wiki/File-Profile_portrait_of_Catherine_II_by_Fedor_Ro
kotov_(1763,_Tretyakov_gallery).jpg

Since the very beginning of her reign, she made an effort to expand the special schools in Moscow and St. Petersburg, namely the universities and military academies. These institutions were almost completely reorganized with the help of Ivan Betskoy, who served as the chief of the Imperial Academy of Arts and was one of the main advisors to the queen on educational matters. Together, Betskoy and Catherine implemented the first public school system in the country, as well as special schools for girls and orphans. This reform proved extremely successful; by the end of the 18th century, there were about 62,000 students enrolled in 550 different institutions. The majority of these students were in military and church schools, but the rest studied in newly-set-up schools. Catherine understood the importance of an educated middle class, so she made sure that many people had access to schools all around the country.

Providing education to the masses also complemented the spread of Enlightenment ideas through different means, like the translation and dissemination of popular Western works, not just in the highest societies of Moscow and St. Petersburg but also in other, more rural parts of the country. The creation of intellectual or literary spheres was greatly encouraged, and many new Russian writers emerged on the local scene. In short, it was a much-needed, effective cultural revolution on a never-before-seen scale. Unlike Peter the Great, who had tried to make Russia look and feel European, Catherine's efforts were directed at making Russia think like Europe.

When it came to administration, Catherine's reign saw a large increase in the number of officeholders and levels of bureaucracy. By the year 1775, there were about two thousand more state officials in administrative institutions with very high, desirable salaries. Interestingly, with the Charter of the Nobility, a decree the Crown issued in 1785, Catherine made it impossible for people of lower classes and incomes to be elected to office. This made it so the nobility dominated the civil service, receiving salaries in addition to their own incomes from their estates, exponentially increasing their wealth and power and, therefore, keenness toward the empress. This decision, which perhaps stemmed from her close relationship with the higher echelons of the Russian elite since her early days, raised efficiency when it came to administrative rule.

On the other hand, a new state council was set up in 1769 to act as an intermediary between the empress and the Senate, the latter of which got most of its functions back and was reorganized after a rather long time of inactivity. Despite this, the Senate never reached the same height of importance it had during Peter the Great's reign. In 1775, most of Peter's colleges were stripped of their functions. Only the colleges of foreign affairs, the admiralty, and the army were kept largely intact and became the most important administrative institutions in the country.

When it came to changing up the system of governance, Catherine's main goal was to combine some of the Western philosophers' concepts of the balance of power with German cameralism (the state's centralization of the economy to work toward the formation of a welfare state, whose benefits the subjects would enjoy). On this front, Catherine tried to separate the executive, legislative, and judicial powers from the institution of the monarchy as much as she could. But when it came to organizing self-sufficient effective middle and lower classes, which was instrumental for a cameralist society, she failed, deeming Russia unready for such a massive transformation.

Catherine the Great also introduced changes that would try to bring the Russian economic system closer to Europe, as the former had been lagging behind significantly. She encouraged foreign migration to Russian lands. Most notably, she welcomed German farmers, who settled in the Volga Valley and became known as the Volga Germans. The Volga Germans possessed modern agricultural technology and knew how to grow new crops that had been introduced to Europe from the New World, helping modernize Russian agriculture and boosting production. Ukraine and later the rest of Russia became well known for their wheat production. Thanks to the expansion of territories, Catherine was also able to grant many peasants new lands, which was a positive step toward increasing the wealth of the lower class and promoting production.

By revising and boosting local manufacturing, international trade flourished, and Russian exports reached the distant markets of the United States and East Asia, again thanks to the territorial gains Russia had acquired by the end of the 18th century. Textiles and metals were the most popular Russian goods, and some estimates suggest the total trade turnover to have quadrupled during Catherine the Great's reign. This contributed to the growth of Russia's ports, not only the one in St. Petersburg, which was the most important one by a large margin, but also the newly acquired ones on the Black Sea.

Financial reform followed, with the first banknotes and paper currency being issued in 1770. The country lacked silver, which it needed to finance wars. The overall economic growth produced more taxes for the state, which the state would often invest in different domestic or foreign projects.

Expansion during Catherine the Great

Not only did Catherine the Great's reign see some of the most influential cultural, political, and social reforms, but it was also characterized by Russia's rather effective territorial expansion and successful participation in different wars. More than 500,000 square kilometers of land were added to the country, including the pivotal regions of Crimea and the northern coast of the Black Sea, the Caucasus, and most of modern-day Eastern Europe.

Russia went to war with the Ottoman Empire once again in 1768 after the latter opened hostilities. The Ottomans were wary of Russia's potential expansion into Crimea or the Balkans now that the country had finally withdrawn from the Seven Years' War. In fact, Catherine had finalized the procedure of pulling Russia out of the war but retained friendly relations with Frederick II of Prussia, something that would come in handy down the line. Throughout the Russo-Turkish War, Catherine's objective was to finally get rid of the Crimean Tatars, who had dwelt on the northern coast of the Black Sea for centuries and who would continuously raid Russian settlements on the border. Catherine was able to defeat the Ottomans, most notably at the crucial naval encounter at Chesme and one of the largest land battles of the 18th century, the Battle of Kagul, where about 45,000 Russians were able to rout an Ottoman force of 150,000 and claim a heroic victory.

In 1774, with the Treaty of Kuchuk-Kainardzhi, Russia gained possession of parts of Crimea and gave Russian merchants free passage through the Turkish straits. More crucially, the Ottomans nominally said Russia was the protector of all the Orthodox subjects living in the empire. The victory against the Turks prompted Catherine to once and for all deal with the Crimean Khanate. Catherine eventually annexed the peninsula and destroyed the khanate in 1783, something that would lead to another war with the Ottomans in 1787. Russia would again emerge victorious five years later.

Catherine also saw success against another Muslim power: Persia. The two sides had their own interests in the extremely important region of the Caucasus, located between the Black and Caspian Seas. In 1783, Catherine managed to establish a protectorate over the Kingdom of Georgia, thanks to both nations being Orthodox Christians. She also pledged to stand behind the Georgians against any threat from the Persians, who had repeatedly invaded the small nation.

In 1796, Catherine was forced to declare war on Persia after it invaded Georgia and sent an army to expel the invading forces from the Caucasus. In the summer of the same year, the Russian army was able to defeat the Persian resistance, first in the northern Caucasus and then in modern-day Azerbaijan, taking the important cities of Baku and Ganja and forcing the enemy to retreat. Unfortunately, Catherine passed away before the conflict came to an end, and her successor, Paul, did not continue the offensive. He instead recalled the troops home.

In the west, Catherine the Great was able to restore Russia's status as a superpower, one whose interests should be taken into consideration during every major geopolitical event. Russia played an active role in the political processes of Central and Eastern Europe during the late 18th century. Russia was also actively involved in Poland's partitions (on all three occasions), something that underlines Russia's importance as a regional actor. Catherine had always recognized the significance of having her western flank secure and proceeded to place a pro-Russian, Stanislaus Augustus Poniatowski, one of her former lovers, on the Polish throne in 1764 before establishing a protectorate over the Polish-Lithuanian Commonwealth in 1768.

This prompted the Polish nationalists to rise up in an insurrection. They declared war on Russia, which persisted until 1772. Catherine and her allies—Prussia and Austria—stood victorious. The three leaders of these victorious nations divided the conquered territories of the Polish-Lithuanian Commonwealth among themselves, stripping the state of about 30 percent of its bordering lands and significantly reducing its influence and power in the region. This was later followed by the Second and Third

Partitions of Poland, where Russia, Prussia, and Austria continued to slowly whittle away the Polish lands until, in 1795, they completely annexed all of Poland-Lithuania. They then shared a three-way border in historical Poland.

A map of the partitions of Poland.

Halibutt, CC BY-SA 3.0 <http://creativecommons.org/licenses/by-sa/3.0/>, via Wikimedia Commons; https://commons.wikimedia.org/wiki/File:Rzeczpospolita_Rozbiory_3.png

Catherine the Great was not a member of the Romanov dynasty by birth, being of German descent. Still, she remains one of the most prominent members of the ruling family of Russia, thanks to her distinct approach to ruling. Catherine's achievements were far-reaching, rivaled perhaps only by those of Peter the Great, so it is more than fitting that these two rulers deserve such a title. Due to Catherine's social and economic reforms, Russia was, for the first time, able to grasp what having a "European soul" meant. Rather than forcing Europeanness upon Russian society like Peter the Great, Catherine was able to significantly close the gap between Russia and the rest of the civilized Western world. Upon her death, one could see that Russia had become much more prosperous and glorious. It was a true empire.

Chapter 6: 19th-Century Romanovs

After Catherine the Great, the Romanov dynasty persisted for about another 120 years, but this period was in no way easy for the ruling family of Russia, nor for the country itself. Russia was confronted with many challenges during the 19th century (it is one of the most interesting periods in world history due to the many important political developments that took place during it). The Romanovs were forced to adapt to the new world order.

Paul I

The reign of Paul I, the son of Catherine the Great and Peter III, was the shortest of the Romanov monarchs after Empress Catherine. Paul replaced his mother after the latter's death in November 1796, and he was only emperor for five years before he fell victim to growing hostile sentiments, just like many of his predecessors.

In fact, Paul had never been on good terms with his mother, something that may be attributed to the fact that he was Catherine's first child with Peter. Perhaps resenting her child because of his relationship with his father, Catherine limited Paul's ability to engage in political matters, instead making him live at a private estate called Gatchina, which was outside of St. Petersburg. There, Paul lived with his second wife, Wilhelmina of Darmstadt (or Nataliya, which was her adopted Russian name), where he mostly devoted his time to reading Western literature and managing his estate. Paul even had his own small court, with whom he would discuss the potential implications of his mother's many policies. He also trained with the members of his personal army, much like Peter the Great had done when he was a child. However, it was clear that Paul was secluded from matters of real importance in St. Petersburg, and for that reason, he never managed to develop a good relationship with his mother.

Paul immediately replaced Catherine upon her death, perhaps fearing that Catherine would name Alexander, his eldest son, as heir, as he had been the queen's favorite. So, to avoid any further complications, one of the first things he made sure to do as emperor was to cancel the decree that said the monarch had the ability to name their successor, something that had been in place since Peter the Great. Instead, in 1797, he asserted the male line of the Romanovs would become the successor. All in all, it can be said that Paul was quite different than his mother, both in his policies and in the ways in which he implemented them. He was much stricter and often threatened those who opposed him in court with all sorts of punishments. His main domestic changes were directed toward suppressing the local elective governmental functions of the nobles, which, in turn, meant more centralization of power.

Paul's foreign policy was much more lackluster, and in the eyes of many historians, his failure to establish a strong foreign policy agenda eventually caused his doom in 1801. Coinciding with the rise of Napoleon, he chose to join the Second Coalition against the French emperor in 1796, which would end disastrously for the allied European nations and cause another coalition to be created in 1803. The failure of the Second Coalition resulted in Russia having unfavorable relations with its former allies, Britain and Austria, as well as with its enemy, France, which made Napoleon's defeat years later much more difficult. Although Paul formally annexed Georgia, which had been a protectorate of Russia since Catherine, he also planned a rather ambiguous and unnecessary invasion of India through Central Asia—a campaign that was the final straw the opposition needed to move against him.

In March 1801, before Paul could proceed with his unrealistic plans, a discontented group of high-ranking officials, including personnel from the military and the government, assassinated Emperor Paul in his chambers. The insurgents, led by St. Petersburg's governor, Peter von Pahlen, had gained the backing of the emperor's son, Alexander, and immediately declared him the new ruler upon Paul's death.

Alexander I: The Promising Emperor

Catherine the Great personally oversaw Alexander's education from a young age. The young Alexander did not live in Gatchina with his father Paul, instead residing with his grandmother, who put the future monarch in the hands of Frédéric-César de La Harpe, a Swiss national. He became one of the closest friends of Alexander and taught him a lot about contemporary politics, which was slowly being dominated by the revolutionary wave that followed the French Revolution. Alexander also received military education from Aleksey Arakcheev, his future minister of war and confidant, making it so that by the time of his accession at the age of twenty-three, he was quite familiar, in theory, with a monarch's duties and the political state of his country.

However, Alexander's reign coincided with a new era in Europe, an era of nationalism and republicanism, and the young tsar would be challenged by the problems that arose with it. Domestically, most of his time would be devoted to resolving the problems associated with imperial serfs. He would also feel the true wrath of Napoleon after his invasion of Russia in 1812.

At least when compared to his father, Paul, Alexander enjoyed much more sympathy from the Russians. Paul's tyrannical and vicious nature was replaced by Alexander's wise and more humane approach, and the young emperor was motivated to work toward making Russia better than it had been for the past five years. His liberal attitude prompted him to release those who had been taken without trial under Paul from exile and jail, a decision that made the public even more sympathetic toward him. Alexander also restored the right to write and publish freely and gave much of the privileges that had been taken from the nobles back to them.

Thanks to his Neglasny Komitet (private committee), which he formed with his most trusted friends to help work on new laws, he developed Russia's public education system. He provided new training facilities for aspiring teachers and built many schools and three new universities in the country. People holding a university degree had more opportunities to find jobs and start working in public office.

Despite acknowledging the fact that emancipating the serfs would help Russia modernize and catch up with its European neighbors, Alexander was much more reserved and opted not to go through with such a radical reform. During his reign, serfs constituted a large majority of the population, and by granting them freedom, Alexander risked his favorable position with the nobility, who provided the emperor with a lot of material and human resources. In hindsight, it was not the best of decisions, as Russia was forced to experience the age of industrialization and modernization much later than the rest of Europe. However, when we consider Alexander's personality and his unrealistic visions for the future of the backward country, which he had adopted from the theoretical concepts of the Enlightenment thinkers, it is not surprising that he refrained from pushing the reform.

The Man Who Defeated Napoleon

Instead, it is Alexander's achievements in foreign policy that really distinguished his reign. Upon his accession, he quickly tried to reverse the mistakes of his father by making Russia actively involved in European politics once again. He allied with Britain and got on good terms with both Prussia and Austria, the two nations he believed were instrumental if Europe hoped for a period of peace. Alexander also started to negotiate with France, but Napoleon Bonaparte, freshly crowned as emperor in 1804, redeclared war on the whole continent in hopes of achieving a total French hegemony and spreading the glorious revolutionary ideals of late-18th-century France.

Thus, in 1804, Russia formally joined the war against Napoleon as an ally of Britain but did not participate before late 1806, as Alexander was planning on waging war against the Ottomans to liberate the Turkish-held northwestern Orthodox territories (a war he did win after six years, in 1812). Alexander looked closely and planned his retaliation after Napoleon decimated Austria at the Battle of Austerlitz in 1805, forcing the Austrians to capitulate and exit the war. Napoleon also conquered Berlin and defeated the Prussians at the Battle of Jena-Auerstedt. Alexander's army would finally feel the wrath of the French at the Battle of Friedland in June 1807, where it suffered double the casualties of Napoleon's forces.

After the defeat at Friedland, Napoleon and Alexander met face to face, and the Russian tsar signed the Treaty of Tilsit, basically declaring that Russia would exit the war. Alexander was also forced to break off his alliance with Britain and join France's Continental System, an economic blockade that served to weaken the British. Napoleon, in turn, promised Russia would be free when it came to its disputes with Sweden and the Ottoman Empire. He also shared his overall vision with Alexander, which reportedly included the domination of most of the world by the two emperors. It was not the best outcome for Alexander, and the treaty would be received by the Russian public as humiliating.

However, the tsar did not plan to give up his struggle against Napoleon, and he sought revenge, not only for his own losses at Friedland but also for the defeats of his allies: Austria and Prussia. The two emperors grew increasingly friendly toward each other, and Napoleon considered Alexander to be his only friend in Europe. Napoleon even supported the Russians in a one-year war against Sweden in 1808/09, where Alexander gained control of Finland and forced Sweden to join the Continental System. It was a very interesting relationship, but Alexander knew it was doomed to fail, mainly due to Napoleon's ambitions of world domination.

Thus, after his defeat at Friedland, Alexander engaged in a rigorous military reform. Aided by his trusted friend Aleksei Arakcheev, the two aimed to strengthen Russia's main army, but military activity did not cease during this time. After Sweden was defeated in 1809, Alexander saw gradual progress against the Ottomans in Moldova. When it came to aiding Napoleon, Alexander refrained on a number of occasions, most importantly during France's war against Austria in 1809, respecting his old relations with the Austrians and refusing to send military help. Alexander also showed his discontent when Napoleon invaded Prussia and annexed Oldenburg, which was the duchy of Alexander's brother-in-law. Alexander could not dissuade Napoleon from forming the Kingdom of Poland out of the newly acquired territories by the French Empire.

As a response and partially due to economic hardships that had come about due to no trade with Britain, Alexander started quietly smuggling goods to Britain and was eventually confronted by Napoleon. It was clear the relationship between the two sides, while cordial for a brief moment, was deteriorating once again. The conflict would reach its peak in 1812, when Napoleon, coming fresh from an array of victories against every major or minor European power, decided to launch a full-scale invasion of Russia.

Six hundred thousand French soldiers set foot upon Russian soil in late June 1812 with the intention of reaching Moscow by late autumn and forcing Russia to capitulate. Alexander knew Napoleon's army was far too strong to meet in an open battle and ordered his generals to avoid head-to-head confrontation as much as possible, instead luring the French deeper into Russia so the Russians could strike at an advantageous time. Alexander appointed General Mikhail Kutuzov as the commander of his armies, and thanks to the strategy the two of them devised together, he led the country through the Patriotic War, as it is called in Russia. During the great retreat, people evacuated major cities while the soldiers burned down everything that Napoleon could use.

An image of the French forces crossing the Nieman River, 1812.
https://commons.wikimedia.org/wiki/File:French_Army_crossing_Nieman_River_1812.PNG

The French emperor defeated the Russians, first at Smolensk and then at Borodino, by September of 1812, but he could not utilize the lands that had been made useless by the retreating Russian forces to his advantage. The French entered a deserted Moscow in mid-September and camped in the city for about a month. Napoleon found it difficult to continue his advance deeper into Russia. As Alexander had hoped, the French were soon forced to retreat, with Napoleon losing tens of thousands of men due to attrition and desertion. The harsh Russian winter had made it impossible for the French to use their superior numbers to their advantage, and Alexander had outsmarted his opponent, marking Napoleon's first major defeat.

After his triumph, Alexander urged the other European leaders to rise up and retaliate against the French. Prussia and Austria soon answered and entered a new coalition. Alexander led the coalition forces in a decisive battle against Napoleon at Leipzig in October 1813, liberating the conquered Europeans on his way west and heavily defeating the French. Then, he pursued the remnants of Napoleon's army, victoriously marching into Paris in March 1814 to cement his victory over Napoleon. Napoleon was forced to abdicate, and the Bourbons were reinstalled as the ruling family of France.

Alexander played a big role in the instrumental Vienna Congress, where the future of Europe was discussed by the victorious nations. Taking Poland as his prized possession, Alexander returned to Russia as one of the most successful leaders the country had seen in a long time. He was widely regarded as the most powerful monarch in Europe and continued to play a pivotal role in the geopolitical developments that shaped the continent for years to come. Just like his grandmother Catherine, Alexander was a new "arbiter of Europe," assuming a dominant position in European power politics.

After defeating Napoleon, Alexander would last about another decade on the throne, dying at the early age of forty-seven. His personality had always been unpredictable and easily influenced, something that showed especially after the tsar's return home from France. Over the course of the war, he had become overly religious and decided to blindly trust Christian traditions over the more liberal viewpoints he had adopted in his early years. Due to his new love of religion, he persuaded the leaders of Austria and Prussia to enter a "Holy Alliance," whose main aim was the promotion of Christian, conservative principles, which greatly influenced the development of republican nationalism in these countries. Alexander himself adopted rather conservative policies in Russia after Napoleon's defeat and further limited the rights of serfs, who had struggled for freedom for many decades. He also set up the so-called military colonies, distributing lands and peasants to his soldiers, perhaps as a reward for their resilience in the war. This policy did not yield any economic or social benefits whatsoever and created further difficulties for the serfs.

There is no denying Alexander I returned to Russia a completely different man, abandoning his idealistic and ambitious liberal views for conservatism, something that rapidly transformed into ruthless actions against the discontented populace. The Russians tried to rise up several times against the tsar, who became more tyrannical as the years passed. As more and more conspiratorial and secret societies emerged in the major cities to oppose Alexander, depression and paranoia took over, which had a grave effect on the tsar's health. After years of struggling with himself and his subjects, he finally met his end in December 1825 after visiting Crimea with his wife and contracting a severe disease, most likely pneumonia.

Nicholas I: The Classic Autocrat

As Alexander I had no heirs of his own, the throne was supposed to go to the heir presumptive, his younger brother, Constantine. However, Alexander's death brought about yet another, albeit this time brief, succession crisis.

Problems arose because Constantine, who never had much desire to rule, had married a Polish woman of common descent in 1820, five years before Alexander's death, and had thus renounced his claim to the throne of Russia. The next in line was the third brother, Nicholas, who was about seventeen years younger than Constantine and nineteen years younger than Alexander.

Alexander had actually chosen him as his successor after Constantine made his choice, but the process of Nicholas's coronation did not go smoothly. Those who had grown wary of Tsar Alexander in his later years saw his death as an opportunity.

There were many high-ranking military officials and members of the upper classes who believed that Alexander had treated them unjustly by sending them off to his newly created colonies after the end of the war with Napoleon. The main goal of this brief but important uprising, which took place on December 26th, 1825 (December 14th in the Old Style Calendar and is known as the Decembrist uprising for that reason), was to convince the troops stationed in the capital to refuse to swear allegiance to Nicholas and to instead install Constantine. The rebels thought Constantine would help them take back the power that had been stripped away by Alexander. In the end, the Decembrists failed miserably, with those loyal to Nicholas quickly defeating them. Most of the rebels were exiled to Siberia or imprisoned during the trials.

Thus, Nicholas became the emperor of Russia. He was a very educated man in every field, including politics, and would quickly become one of the most conservative autocrats of the 19th century, reasserting the tsar's position as being superior to all bureaucratic or administrative institutions. Nicholas hated the concept of revolution and disloyalty toward the Crown, so he became an excellent embodiment of conservative, autocratic rule, which was slowly becoming old-fashioned in the rest of Europe. His contemporaries often remarked that he brought a sort of firmness and orderliness to his position that greatly resembled a seasoned army general.

And Nicholas was certainly experienced when it came to military matters, having been raised during the Napoleonic Wars. He was also a true royal, being engaged in high politics from a very young age. The best example of this is the fact that he married Princess Charlotte (Alexandra), the daughter of King Frederick William III of Prussia, and made sure the Russo-Prussian bond grew stronger than ever. His strict personality, which valued productivity, had developed after years of traveling in different European nations, of which England had made the biggest impression. In short, by the time Nicholas became emperor, he had almost all of the characteristics of a classic ruler; it was just a matter of how he would use them to benefit his country.

Emperor Nicholas I.
https://commons.wikimedia.org/wiki/File:Botman_-_Emperor_Nicholas_I_(cropped).jpg

All of these influences played a big role when it came to the nature of Nicholas's reign. It can perhaps be best summarized by the official decree that was made in 1833 by the Russian minister of education, Sergei Uvarov. He proclaimed, on behalf of the king, the doctrine of "Official Nationality." The doctrine encapsulated three aspects that came to be the defining characteristics of Nicholas's rule: Orthodoxy (the holy source of the nation's morals and ethical conduct), autocracy (asserting the absolute dominance of the monarch), and nationality (an abstract concept of *narodnost*, which claimed the Russian people's ideal, traditional nature was characterized by their unwavering support of the monarchy and the royal family). Nicholas would force his subjects to live by these principles and would punish those who refused.

When it came to ruling, Tsar Nicholas I was very specific and demanding in his approach. He wished to personally be aware of everything that was going on in his vast empire and surrounded himself with ex-military members to enforce his strict attitude. He personally recruited all of his immediate subordinates, who acted as his personal assistants, and embedded them in all of the major administrative institutions.

Still, when it came to official meetings and ceremonies, Nicholas rarely showed up, thus diminishing the importance of many important structures set up by his predecessors, like the Senate or the state council. The emperor made sure his most trusted men, who embodied the emperor himself as if they were Nicholas's extensions, took care of the most vital matters in different parts of Russia and ensured productivity and maximum obedience. Nicholas believed he could maintain a strong grip on the country by doing this, though, due to his lack of initiative to implement actual changes that would affect the lives of millions of people, corruption reached high levels, with different state officials confused as to what their actual purpose was.

Nicholas I's biggest mistake undoubtedly was his refusal to liberate the serfs, as many European nations had already done. Fearing that it would result in a revolution that would topple the dominance of the royal family, as it had during the 1840s in other nations, Nicholas I further restricted the limited freedoms the serfs had. He was reluctant to adopt reforms that would grant society more liberties for that same reason. So, instead of trying to modernize the different social strata of Russia, he implemented different chanceries. The Third Department of the Chancery, for example, was essentially a personal police force, operating closely with the newly formed Gendarme Corps and making sure that every suspicious person was immediately dealt with. The Third Department's duties also included mass surveillance, enforcing censorship, and arresting criminals. Meanwhile, its leaders became very close to the emperor himself, who had grown increasingly wary of his potential opposition.

The final years of Nicholas I's rule saw the country dragged into the Crimean War, which would end disastrously for Russia. Now, Nicholas's foreign policy had never been strong, but he was generally on good terms with the more conservative European nations. Adamant about "protecting" the Orthodox subjects in the Ottoman Empire, Nicholas ordered his forces to occupy the province of Danubia, modern-day Romania, which was under Turkish rule, in June 1853. The Ottomans, with the support of the

British and, later, the French, retaliated, declaring war in October and launching an offensive to get rid of the Russian forces in the province. Britain and France sent their fleets to the Black Sea to support the Ottomans (both countries had grown unfriendly with Russia, with Britain wanting a strong Ottoman Empire as a means of preserving the balance of power in Europe, while France had ongoing disputes with the Orthodox Church over the rights of Catholics in Ottoman-held Palestine).

All in all, the conflict was devastating from the very beginning for Nicholas, as the Anglo-Franco-Turkish alliance forced him to retreat his forces from Danubia. And if that was not enough, he had to deal with another offensive on the Crimean Peninsula, where the allies established a beachhead. By the end of autumn 1854, the French and the British had defeated the Russians at the Battles of Inkerman and Balaclava and had taken the crucial port of Sevastopol after a month-long siege.

It was all coming crashing down on the Russian tsar, who was quickly overcome by stress and paranoia and experienced severe health problems. By February 1855, his condition had reached the point of no return, and Nicholas I passed away. Some historians have suggested that he took his own life—an explanation that is not entirely unlikely, considering his distorted psychology and the toll of the Crimean War.

Nicholas I, who was a classic autocrat in every sense of the word, made many mistakes during his reign. He was reluctant to give up old traditions and encourage change in Russia. Who knows what would have happened had he loved Russia in a different manner. Would that have changed the way history would remember him?

Alexander II: The Liberator

The late Tsar Nicholas I was succeeded by his eldest son, thirty-six-year-old Alexander, who became Emperor Alexander II upon his accession to the throne. Alexander's reign would be much different than his father's rule, something that can be attributed to his early years, as the future heir had been educated by Vasily Zhukovsky, who possessed strong liberal and romantic views. Alexander had experienced the harsh autocratic rule of Nicholas firsthand and, due to the influence of Zhukovsky, had sort of become a liberal. Although Alexander was not as smart or hard-working as his father, he nevertheless realized the problems Russia was facing and decided to address them as soon as possible.

Alexander sued for peace in the Crimean War soon after becoming tsar, realizing the Russian military would not be able to defeat the combined forces of the Ottomans, French, and British. He preferred to accept defeat to buy more time to work on his domestic reforms to help Russia catch up with the rest of the European powers. Alexander signed the Treaty of Paris in March 1856 and was fortunate enough that he was not forced to give up any territories. Instead, the terms of the peace agreement forbade Russia from having warships in the Black Sea and also granted the disputed territories in Ottoman-held Romania a degree of autonomy. Christians throughout the Ottoman Empire gained more recognition. All in all, the aftermath of the Crimean War was not as disastrous as the military operations themselves, giving the new tsar a rather desirable outcome.

Once peace was established, Alexander started working on addressing some of the most immediate problems. One of the first reforms included the establishment of a brand-new railway system, which was very much needed in an empire as vast as Russia. Before Alexander, the only railway line connected Moscow to St. Petersburg. By the end of his reign, railways had been set up in most of the Russian provinces, amounting to more than twenty-two thousand kilometers (fourteen thousand miles) in total. The project of building a stable railway system was challenging, but it paid dividends, as it improved almost every aspect of Russian life. It helped with the flow of goods and labor, thus increasing trade effectiveness. It also helped with the transportation of the military in case war broke out once again.

The reform for which Alexander II is best known is his decision to finally abolish serfdom, freeing millions of people from essentially being slaves of landowners and giving them the opportunity to pursue independent lives and accumulate their own wealth. Despite opposition from the nobility, Alexander signed the Emancipation Act in 1861, which even included a decree about gradually granting the serfs small pieces of land so they could own something after they became free. Russia still lagged behind in overall industrialization and modernization when compared with

Europe's best, but freeing the serfs was a massive step toward a more stable Russia and signaled the country was ready to abandon many of its old-fashioned standards. To the disappointment of the nobility, emancipation did not cause a severe economic crisis. Instead, it presented millions of people with new opportunities and is the reason Alexander II is often referred to as "the Liberator."

After the abolition of serfdom, Alexander reformed Russia's judicial system, which had essentially been in place unchanged for more than one hundred years. The new system was loosely remodeled and based on the one in France and was yet another step toward adhering to modern principles. Administrative changes included a subtle decentralization of power in 1864 in favor of locally elected assemblies, which came to increase the quality of life in the different provinces. Education was also revisited, and the government funded the construction of new schools all around the country, greatly increasing the literacy rate of its citizens, especially of newly freed serfs in the countryside.

In tandem with his minister of war, Dmitry Milyutin, Alexander reorganized the Russian military, which had shown its obvious flaws during the Crimean War. The two men focused not only on improving the training of regiments and introducing new technologies and strategies but also on making military education institutions significantly more effective. The military reform ended with the introduction of conscription in 1874, which was the "modern standard" of late-19th-century European militarism.

Alexander II was much more relaxed and tolerant when it came to minority groups, granting them different freedoms and rights. However, measures like releasing political prisoners from exile and imprisonment, recognizing Jewish and other religious minorities, and encouraging the creation of local institutions came to be a thorn in the tsar's side for the second half of his rule. As much as he had tried to liberalize Russia, Alexander had perhaps introduced a lot of important changes too quickly, something that inspired many to push for more freedoms in different ways, like organizing protests to gain more power or establishing secret societies where intellectuals would assemble to discuss ways of ending Alexander's conservative rule. Although he was much more liberal than his predecessor, Alexander was still an old-fashioned emperor in the eyes of many people, especially considering the fact that other European countries had slowly diminished the power of their ruling families.

Better education and more freedoms and rights to express their opinions caused the Russian youth to become increasingly anti-conservative, and members of the radical liberal opposition even tried to assassinate the tsar on a number of occasions during his reign. On the other hand, due to Alexander's more relaxed rule, the incorporated peoples, like the Poles, tried revolting on a number of occasions, forcing Alexander to brutally suppress their demands for freedom and an end to the monarchy. In a way, these developments made Alexander more conservative, pushing him away from his liberal views to protect his position as emperor. He made sure to reassert that the emperor was the single most important person in Russia, saying he had been granted his position from God, a characteristic thing that classic authoritarians say. It also had a great effect on his mental health, with Alexander becoming less communicative toward his family. He actually started an affair that would greatly influence his conduct over the next few years.

The late 1870s proved to be the most difficult for Alexander II, as the Orthodox Slavs in the Ottoman Empire increasingly started viewing him as their supreme protector, dragging Russia into another war with the Ottomans in 1877. Alexander had been reluctant to go to war but refused to leave the rebels on their own. The Balkan nations of Serbia, Montenegro, Romania, and Bulgaria, all of them supported by Tsar Alexander and mighty Russia, were able to defeat the Muslim Ottomans and largely drive them out of the Balkans. After one year of fighting, with the coalition pushing the Ottomans all the way to Constantinople, the Balkan nations sued for peace and achieved victory. Serbia, Montenegro, and Romania declared independence, while Bulgaria was established as a special autonomous region. In fact, Alexander is still revered in Sofia as the great liberator of Bulgarian people from the tyrannical Ottoman rule.

Despite Alexander's triumph in the war against the Ottomans, public sentiment at home had grown to be very anti-conservative. Secret terrorist societies that favored revolution had spread throughout all of the major Russian cities and posed a serious threat to the tsar and the monarchy's future. Alexander entrusted his interior minister, Mikhail Loris-Melikov, with the task of dealing with this problem, but the attempts to assassinate the emperor only grew. The terrorist groups tried everything to get rid of their monarch but were unsuccessful on multiple occasions. Finally, Alexander felt he had to give in, at least partially, to what the people wanted.

In January 1881, the Loris-Melikov Constitution was drawn up by his interior minister. The document would introduce two new constitutional bodies, allowing Russia to take its first step toward becoming a constitutional monarchy. However, the tsar was never able to officially issue the constitution, as he finally fell victim to assassins from the radical terrorist organization called People's Will. In March, on the same day the tsar approved the constitution, four assassins threw nitroglycerin and pyroxylin bombs at Alexander's closed carriage. The bombs mortally wounded the tsar.

Alexander III: The Peacemaker

Alexander II's second eldest son, also named Alexander, became the next emperor upon his father's death in 1881. Alexander III's older brother, Nicholas Alexandrovich, the heir presumptive, had tragically passed away in 1865, making him the next in line for the throne. Alexander III had been married to Princess Dagmar of Denmark since 1866, although the princess had initially been engaged to Nicholas (Alexander III's older brother) but was unable to go through with the marriage because of his death. Alexander III was the penultimate Romanov ruler of Russia and would rule until 1894. His reign would be completely different than that of his predecessor.

Deviating from his father's relaxed attitude and keenness of liberal thought, Alexander III made sure the monarchy retained its supreme power amidst the political turmoil of Europe. Being more than familiar with royal conduct and principles of law and administration, Alexander had, from a young age, developed a sense of distrust toward a representative structure of governance, firmly believing that it caused chaos and instability. Instead, he favored the traditional approach to rule, being heavily inspired by his grandfather, Nicholas I, and placing preference in the principles of autocracy, Orthodoxy, and *narodnost.*

Thus, Alexander had developed beliefs that clashed quite significantly with those of his father, and they would demonstrate themselves the most when it came to his change in the direction of foreign policy. In the late 19th century, Europe was quickly transforming geopolitically, and Alexander believed Russia had to keep up with the latest developments and assume its long-held position as the "arbiter of Europe." The most influential occurrences of the time included the Franco-Prussian War and the subsequent birth of a unified German state, the unification of Italy for the first time in centuries, thanks to the nationalistic movements, and the existence of a wavering conservative monarchy in Austria-Hungary.

Years of political maneuvering between these nations almost forced Alexander into an alliance with France in 1890 to balance against the Austro-Germanic partnership, which had been pushed by the new chancellor of Germany, Otto von Bismarck. This marked a deviation from the League of the Three Emperors, the previous alliance system between Austria, Germany, and Russia that had been agreed upon during Alexander II's reign due to his friendly attitude toward Bismarck. Although Alexander III's reign did not see Russia engage in any major wars, foreign policy developments played a crucial role when it came to establishing a new balance of power in Europe and, ultimately, became relevant at the beginning of World War I.

The League of the Three Emperors meets at Skierniewiece.
https://commons.wikimedia.org/wiki/File:The_League_of_the_Three_Emperors.png

When it came to domestic policies, Alexander would again transform the country's political landscape. He canceled the constitution his father had planned to officially issue and declared that his reforms would be directed toward revisiting some of the problematic characteristics of his father's reign. Alexander III firmly believed that restructuring Russia to include modern European principles harmed the country and his people. He instead promoted the revival of the three doctrines that had served the country for so long: autocracy, Orthodoxy, and *narodnost.*

Alexander III would start the process of Russification, enforcing the practice of one religion and speaking one language. He also spread the idea that the Russian sense of nationality stood higher than that of other Europeans. For a diverse empire like Russia, which included a large number of people of different ethnicities, faiths, and nationalities, this seemed pretty problematic. The tsar completely diminished the importance of the autonomous structures established by his father by reducing their ability to have a say in major decisions.

During Alexander III's reign, Slavophiles—individuals who preached Russian and Orthodox superiority over their Western counterparts—enjoyed their most influential period. Alexander was a robust Slavophile in every sense of the word, and Russia would assume the role of the protector of all the Slavic Orthodox nations in the Balkans, which was yet another prerequisite for World War One.

Alexander III of Russia.
https://commons.wikimedia.org/wiki/File:Alexander_III_of_Russia_1892.jpg

All in all, Alexander III is referred to as "the Peacemaker" since Russia was not involved in any wars during his reign. His reign, in general, was rather uneventful, and while efforts were made to backtrack some of the liberal policies introduced by his father, Alexander III, as time would tell, was just trying to avoid the inevitable. Russia's conservative monarchy was outdated, and public sentiment had changed so much that a Slavophile emperor could not singlehandedly reverse it in his favor. Although some improvements were made when it came to infrastructure and technological advancements, mostly thanks to the generous funds that flowed into the country from its French alliance, Alexander III was unable to build on the liberal foundations his father had already created. He died of an illness in the Maly Palace in Crimea at the young age of forty-nine in November 1894, making his son, Nicholas, the new tsar of Russia.

Chapter 7: Nicholas II, the Last Romanov

It is now time to take a look at the last tsar of Russia: Nicholas II Romanov. He ascended to the throne in 1894 after the death of his father and had to lead the country during one of the most difficult times in history. Although the Russian monarchy was already in a pretty rough state at the time of his coronation as tsar, few could have predicted the harsh ending the Romanovs would experience by 1917.

This chapter will explore Nicholas II's reign and talk about the most impactful events that transpired during his twenty-three-year rule, including the Russo-Japanese War, World War I, and the Russian Revolution. These major events are significant enough to be discussed on their own, so this book will only mention them in relation to the last Romanov tsar.

Accession of Nicholas II

Nicholas II was the eldest son of Alexander III, making him the heir apparent to the Russian throne. However, young Nicholas was neither particularly interested in ruling nor fit to become a tsar. He had mostly received a military education and, unlike his predecessors, lacked intellect and strength of character. This would prove problematic for Nicholas II, as his reserved personality was easily affected by the powerful people with whom he surrounded himself.

Although he deeply loved his wife, Alexandra, she possessed a much stronger nature and sense of resilience than her husband, which was difficult for the emperor to bear. Because Nicholas preferred spending time with his inner circle, Alexandra managed to quickly assert her dominance. Because of her, Nicholas's reign would be plagued by external influences, most importantly by Grigori Rasputin. Rasputin was introduced to the royal couple as a healer to help their ill son, but over time, he became heavily involved in Russian politics. He slowly climbed the ranks in Nicholas's court, thanks to his cunning nature. Rasputin gained the royal couple's trust before essentially becoming an unofficial ruler of Russia during World War One since Nicholas was often absent. Although Rasputin was eventually dealt with by those loyal to the tsar, the scandals that surrounded Rasputin had a great effect on Nicholas's reign.

The truth of the matter was Nicholas was deeply insecure and indecisive, which caused him to grow apart from the officials under him, whom he considered to be more experienced in governance and politics. In trying to uphold his position as tsar, Nicholas almost forcibly followed the principles of Orthodoxy, autocracy, and *narodnost* and severely punished those who had liberal tendencies and rose up against his rule. Local police forces became a tool for him to brutally repress "conspirators," the people who dared to go against his regime. All in all, one might argue his weak personality was the root cause of the many problems he faced over the years.

Nicholas II.

Nicholas II's indecisiveness would show when it came to both domestic and foreign policies, as he could not keep his focus on one particular aspect. Despite the ever-so-strong anti-royal public sentiment, he tried to further centralize the monarchy's power by limiting the agency of local political institutions. His contemporaries, including emissaries from the European countries, urged Nicholas to adopt more liberal policies, but the emperor never agreed with them.

He also could not decide where it was best for Russia to expand. During his father's reign, Russia had practically been declined the opportunity to have any colonies after the Berlin Conference, where the other European nations divided the world between them. This had a grave effect on the already insecure tsar, who believed Russia should maintain its influence on multiple bordering regions, including the Orthodox Balkans (which still regarded Russia as its sole protector), Central Asia, and, most importantly, Korea. The construction of the Trans-Siberian Railway signaled that Nicholas was ready to make an effort to increase Russia's power over Korea and to potentially gain access to its ports in the warm waters, which would not freeze come winter.

However, Nicholas II's interests clashed with those of Japan, another nation that was rapidly industrializing and growing its power in East Asia. After being unable to settle their disputes diplomatically, Nicholas was manipulated by his expansionist court to start a conflict with the Japanese over establishing a sphere of influence in Korea. The tensions reached new highs in early 1904 when the Japanese, who were also expansionists, suddenly attacked a Russian port in East Asia. By doing this, they declared war. The world watched closely as a mighty European nation engaged with a rising Asian power. Nations were curious about the outcome since a lot of new military technology was essentially being tested in the war.

To the surprise of many, Russia was heavily defeated, as its army was totally outclassed by the Japanese, who had made significant progress when it came to military innovations. Nicholas and his outdated and humiliated forces sued for peace and gave up Russian control of the province of Manchuria. Korea was quickly taken over by the Japanese by late 1905.

A quick defeat in a war against a weaker nation was the last thing Nicholas needed on his plate. The Russian public was outraged by the Russian military's humiliating showing. People took to the streets and demanded more freedoms, which they hoped would increase their quality of life. The tsar gave in, agreeing to set up a national assembly, the Russian Duma, and drew up a declaration that claimed no new laws would be implemented without the Duma's approval, essentially setting up a constitutional monarchy.

However, in classic autocratic fashion, Nicholas reversed these changes a year later in 1906 with the introduction of his infamous Fundamental Laws, which gave the sovereign complete control of the Duma. Nicholas could now act as the Duma when it was not in session or could even dissolve it if he so pleased. The Fundamental

Laws also reasserted his position as the supreme commander of the Russian military forces and gave him immense powers to change the electoral system.

Instead of progress, Russia had taken another step backward.

World War One

In Russia, the 1910s was a period of instability and chaos. Nicholas blamed everyone but himself for his unsuccessful reign and replaced high-ranking officials often. He brutally repressed anyone who dared oppose him and still considered himself as being ordained by God. In reality, the influence of external personas on him would reach its peak. In short, Nicholas hoped for a breath of fresh air, as the duties of the monarch were making him experience stress and doubt.

An opportunity arose with the assassination of Austrian Archduke Franz Ferdinand in June 1914 by radical Serbian nationalists in Sarajevo. The assassination kicked off a series of events that would eventually culminate in World War One. Russia and all the major European powers were dragged into the conflict. Now, it is impossible to analyze the political complexities that were in place at the time of the archduke's assassination, but we will cover how Nicholas became involved in the war.

After the assassination of Franz Ferdinand, who was the heir to the Austro-Hungarian Empire, Austria-Hungary declared war on Serbia. At the time, Serbia was a small nation that had been struggling to maintain its independence from the conservative Austrians. Russia, as the traditional protector of all Orthodox Slavs, had guaranteed Serbian independence for quite some time and was thus forced to come to the aid of its ally when Austrian troops crossed the border and launched an offensive. But declaring war on Austria meant declaring war on Germany since the two were close allies. Fortunately for Nicholas, France joined the war on the side of Russia and Serbia, with the Great War kicking off in late July 1914.

Each belligerent had its own justifications and goals, including Russia. Although Nicholas tried his best to mediate the ensuing conflict between Austria and Serbia for about a month after the assassination of Franz Ferdinand, his court made him realize that the war was a sort of a blessing in disguise. If Russia could emerge victorious in a war against the great European nations, the people's trust in the monarchy would be restored, and the revolutionaries would be forced to give up their dreams of a revolution. It was now or never for Nicholas II Romanov.

Russia entered the war, hopeful that Austria and Germany would be defeated. Nicholas was confident the Central Powers could not withstand an attack on both fronts. And the Russians united behind the monarch and were ready to fight for the country's honor. However, soon enough, the truth was presented to Nicholas. The Russian military, which the tsar had refused to adequately mobilize during the July Crisis before the war broke out, was of no match to the Germans, who wielded superior technology and were familiar with new tactics.

The Russian army was undisciplined and lacked motivation. The only advantage Nicholas had was superior numbers, but it did not amount to much because of the use of trench warfare and the might of machine guns. Although the Russian offensive had made some progress against the German and Austrian forces, a quick response from the Germans, who had entered a stalemate in the west against the French and the British and were able to transfer the majority of their forces to the east, pushed Nicholas's troops back to their original front lines.

Back home, people grew more distrustful of Nicholas, as the tsar devoted all of his time, energy, and resources to the war effort and further neglected the already troubled populace. Influenced by his wife and stressed by the war, Nicholas replaced the commander of his forces and assumed total control himself, leaving St. Petersburg to go and fight on the front lines. This proved to be the final straw. The government deteriorated in the absence of the tsar, and Queen Alexandra and Rasputin essentially became absolute rulers. People took to the streets, and even those who were traditionally conservative disproved of Nicholas's actions. Many planned his murder in hopes of saving the royal family. However, it was all in vain.

The Last Tsar

Russia continued to slowly lose the war. Meanwhile, the tsar was not in the country, and the situation reached its absolute worst point by 1917. With new fronts opening with the Ottomans in the south and the Germans and Austrians pushing farther into Russian territories, the war effort seemed doomed for Nicholas, but he nevertheless continued to pour resources into the war to keep it going. Major Russian cities experienced constant protests organized by upset citizens. Most of these protests would last for a day or two and eventually fade out without a reaction from the government.

Crucially, on March 8th, 1917 (February 23rd in the Old Style), more than 100,000 factory workers took to the streets of St. Petersburg, demanding higher wages for the hours they had spent working in different industries for Nicholas's war. Joined by numerous female demonstrators celebrating Women's International Day, the people protested throughout the day, failing to get a reaction from the government. However, the strike did not die out the next day; instead, it became a general strike, growing to include nearly a third of St. Petersburg's workers, and it was slowly gaining more and more traction.

The demonstrators turned to violence, raiding different shops, police stations, and factories and overcoming the city police. The workers on strike protested largely against the monarchy, alerting the government, which was prompted to act to stop a full-on revolution from toppling the regime.

It was too late, though. The chain of command was confusing due to the absence of Nicholas and the Duma's inability to deal with the protesters. What became even more worrying for the tsar was the fact the Cossack police switched sides after seeing the magnitude of the protests. Instead of preventing further escalation, they joined the demonstrators.

Nicholas desperately ordered Officer Sergey Khabalov to return from the front lines to reinforce the city with a thousand men, but once Khabalov returned, his men also mutinied. They were tired of fighting a losing war and fed up with the high command's incompetence. They were soon followed by the Imperial Guard, who basically let the revolutionaries into the White Palace. By late February (early March in the New Style), it was clear the government could do no more. Nicholas had a revolution on his hands.

Bolshevik Red Guards at Vulkan Factory, St. Petersburg, October 1917.
https://commons.wikimedia.org/wiki/File:Red_Guard_Vulkan_factory.jpg

The revolutionaries effectively took control of St. Petersburg and organized themselves into the Petrograd Soviet. They held their first plenary session in late February (or early March if you go by the New Style calendar), discussing the goals of the revolution and setting up committees to carry out different tasks. Then, the Soviet started discussing the possibility of setting up a provisional government with the Duma. During the negotiations, another rather valid question arose: what exactly was going to happen to Nicholas and the royal family? The revolutionaries were anti-monarchy, but the Duma mainly constituted of conservatives who supported the tsar. As for Nicholas, he resided in Pskov. The country was completely paralyzed, having likely realized the impending doom and awaiting the decision of the Soviet and the Duma.

Nicholas II was finally approached on March 1st (March 14th in the New Style) by the Duma representatives, who painted a clear picture of the situation to the tsar. They had come to the conclusion that the heads of the Petrograd Soviet, which represented the revolutionaries in the country, would be content if Nicholas gave the throne to his son, Alexei. Since Alexei had not yet come of age, Nicholas's brother, Michael, would serve as regent. What they essentially proposed to Nicholas was a constitutional monarchy, where the Romanovs would still be recognized as the ruling family but would lose most of their powers and instead play a symbolic role, with the country being controlled by other institutions.

Since Nicholas had no other choice, he abdicated the throne. He also declined the throne on behalf of his young son, as he did not want Alexei to go through the trouble of being the emperor one day. The onus was now on Michael to act. He was approached days later by the very same members of the Duma. However, instead of encouraging him to take the throne and become tsar, they convinced Michael to refuse it before the provisional government came up with a new constitution for the country.

Michael Romanov would never get the chance to formally accept the role, as the Petrograd Soviet and the far-left Bolshevik Party, which controlled Russia soon after the February Revolution, adopted an anti-Romanov policy. The Bolsheviks, who rallied behind their leader Vladimir Lenin, sent the royal family to the Tsarskoe Selo, an estate near St. Petersburg, effectively detaining them there for an indefinite time. Russia would tear itself apart, as the Bolsheviks fought with the Mensheviks, royalist "White Russians," for dominance of the country.

To keep the royal family away from the Mensheviks, they were sent to Ekaterinburg, where Nicholas Romanov, the last tsar of Russia, his wife Alexandra, his four daughters, and his one son would spend the rest of their days. In July 1918, as the Mensheviks tried to free the tsar from captivity, the guards watching over the royal family were ordered to shoot the family and their staff before burning their bodies and secretly burying their remains. It was the most gruesome death that could be imagined.

The guards were planning on a quick execution, as the family would be caught entirely unaware. However, the family believed they were going to be rescued any day now. They sewed jewels and other items into their garments for that very occasion. After the gunfire died down, all of the children were still alive. So, the guards shot, stabbed, and beat them until they finally died.

Although several imposters popped up as the years passed (most notably Anastasia), it has been proven that the entire Romanov family died that day. They buried the bodies in two separate graves. One grave was found in 1991; the other one, which contained the bodies of Maria and Alexei, was uncovered in 2007.

The Romanov dynasty had ended. Tsar Nicholas II, the final emperor of Russia, was defeated by the will of the people. Russia was no longer a monarchy.

Conclusion

The Romanovs are one of the most famous ruling families in European history. Succeeding the Rurikids as the main dynasty of Russia, they managed to stay in control of the country for about three hundred years and contributed greatly to its development. From Mikhail Romanov, who ascended the throne rather unexpectedly after the Time of Troubles, to Nicholas II, whose reign was cut short by the Russian Revolution, there is no denying the Romanov dynasty remains very influential, not only to historians but also to people who are simply curious about history.

Perhaps what makes the Romanovs so special is the fact that each of the tsars or empresses who came to rule Russia was different. They all possessed completely different personalities and strove to achieve different goals for the country's prosperity. Fundamentally, however, they all defined and embodied absolutism, albeit to varying degrees. The circumstances under which the Romanovs came to power in the first place explains this fact the best, as Russia, as a political entity, was much more diverse and complex than its European neighbors. The Romanovs mostly centered their rule around the principles of autocratic rule, Orthodoxy, and the importance of "Russianness" and thus were able to persevere during the hardest of times.

Peter the Great and Catherine the Great are undoubtedly the two Romanov rulers who are largely regarded to be the most successful. Thanks to their strong personas, they were able to maximize their power and lead Russia into a period of greatness and prosperity. That is why they are the only two who are referred to as "the Great." On the other hand, the last few Romanov rulers are considered to be weaker than their predecessors simply based on the fact they were unable to repeat or top the achievements of Peter and Catherine. What made the rule of those like Nicholas II extremely difficult were the unfortunate periods with which their reign coincided. The time of radical change in Europe did not favor the older, traditional system of the monarchy.

Still, it has to be said that the Romanovs did not deserve the abrupt and brutal end they received. Today, historians recognize many of the Romanov dynasty's pivotal contributions to Russian society. The Romanovs deserve their place as one of the most legendary ruling families in European history.

Here's another book by Enthralling History that you might like

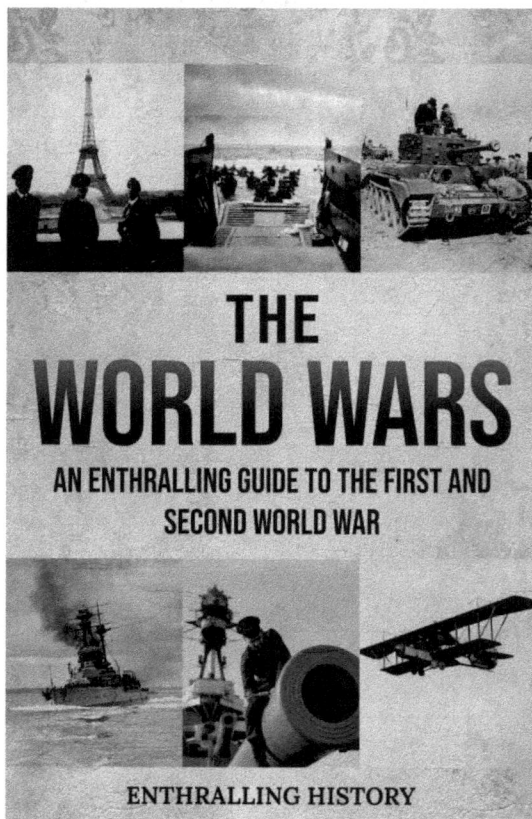

THE

WORLD WARS

AN ENTHRALLING GUIDE TO THE FIRST AND
SECOND WORLD WAR

ENTHRALLING HISTORY

Free limited time bonus

Stop for a moment. We have a free bonus set up for you. The problem is this: we forget 90% of everything that we read after 7 days. Crazy fact, right? Here's the solution: we've created a printable, 1-page pdf summary for this book that you're reading now. All you have to do to get your free pdf summary is to go to the following website:

https://livetolearn.lpages.co/enthrallinghistory/

Once you do, it will be intuitive. Enjoy, and thank you!

We forget 90% of everything that we've read in 7 days...

Get the free printable pdf summary of the book you've read AND much, much more... shhhh...

Enter Your Most Frequently Used Email to Get Started

DOWNLOAD FREE PDF SUMMARY

©Enthralling History

Bibliography

- Title: Russia: A Timeline
Date Accessed: 11/8/2022
Link: https://www.history.com/topics/russia/russia-timeline
- Title: Slavs and the Early Slav Culture
Date Accessed: 11/8/2022
Link: https://www.encyclopedia.com/humanities/encyclopedias-almanacs-transcripts-and-maps/slavs-and-early-slav-culture
- Title: Slavs
Date Accessed: 11/8/2022
Link: https://www.worldhistory.org/Slavs/
- Title: When Viking Kings and Queens Ruled Medieval Russia
Date Accessed: 11/8/2022
Link: https://www.history.com/news/vikings-in-russia-kiev-rus-varangians-prince-oleg
- Title: Kievan Rus'
Date Accessed: 11/8/2022
Link: https://www.worldhistory.org/Kievan_Rus/
- Title: Khazars
Date Accessed: 11/8/2022
Link: https://cs.mcgill.ca/~rwest/wikispeedia/wpcd/wp/k/Khazars.htm

- Title: The Rise and Fall of Kievan Rus'

Date Accessed: 11/8/2022

Link: https://www.themaparchive.com/the-rise-and-fall-of-kievan-rus/

- Title: Olga of Kiev: One Saint You Do Not Want to Mess With

Date Accessed: 11/8/2022

Link: https://www.historyanswers.co.uk/medieval-renaissance/olga-of-kiev-one-saint-you-do-not-want-to-mess-with/

- Title: The Great Migration and Early Slavic History

Date Accessed: 11/8/2022

Link: https://about-history.com/the-great-migration-and-early-slavic-history/

- Title: The Slavs and Byzantium

Date Accessed: 11/8/2022

Link: https://unesdoc.unesco.org/ark:/48223/pf0000046109

- Title: Vladimir I and Christianization

Date Accessed: 12/8/2022

Link: https://courses.lumenlearning.com/atd-herkimer-westerncivilization/chapter/vladimir-i-and-christianization/

- Title: Eastern Orthodox Church

Date Accessed: 12/8/2022

Link: https://www.bbc.co.uk/religion/religions/christianity/subdivisions/easternorthodox_1.shtml#:~:text=The%20Orthodox%20tradition%20developed%20from,sometimes%20called%20'Byzantine%20Christianity'.

- Title: Christianity and the Slavic Folk Culture: The Mechanisms of Their Interaction

Date Accessed: 12/8/2022

Link: https://www.mdpi.com/2077-1444/12/7/459/htm

- Title: Who Were the Mongols?

Date Accessed: 12/8/2022

Link: https://www.nationalgeographic.com/culture/article/mongols

- Title: The Mongol Threat

  Date Accessed: 12/8/2022

  Link: https://courses.lumenlearning.com/atd-herkimer-westerncivilization/chapter/the-mongol-threat/

- Title: Golden Horde

  Date Accessed: 12/8/2022

  Link: https://www.worldhistory.org/Golden_Horde/

- Title: Ivan I and the Rise of Moscow

  Date Accessed: 12/8/2022

  Link: https://courses.lumenlearning.com/atd-herkimer-westerncivilization/chapter/ivan-i-and-the-rise-of-moscow/

- Title: Alexander Nevsky

  Date Accessed: 12/8/2022

  Link: https://www.thoughtco.com/alexander-nevsky-profile-p2-1788255

- Title: Grand Duchy of Moscow

  Date Accessed: 22/8/2022

  Link: https://courses.lumenlearning.com/suny-fmcc-boundless-worldhistory/chapter/the-grand-duchy-of-moscow/

- Title: Ivan III of Russia

  Date Accessed: 22/8/2022

  Link: https://www.newworldencyclopedia.org/entry/Ivan_III_of_Russia

- Title: Why Was Ivan So Terrible?

  Date Accessed: 22/8/2022

  Link: https://www.history.co.uk/articles/why-was-ivan-so-terrible

- Title: Three Terrible Things Ivan the Terrible Did

- Title: Rurikid Dynasty

  Date Accessed: 22/8/2022

  Link: https://www.encyclopedia.com/history/encyclopedias-almanacs-transcripts-and-maps/rurikid-dynasty

- Title: Michael Romanov (Russia) (1596-1645; ruled 1613-1645)

  Date Accessed: 22/8/2022

Link: https://www.encyclopedia.com/history/encyclopedias-almanacs-transcripts-and-maps/michael-romanov-russia-1596-1645-ruled-1613-1645

- Title: The Romanov

Date Accessed: 22/8/2022

Link: https://courses.lumenlearning.com/suny-hccc-worldcivilization/chapter/the-romanovs/

- Title: Peter the Great

Date Accessed: 22/8/2022

Link: https://www.rmg.co.uk/stories/topics/peter-great

- Title: Russo-Persian Wars

Date Accessed: 22/8/2022

Link: https://www.encyclopedia.com/history/encyclopedias-almanacs-transcripts-and-maps/russo-persian-wars

- Title: Peter the Great and his Legacy (1682-1762)

Date Accessed: 22/8/2022

Link: http://web-static.nypl.org/exhibitions/russia/level3.html

- Title: Peter the Great

Date Accessed: 22/8/2022

Link: https://www.biography.com/political-figure/peter-the-great

- Title: Peter the Great Dies

Date Accessed: 24/8/2022

Link: https://www.history.com/this-day-in-history/peter-the-great-dies

- Title: The Brief Reign of Peter III

Date Accessed: 24/8/2022

Link: https://courses.lumenlearning.com/suny-hccc-worldhistory2/chapter/the-brief-reign-of-peter-iii/

- Title: Catherine the Great (1729-1796)

Date Accessed: 24/8/2022

Link: https://www.bbc.co.uk/history/historic_figures/catherine_the_great.shtml

- Title: How Did Catherine the Great's Reign Shape Imperial Russian History

Date Accessed: 24/8/2022

Link: https://www.thebritishacademy.ac.uk/blog/how-did-catherine-the-great-reign-shape-imperial-russian-history/

- Title: 10 Facts About the Russian Enlightenment

Date Accessed: 24/8/2022

Link: https://www.historyhit.com/facts-about-the-russian-enlightenment/

- Title: Pugachev's Rebellion: 5 Questions about the biggest uprising in Russia's history

Date Accessed: 24/8/2022

Link: https://www.rbth.com/history/326277-5-questions-about-pugachevs-rebellion

- Title: The Imperial Russian Army 1725-1796

Date Accessed: 24/8/2022

Link: https://link.springer.com/chapter/10.1007/978-0-230-10822-6_4

- Title: Orthodox Russia

Date Accessed: 24/8/2022

Link: https://www.psupress.org/books/titles/0-271-02349-X.html

- Title: Russian Northern Expeditions (18th-19th Centuries)

Date Accessed: 24/8/2022

Link: https://www.whoi.edu/beaufortgyre/history/history_russian1819.html

- Title: What Really Happened After Peter the Great Died?

Date Accessed: 24/8/2022

Link: https://www.grunge.com/716399/what-really-happened-after-peter-the-great-died/

- Title: Peter II

Date Accessed: 24/8/2022

Link: http://www.saint-petersburg.com/royal-family/peter-ii/

- Title: Why Peter the Great Tortured and Killed His Own Son

Date Accessed: 24/8/2022

Link: https://www.history.com/news/peter-the-great-tortured-killed-own-son#:~:text=But%20even%20those%20royals%20might,for%20allegedly%20conspiring%20against%20him.

- Title: The Seven Years War 1756-1763

Date Accessed: 24/8/2022

Link: https://www.thoughtco.com/the-seven-years-war-1756-1763-1222020

- Title: Jun 24, 1812 CE: Napoleon Invades Russia

Date Accessed: 25/8/2022

Link: https://education.nationalgeographic.org/resource/napoleon-invades-russia

- Title: Why Napoleon's Invasion of Russia Was the Beginning of the End

Date Accessed: 25/8/2022

Link: https://www.history.com/news/napoleons-disastrous-invasion-of-russia

- Title: Napoleon Defeated at Waterloo

Date Accessed: 25/8/2022

Link: https://www.history.com/this-day-in-history/napoleon-defeated-at-waterloo

- Title: Nicholas I of Russia

Date Accessed: 25/8/2022

Link: https://www.newworldencyclopedia.org/entry/Nicholas_I_of_Russia

- Title: The Decembrist Revolt

Date Accessed: 25/8/2022

Link: https://courses.lumenlearning.com/suny-hccc-worldhistory2/chapter/the-decembrist-revolt/

- Title: The Russo-Turkish War, 1828-1829

Date Accessed: 25/8/2022

Link: https://academic.oup.com/british-academy-scholarship-online/book/35530/chapter-abstract/305708973?redirectedFrom=fulltext#no-access-message

- Title: Poland's 'largest uprising' EVER took place 153 years ago today

Date Accessed: 25/8/2022

Link: https://www.thefirstnews.com/article/polands-largest-uprising-ever-took-place-153-years-ago-today-4354

- Title: Russo-Persian Wars

Date Accessed: 25/8/2022

Link: https://www.encyclopedia.com/history/encyclopedias-almanacs-transcripts-and-maps/russo-persian-wars

- Title: The Westerners and the Slavophiles

Date Accessed: 25/8/2022

Link: https://courses.lumenlearning.com/suny-hccc-worldhistory2/chapter/the-westerners-and-the-slavophiles/

- Title: Crimean War

Date Accessed: 25/8/2022

Link: https://www.history.com/topics/british-history/crimean-war

- Title: The Outcome of the Crimean War

Date Accessed: 25/8/2022

Link: https://www.historic-uk.com/HistoryUK/HistoryofBritain/Outcome-Crimean-War/#:~:text=On%2030th%20March%201856%2C%20the,the%20Ottoman%20Empire%20and%20Sardinia.

- Title: Alexander II of Russia

Date Accessed: 25/8/2022

Link: https://www.newworldencyclopedia.org/entry/Alexander_II_of_Russia

- Title: The Emancipation of the Russian Serfs, 1861

Date Accessed: 25/8/2022

Link: https://www.historytoday.com/archive/emancipation-russian-serfs-1861

- Title: Russo-Turkish War

Date Accessed: 25/8/2022

Link: https://www.encyclopedia.com/history/encyclopedias-almanacs-transcripts-and-maps/russo-turkish-war

---

- Title: U.S takes possession of Alaska

  Date Accessed: 25/8/2022

  Link: https://www.history.com/this-day-in-history/u-s-takes-possession-of-alaska

- Title: Czar Alexander II assassinated in St. Petersburg

  Date Accessed: 25/8/2022

  Link: https://www.history.com/this-day-in-history/czar-alexander-ii-assassinated

- Title: Alexander III of Russia

  Date Accessed: 25/8/2022

  Link: https://www.newworldencyclopedia.org/entry/Alexander_III_of_Russia

- Title: May Laws

  Date Accessed: 25/8/2022

  Link: https://www.encyclopedia.com/religion/encyclopedias-almanacs-transcripts-and-maps/may-laws

- Title: Review: The Franco-Russian Alliance

  Date Accessed: 25/8/2022

  Link: https://www.jstor.org/stable/45336751

- Title: Trans-Siberian Railroad

  Date Accessed: 25/8/2022

  Link: https://www.britannica.com/topic/Trans-Siberian-Railroad

- Title: Nicholas II (1868-1918)

  Date Accessed: 27/08/2022

  Link: https://www.bbc.co.uk/history/historic_figures/nicholas_ii.shtml

- Title: 1905 Russian Revolution

  Date Accessed: 27/08/2022

  Link: https://www.newworldencyclopedia.org/entry/1905_Russian_Revolution

- Title: Bloody Sunday Massacre in Russia

  Date Accessed: 27/08/2022

  Link: https://www.history.com/this-day-in-history/bloody-sunday-massacre-in-russia

- Title: The Duma in Russian History
Date Accessed: 27/08/2022
Link: https://www.thoughtco.com/duma-in-russian-history-1221805

- Title: Russo-Japanese War
Date Accessed: 27/08/2022
Link: https://www.history.com/topics/japan/russo-japanese-war

- Title: How World War I Fueled the Russian Revolution
Date Accessed: 27/08/2022
Link: https://www.history.com/news/world-war-i-russian-revolution

- Title: Grigori Rasputin
Date Accessed: 27/08/2022
Link: https://www.newworldencyclopedia.org/entry/Grigori_Rasputin

- Title: Russian Revolution
Date Accessed: 27/08/2022
Link: https://www.history.com/topics/russia/russian-revolution

- Title: Why Czar Nicholas II and the Romanovs Were Murdered
Date Accessed: 27/08/2022
Link: https://www.history.com/news/romanov-family-murder-execution-reasons

- Title: Vladimir Lenin
Date Accessed: 30/08/2022
Link: https://www.history.com/topics/russia/vladimir-lenin

- Title: Leon Trotsky
Date Accessed: 30/08/2022
Link: https://www.biography.com/scholar/leon-trotsky

- Title: Russian Revolution
Date Accessed: 30/08/2022
Link: https://www.history.com/topics/russia/russian-revolution

- Title: Nov 7, 1917, CE: October Revolution

  Date Accessed: 30/08/2022

  Link: https://education.nationalgeographic.org/resource/october-revolution

- Title: Bolsheviks Revolt in Russia

  Date Accessed: 30/08/2022

  Link: https://www.history.com/this-day-in-history/bolsheviks-revolt-in-russia

- Title: An Anti-Bolshevik Alternative

  Date Accessed: 30/08/2022

  Link: https://uwpress.wisc.edu/books/5573.htm

- Title: The Russian Civil War

  Date Accessed: 30/08/2022

  Link: https://courses.lumenlearning.com/suny-hccc-worldhistory2/chapter/the-russian-civil-war/

- Title: Karl Marx

  Date Accessed: 30/08/2022

  Link: https://www.history.com/topics/germany/karl-marx

- Title: Joseph Stalin

  Date Accessed: 30/08/2022

  Link: https://www.history.com/topics/russia/joseph-stalin

- Title: Formation of the Soviet Union

  Date Accessed: 30/08/2022

  Link: https://courses.lumenlearning.com/suny-hccc-worldhistory2/chapter/formation-of-the-soviet-union/

- Title: The New Economic Policy

  Date Accessed: 30/08/2022

  Link: https://alphahistory.com/russianrevolution/new-economic-policy-nep/#:~:text=The%20NEP%20replaced%20war%20communism,the%20sale%20of%20surplus%20goods.

- Title: Soviet Union

  Date Accessed: 30/08/2022

  Link: https://www.history.com/topics/russia/history-of-the-soviet-union

- Title: Soviet Policy on Nationalities, 1920's-1930s

  Date Accessed: 30/08/2022

  Link: https://www.lib.uchicago.edu/collex/exhibits/soviet-imaginary/socialism-nations/soviet-policy-nationalities-1920s-1930s/

- Title: Joseph Stalin's Show Trials: A Short Summary

  Date Accessed: 30/08/2022

  Link: https://www.historyonthenet.com/stalin-show-trials-summary

- Title: Great Purge

  Date Accessed: 30/08/2022

  Link: https://www.history.com/topics/russia/great-purge

- Title: Kronstadt Rebellion

  Date Accessed: 31/08/2022

  Link: https://alphahistory.com/russianrevolution/kronstadt-rebellion/

- Title: What Were Stalin's Five-Year Plans?

  Date Accessed: 31/08/2022

  Link: https://www.historyhit.com/first-five-year-plan-begins/

- Title: The Invasion of the Soviet Union

  Date Accessed: 31/08/2022

  Link: https://www.facinghistory.org/holocaust-and-human-behavior/chapter-8/invasion-soviet-union

- Title: Operation Barbarossa

  Date Accessed: 31/08/2022

  Link: https://www.history.com/topics/world-war-ii/operation-barbarossa

- Title: Auschwitz is Liberated

  Date Accessed: 31/08/2022

  Link: https://www.history.com/this-day-in-history/soviets-liberate-auschwitz

- Title: Soviets Declare War on Japan, Invade Manchuria

  Date Accessed: 31/08/2022

  Link: https://www.history.com/this-day-in-history/soviets-declare-war-on-japan-invade-manchuria

- Title: What Will Russia Do After the War?

Date Accessed: 31/08/2022

Link: https://www.nationalww2museum.org/war/articles/what-will-russia-do-after-war

- Title: Cold War History

Date Accessed: 31/08/2022

Link: https://www.history.com/topics/cold-war/cold-war-history

- Title: Berlin Blockade

Date Accessed: 31/08/2022

Link: https://www.history.com/topics/cold-war/berlin-blockade

- Title: The Warsaw Pact is Formed

Date Accessed: 31/08/2022

Link: https://www.history.com/this-day-in-history/the-warsaw-pact-is-formed

- Title: Cuban Missile Crisis

Date Accessed: 31/08/2022

Link: https://www.history.com/topics/cold-war/cuban-missile-crisis#:~:text=During%20the%20Cuban%20Missile%20Crisis,90%20miles%20from%20U.S.%20shores.

- Title: Arms Race, Space Race

Date Accessed: 31/08/2022

Link: https://www.khanacademy.org/humanities/whp-origins/era-7-the-great-convergence-and-divergence-1880-ce-to-the-future/x23c41635548726c4:other-materials-origins-era-7/a/arms-race-space-race

- Title: SALT Treaties

Date Accessed: 31/08/2022

Link: https://www.encyclopedia.com/history/encyclopedias-almanacs-transcripts-and-maps/salt-treaties

- Title: The Space Race

Date Accessed: 31/08/2022

Link: https://www.history.com/topics/cold-war/space-race

- Title: The Anti-Ballistic Missile (ABM) Treaty at a Glance

Date Accessed: 31/08/2022

Link: https://www.armscontrol.org/factsheets/abmtreaty

- Title: Nikita Khrushchev
Date Accessed: 5/09/2022
Link: https://www.history.com/topics/cold-war/nikita-sergeyevich-khrushchev
- Title: De-Stalinization
Date Accessed: 5/09/2022
Link: https://www.encyclopedia.com/history/encyclopedias-almanacs-transcripts-and-maps/de-stalinization
- Title: Stagnation in the Soviet Union
Date Accessed: 5/09/2022
Link: https://alphahistory.com/coldwar/stagnation-soviet-union/
- Title: From Sputnik to Spacewalking: 7 Soviet Firsts
Date Accessed: 5/09/2022
Link: https://www.history.com/news/from-sputnik-to-spacewalking-7-soviet-space-firsts
- Title: Mikhail Gorbachev
Date Accessed: 5/09/2022
Link: https://www.nobelprize.org/prizes/peace/1990/gorbachev/biographical/
- Title: Perestroika
Date Accessed: 5/09/2022
Link: https://www.history.com/topics/cold-war/perestroika-and-glasnost
- Title: The Chernobyl disaster: What happened, and the long-term impacts
Date Accessed: 5/09/2022
Link: https://www.nationalgeographic.com/culture/article/chernobyl-disaster
- Title: Boris Yeltsin
Date Accessed: 5/09/2022
Link: https://www.history.com/topics/russia/boris-yeltsin
- Title: Vladimir Putin
Date Accessed: 5/09/2022
Link: https://www.forbes.com/profile/vladimir-

putin/?sh=5870d016fc58

- Title: Chronicles of the First and Second Chechen Wars

Date Accessed: 5/09/2022

Link: https://www.academicapress.com/node/415

- Title: Vladimir Putin

Date Accessed: 5/09/2022

Link: https://www.britannica.com/biography/Vladimir-Putin

- Title: Collapse of the Soviet Union

Date Accessed: 06/09/2022

Link: https://www.history.com/topics/cold-war/fall-of-soviet-union

- Title: Berlin Wall

Date Accessed: 06/09/2022

Link: https://www.history.com/topics/cold-war/berlin-wall#:~:text=at%20high%20speeds.-,The%20Berlin%20Wall%3A%20The%20Fall%20of%20the%20Wall,to%20cross%20the%20country's%20borders.

- Title: Pyotr Ilyich Tchaikovsky

Date Accessed: 06/09/2022

Link: https://www.britannica.com/biography/Pyotr-Ilyich-Tchaikovsky

- Title: Sergey Rachmaninoff

Date Accessed: 06/09/2022

Link: https://www.britannica.com/biography/Sergey-Rachmaninoff

- Title: Nikolai Rimsky-Korsakov

Date Accessed: 06/09/2022

Link: https://www.abt.org/people/nikolai-rimsky-korsakov/

- Title: Dmitri Shostakovich: A Life

Date Accessed: 06/09/2022

Link:
https://www.classicfm.com/composers/shostakovich/guides/dmitri-shostakovich-life/

- Title: Igor Stravinsky

Date Accessed: 06/09/2022

Link: https://www.newworldencyclopedia.org/entry/Igor_Stravinsky

- Title: Leo Tolstoy

Date Accessed: 06/09/2022

Link: https://www.biography.com/scholar/leo-tolstoy

- Title: Alexander Pushkin

Date Accessed: 06/09/2022

Link: https://www.poetryfoundation.org/poets/alexander-pushkin

- Title: Fyodor Dostoevsky

Date Accessed: 06/09/2022

Link: https://www.newworldencyclopedia.org/entry/Fyodor_Dostoevsky

- Title: Maxim Gorky

Date Accessed: 06/09/2022

Link: https://www.britannica.com/biography/Maxim-Gorky

- Title: Nikolai Gogol

Date Accessed: 06/09/2022

Link: https://www.newworldencyclopedia.org/entry/Nikolai_Gogol

- Title: Anton Chekhov

Date Accessed: 06/09/2022

Link: https://www.britannica.com/biography/Anton-Chekhov

- Title: Alexander Solzhenitsyn

Date Accessed: 06/09/2022

Link: https://www.nobelprize.org/prizes/literature/1970/solzhenitsyn/biographical/

- Title: Dmitri Mendeleev

Date Accessed: 06/09/2022

Link: https://www.khanacademy.org/humanities/big-history-project/stars-and-elements/knowing-stars-elements/a/dmitri-mendeleev

- Title: Ivan Pavlov

Date Accessed: 06/09/2022

Link: https://www.thoughtco.com/ivan-pavlov-biography-4171875

- Title: Mikhail Lomoncsov

Date Accessed: 06/09/2022

Link:
https://www.newworldencyclopedia.org/entry/Mikhail_Lomonos
ov

Sources

1. Bushkovitch, P. (2001). *Peter the Great: The Struggle for Power, 1671-1725* (Ser. New Studies in European History). Cambridge University Press.

2. Clements, B. E. (2012). *A History of Women in Russia: From Earliest Times to the Present.* Indiana University Press.

3. Dmytryshyn, B. (1991). *Medieval Russia: A Source Book, 850-1700* (3rd ed.). Holt, Rinehart and Winston.

4. Dukes, P. (1990). *A History of Russia: Medieval, Modern, Contemporary* (2nd ed.). Duke University Press.

5. DUNNING, C. (1995). "Crisis, Conjuncture, and the Causes of the Time of Troubles." *Harvard Ukrainian Studies, 19,* 97-119. http://www.jstor.org/stable/41036998.

6. Ellison, H. J. (1965). "Economic Modernization in Imperial Russia: Purposes and Achievements." *The Journal of Economic History, 25*(4), 523-540. http://www.jstor.org/stable/2116126.

7. Esthus, R. A. (1981). "Nicholas II and the Russo-Japanese War." *The Russian Review, 40*(4), 396-411. https://doi.org/10.2307/129919.

8. Heilbronner, H. (1961). "Alexander III and the Reform Plan of Loris-Melikov." *The Journal of Modern History, 33*(4), 384-397. http://www.jstor.org/stable/1877215.

9. Leontovitsch, V., & Solzhenitsyn Aleksandr Isaevich. (2012). *The History of Liberalism in Russia.* (P. Leontovitsch, Trans.) (Ser. Series in Russian and East European Studies). University of Pittsburgh Press.

10. Lewitter, L. R. (1958). "Peter the Great, Poland, and the Westernization of Russia." *Journal of the History of Ideas, 19*(4), 493–506. https://doi.org/10.2307/2707919.

11. Markevich, A., & Zhuravskaya, E. (2018). "The Economic Effects of the Abolition of Serfdom: Evidence from the Russian Empire." *The American Economic Review, 108*(4-5), 1074–1117. https://www.jstor.org/stable/26527998.

12. Meehan-Waters, B. (1975). "Catherine the Great and the Problem of Female Rule." *The Russian Review, 34*(3), 293–307. https://doi.org/10.2307/127976.

13. Okenfuss, M. J. (1997). "Catherine II's Restored Image and the Russian Economy in the Age of Catherine the Great." *Jahrbücher Für Geschichte Osteuropas, 45*(4), 521–525. http://www.jstor.org/stable/41049995.

14. PEREIRA, N. G. O. (1980). "Alexander II and the Decision to Emancipate the Russian Serfs, 1855-61." *Canadian Slavonic Papers / Revue Canadienne Des Slavistes, 22*(1), 99–115. http://www.jstor.org/stable/40867679.

15. Rieber, A. J. (1978). "Bureaucratic Politics in Imperial Russia." *Social Science History, 2*(4), 399–413. https://doi.org/10.2307/1171155.

16. Wortman, R. (2013). "Nicholas II and the Revolution of 1905." In *Russian Monarchy: Representation and Rule* (pp. 199–218). Academic Studies Press. https://doi.org/10.2307/j.ctt21h4wbq.14.